Summary of Contents

P9-CKS-994

JAVASCRIPT: NOVICE TO NINJA

BY DARREN JONES

JavaScript: Novice to Ninja

by Darren Jones

Product Manager: Simon Mackie **English Editor:** Kelly Steele

Technical Editor: Craig Buckler **Cover Designer:** Alex Walker

Published by SitePoint Pty. Ltd.

48 Cambridge Street Collingwood
VIC Australia 3066
Web: www.sitepoint.com
Email: business@sitepoint.com

ISBN 978-0-9924612-2-5 (print)

ISBN 978-0-9924612-1-8 (ebook)
Printed and bound in the United States of America

About Darren Jones

Darren has been playing around with programming and building websites for over a decade. He wrote the SitePoint book *Jump Start Sinatra,* and also produced the *Getting Started With Ruby* video tutorials for Learnable, as well as writing a number of articles published on SitePoint.

In recent years, having seen just how powerful the language can be, Darren has started to use JavaScript much more heavily. He believes that JavaScript will be the most important programming language to learn in the future.

About SitePoint

SitePoint specializes in publishing fun, practical, and easy-to-understand content for web professionals. Visit http://www.sitepoint.com/ to access our blogs, books, newsletters, articles, and community forums. You'll find a stack of information on JavaScript, PHP, Ruby, mobile development, design, and more.

To my two favourite super heroes,
Zac & Sienna — love you loads x

Table of Contents

Chapter 2 Programming Basics 19

Chapter 3 Arrays, Logic, and Loops 55

Chapter 9 **The Window Object**

Chapter 10 Testing and Debugging

Chapter 13   Ajax

Chapter 16   **Next Steps**

Preface

The aim of this book is to introduce you to programming using the JavaScript language, eventually helping you to develop into a JavaScript ninja.

This is an exciting time to be learning JavaScript, having finally outgrown its early reputation as a basic scripting language used to produce cringeworthy effects on web pages. Today, JavaScript is used to produce professional and powerful web applications. Modern browsers are now capable of running JavaScript code at lightning speed, and Node.js has helped to revolutionize it by facilitating its use in other environments. This has led to a much more professional and structured approach to building JavaScript applications, where it is now considered a full-fledged programming language. In short, JavaScript has grown up.

JavaScript has a number of cool features that make it stand out from other languages, such as callbacks, first-class functions, prototypal inheritance, and closures. Its event-based model also makes it a very good choice for modern web application development. JavaScript's ace in the pack, though, is something of which every language is envious—its *ubiquity*. JavaScript is available almost everywhere; anybody who has access to a browser can use it. And this is increasing every year as it becomes more readily available outside the browser environment. This translates into JavaScript's reach being immense: it is already the most popular language on GitHub.[1] I can only see JavaScript growing even more popular in the future as it becomes the language of choice for the Internet of Things[2]—helping to control household appliances, even program robots.

Before I get carried away, though, I should point out that JavaScript is far from perfect, having a number of flaws. It is missing some important programming constructs, such as modules and private functions, that are considered standard in many modern programming languages. Yet it's also an unbelievably flexible language, where many of these gaps can be filled using the tools that it provides. In addition, many libraries have sprung into existence that help to extend JavaScript so that it's now able to reach its full potential.

---

[1] https://www.asad.pw/blog/2014/11/04/github-language-popularity-statistics/
[2] http://en.wikipedia.org/wiki/Internet_of_Things

This book starts off with the basics, assuming no programming or JavaScript knowledge, but quickly gets up to speed covering all the main topics in great depth such as functions, objects, and DOM manipulation. More advanced topics such as error handling and testing, functional programming, and OOP are then introduced after the basics have been covered. There have been some exciting new developments in the world of JavaScript over the last few years such as Ajax, HTML5 APIs, and task runners, and these are covered in the last part of the book. There's also a practical project to build a quiz application that is developed throughout the book towards the end of each chapter. I've written with developing for modern browsers in mind, so I've always tried to use the most up-to-date methods in the examples. Having said that, I've also tried to acknowledge if something might not work in an older browser, or if a workaround is needed.

It's a long way ahead—16 chapters, to be precise. But remember, every ninja's journey starts with a single page (or something like that, anyway). So, turn the page and let's get started!

Who Should Read This Book

This book is suitable for beginner-level web designers and developers. Some knowledge of HTML and CSS is assumed, but no previous programming experience is necessary.

Conventions Used

You'll notice that we've used certain typographic and layout styles throughout this book to signify distinct types of information. Look out for the following items.

Code Samples

Code in this book will be displayed using a fixed-width font, like so:

```
<h1>A Perfect Summer's Day</h1>
<p>It was a lovely day for a walk in the park. The birds
were singing and the kids were all back at school.</p>
```

If the code is to be found in the book's code archive, the name of the file will appear at the top of the program listing:

```
example.css
.footer {
  background-color: #CCC;
  border-top: 1px solid #333;
}
```

If only part of the file is displayed, this is indicated by the word *excerpt*:

```
example.css (excerpt)
  border-top: 1px solid #333;
```

If additional code is to be inserted into an existing example, the new code will be displayed in bold:

```
function animate() {
  new_variable = "Hello";
}
```

Where existing code is required for context, rather than repeat all of it, a ⋮ will be displayed:

```
function animate() {
  ⋮
  return new_variable;
}
```

Some lines of code are intended to be entered on one line, but we've had to wrap them because of page constraints. A ➥ indicates a line break that exists for formatting purposes only, and should be ignored.

```
URL.open("http://www.sitepoint.com/responsive-web-design-real-user-
➥testing/?responsive1");
```

Tips, Notes, and Warnings

 Hey, You!

Tips will give you helpful little pointers.

Ahem, Excuse Me ...

Notes are useful asides that are related, but not critical, to the topic at hand. Think of them as extra tidbits of information.

Make Sure You Always ...

... pay attention to these important points.

Watch Out!

Warnings will highlight any gotchas that are likely to trip you up along the way.

Supplementary Materials

http://www.learnable.com/books/jsninja1/
> The book's website, which contains links, updates, resources, and more.

https://github.com/spbooks/jsninja1/
> The downloadable code archive for this book.

http://community.sitepoint.com/category/javascript
> SitePoint's forums, for help on any tricky web problems.

books@sitepoint.com
> Our email address, should you need to contact us for support, to report a problem, or for any other reason.

Want to Take Your Learning Further?

Thanks for buying this book—we appreciate your support. Do you want to continue learning? You can now gain unlimited access to courses and ALL SitePoint books at Learnable for one low price. Enroll now and start learning today! Join Learnable and you'll stay ahead of the newest technology trends: http://www.learnable.com.

Hello JavaScript

Now it's time to start learning JavaScript. In this chapter, we're going to introduce the language, as well as set up a programming environment. We'll also write our first programs in JavaScript.

Here's what this chapter will cover:

- programming

- the history of JavaScript

- the tools that are needed to program in JavaScript

- Hello, World!—your first JavaScript program

- JavaScript in the console

- JavaScript in the web browser

- another more complicated JavaScript program

Programming

Programming is about making computers do what you want. A computer program is basically a series of instructions that tell your computer how to perform a task. Unfortunately, though, computers don't speak the same language as us—they only use 1s and 0s. The first computers were programmed using punched cards, with a hole representing a 1 and no hole representing 0. Machine code and assembly language are low-level programming languages that are closely associated with a computer's hardware. These can be difficult in which to program because they involve writing very abstract code that is heavily tied to a computer's architecture.

Alternatively, high-level programming languages allow abstractions such as functions and logical statements to be used, making code easier for humans to read and write. Programs are written in a language such as C, C++ or Java, which is then compiled into machine code and executed. These programs are usually very fast and are often used to write games and professional business software where speed is important.

Interpreted high-level languages that are translated into machine code at run time are often referred to as **scripting languages**. They typically run slower than compiled languages, although interpreters are becoming more and more sophisticated, increasingly blurring the line between compiled and interpreted languages.

JavaScript

The language we'll be learning in this book is **JavaScript**, often referred to as the language of the Web. Nearly all web browsers can run JavaScript, making it one of the most popular programming languages in the world. It has a low barrier to entry—all you need to program in JavaScript is a text editor and a web browser. Although it is easy to get started, JavaScript can be a tricky language to grasp as it has some unique features and interesting quirks. Once you have mastered it, though, you'll find it is a very flexible and expressive language that can create some powerful applications.

JavaScript is a high-level language that is compiled at run time. This means that it requires an engine that is responsible for interpreting programs and running them. The most common JavaScript engines are found in browsers such as Firefox, Chrome, or Internet Explorer, although JavaScript can be run without a browser. Many modern JavaScript engines use a Just-in-time (JIT) interpreting process, which considerably speeds up the compilation process, making the programs run faster.

JavaScript is also a dynamic language, which means that elements of a program can change while it is running.

The History of JavaScript

The World Wide Web was originally a bunch of pages linked together by hyperlinks. Soon people wanted more interaction and so Netscape (an early browser vendor) asked Brendan Eich to develop a new language for their Navigator browser. This needed to be done quickly because of the intense competition between Netscape and Microsoft to be first to market, and Eich managed to create a prototype language in just ten days. In order to do this, he borrowed various elements from other languages, including AWK, Java, Perl, Scheme, HyperTalk, and Self. The new language was originally called LiveScript, but was hastily rebranded as JavaScript so that it could benefit from the publicity that the Sun Microsystem's Java language was attracting at the time. This name has often caused some unfortunate confusion, with JavaScript often thought of as a lighter version of Java; the two languages are unrelated, although JavaScript does share some syntax with Java.

JavaScript made its debut in version 2 of Netscape's Navigator browser in 1995. The following year, Microsoft reverse-engineered JavaScript to create their own version, called JScript to avoid copyright issues with Sun Microsystems who owned the Java trademark and had licensed it to Netscape. JScript shipped with version 3 of the Internet Explorer browser and was almost identical to JavaScript—it even included all the same bugs and quirks—but did have some extra Internet Explorer-only features. Microsoft included another scripting language called VBScript with Internet Explorere at the same time, although this never really caught on.

JavaScript (and JScript) was immediately popular. It had a low barrier to entry and was relatively easy to learn, which meant an explosion in its usage making web pages dynamic and more interactive. Unfortunately, its low barrier was also a curse as it meant that people could write snippets of code without much understanding of what they were actually doing. Code could be easily copied and pasted and was often used incorrectly, leading to lots of poor code examples appearing all over the Web. JavaScript was also frequently used to create annoying pop-up adverts and for **browser sniffing** (the process of detecting which browser was being used to view a web page), and it started to gain a negative reputation.

Netscape and Sun Microsystems decided to standardize the language along with the help of the European Computer Manufacturers Association, who would host the standard. This standardized language was called ECMAScript, again, to avoid infringing on Sun's Java trademark. This caused even more confusion, but eventually ECMAScript was used to refer to the specification, and JavaScript was (and still is) used to refer to the language itself.

The ECMAScript standard can be difficult to interpret in places, so the implementations of JavaScript can vary in assorted JavaScript engines. This is why some web browsers behave differently when running JavaScript programs.

The Browser Wars

By the time Netscape Navigator 4 and Internet Explorer 4 were released, JavaScript had become incredibly popular. Microsoft had started a lot of hype about the term Dynamic HTML, or DHTML for short, to refer to the use of JavaScript to make HTML more interactive and dynamic. In an attempt to seize upon this popularity, Netscape and Microsoft tried to add new proprietary features, which lead to different syntaxes being used. This "arms race" of adding new features to compete became known as the Browser Wars. The unfortunate downside was that programmers had to write two versions of code to achieve the same results in each browser. Professional programmers often dismissed JavaScript as a toy language unsuitable for any serious programming, but this was unfair criticism—the language wasn't the problem, it was the way it was being implemented and used.

Eventually, Microsoft won the browser wars and Internet Explorer emerged as the dominant browser. Support for standards had also increased, helped largely by the efforts of the Web Standards Project (WaSP). Developer and browser vendors started to work together and embrace the standards laid out by the World Wide Web Consortium (W3C) and ECMA.

The open source web browser Firefox debuted in 2002 and Apple launched the Safari browser in 2003. These both had strong standards support, which meant that developers were able to produce better web applications using JavaScript that behaved consistently across different browsers.

Web 2.0

In 2005, sites such as Google Maps, Flickr, and Gmail started to appear and success-fully demonstrated that JavaScript was capable of creating rich internet applications that looked and behaved like native desktop applications. At around the same time, the term **Ajax**, short for Asynchronous JavaScript And XML, was coined by Jesse James Garrett. This described a technique of obtaining data from a server in the background and updating only the relevant parts of the web page without the need for a full page reload, enabling the user to still interact with the rest of the page. This created a more seamless experience for users where it was used extensively in many Web 2.0 applications. As a result a lot of professional programmers took more notice of JavaScript and it began to be seen as a powerful and flexible program-ming language, capable of producing high-quality code.

Standards

As JavaScript became used for more sophisticated applications and browsers em-braced standards, the JavaScript landscape changed. A new browser war started, but this time it was about seeing which browser could be the most standards-com-pliant. There has also been competition to increase the speed of the JavaScript engine that is built into the different browsers. This started in 2008 when engineers at Google developed the V8 engine to run inside the Chrome browser. It was signific-antly faster than previous JavaScript engines and signalled another arms race as other browser vendors responded by increasing the speed of their engines. JavaScript now runs significantly faster in modern browsers and the pace of improvement shows no sign of slowing down.

HTML5

HTML5 is the latest HTML specification, although it is actually more of an umbrella term for all the latest technologies that are used on the Web. This includes HTML, CSS3 modules, and lots of APIs that use JavaScript to interact with web pages. These will be covered in more detail in Chapter 10.

HTML5 has proven to be very popular and is emerging as a dominant standard for web development. JavaScript is a key feature in how some of its more interesting aspects work.

Node.js

In 2009, Ryan Dahl developed Node.js, which allows server-side applications to be written in JavaScript. It is based on the Google's V8 engine and implements non-blocking input and outputs in an event-driven environment. This allows the creation of fast and powerful real-time web applications written exclusively in JavaScript. It has also lead to many applications and JavaScript libraries that don't use the browser at all. Node JS has proven to be exceptionally popular and its usage continues to grow. This has increased the interest in and use of JavaScript as it starts to appear in many environments.

The popularity of Node,js has lead to an interesting development known as **Iso-morphic JavaScript**. This involves having the same JavaScript code that can be run either on the client- or server-side: if a browser is unable to run the code, it can be run on the server and downloaded, or if the server is unavailable, the code can be run on the client.

The Future of JavaScript

These are exciting times for JavaScript as it is being used for more and more applications beyond simply making web pages interactive. A big growth area at the moment is **Single Page Applications**. These applications run in the browser and rely heavily on JavaScript. HTML5 games that use JavaScript extensively are also becoming increasingly popular, especially as the graphical ability of browsers continues to improve.

JavaScript and HTML5 technologies can be used to develop browser extensions, Windows 8 desktop widgets, and Firefox OS and Chrome OS applications. Many non web-related applications also use JavaScript as their scripting language. It can be used to add interactivity to PDF documents, create HTML templates (Mustache), interact with a database (MongoDB), and even control robots (Cylon.js)!

It certainly seems like JavaScript has a bright future. As the web platform continues to evolve and mature and its usage grows beyond the browser, JavaScript is sure to remain a central part of future developments.

A Ninja Programming Environment

A ninja needs very little to program JavaScript. All one needs is a text editor and a web browser such as Firefox, Opera, Internet Explorer, Safari, or Chrome.

JavaScript Version

We'll be using version 5 of ECMAScript in this book and assume that you are using a modern browser (try to update to the latest version of whichever is your favorite). You can't always rely on users to have the latest version, though, so we'll also try to point out when some of the code will fail to work in older browsers.

Text Editors

If you are using Windows, Notepad will work just fine. If you find it a bit too basic, you might want to try Notepad++[1], E Text Editor[2], UltraEdit[3], or Sublime Text[4].

If you are using a Mac, options include the built-in TextEdit, Text Wrangler[5], TextMate[6], or Atom text editor[7]. You could also use Sublime Text[8].

If you are using Linux, you'll be fine with the built-in text editor (such as Gedit, Genie, Kate, Vim, or Emacs), or you could also use E Text Editor[9] or Sublime Text[10].

You can also consider an Integrated Development Environment (IDE) such as Eclipse[11], Coda[12], NetBeans[13], or the online Cloud 9[14].

---

[1] http://notepad-plus-plus.org/
[2] https://github.com/etexteditor/e
[3] http://www.ultraedit.com/
[4] http://www.sublimetext.com/
[5] http://www.barebones.com/products/textwrangler/
[6] http://macromates.com/
[7] https://atom.io/
[8] http://www.sublimetext.com/
[9] https://github.com/etexteditor/e
[10] http://www.sublimetext.com/
[11] http://www.eclipse.org/webtools/jsdt/
[12] https://panic.com/coda/
[13] https://netbeans.org/
[14] https://c9.io/

Another interesting option is Brackets[15], which is free, cross-platform, and even written in JavaScript!

Browser Console

Nearly every browser can run JavaScript and most modern browsers now include a JavaScript console that can be used to run snippets of JavaScript code. Here are some instructions on how to launch a JavaScript console in some of the more popular browsers:

Chrome

View > Developer > JavaScript Console, or press **Command + Option + J** (Mac) or **Control + Shift + J** (Windows/Linux)

Safari

Press **Command + Option + I**

Internet Explorer

Press **F12** to open the developer tools. Click the **Console** tab.

FireFox

Press **CTRL + SHIFT + K** to open the web console (on Windows) or **COMMAND + SHIFT + K** (on Macs).

Alternatives

You could install the Firebug add-on[16], press **F12** to open Firebug, and click on the **Console** tab.

Another option is to use the excellent JS Console[17] website. This allows you to enter JavaScript commands directly into the browser and see the results. I have used this console to run most of the code snippets in this book.

---

[15] http://brackets.io/

[16] https://getfirebug.com/

[17] http://jsconsole.com/

Your First JavaScript Program

That's enough talk about JavaScript—it's time to write your first program!

It is a tradition when learning programming languages to start with a "Hello world!" program. This is a simple program that outputs the phrase "Hello world!" to announce your arrival to the world of programming. We're going to stick to this tradition and write a "Hello world" program in JavaScript.

Go to JS Console in your browser and enter the following line of code:

```
console.log("Hello World!");
```

If all went to plan you should see a line in your console saying "Hello World!", similar to the screenshot in Figure 1.1.

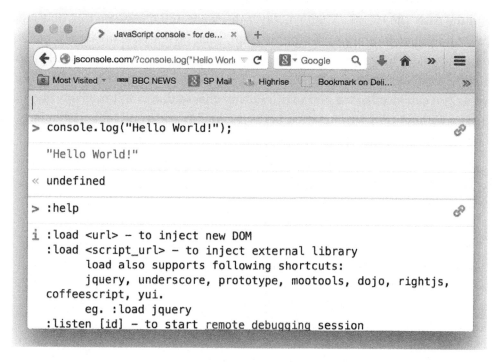

Figure 1.1. "Hello, world!"

The program is a single statement that instructs the console to log the statement "Hello World!" to the console.

Congratulations, you've just written your first JavaScript program. It might not look like much, but remember that every ninja's journey begins with a single step!

JavaScript in the Browser

JavaScript is an interpreted language and needs a host environment to run. Because of its origins, the main environment that JavaScript runs in is the browser, although it can be run in other environments; for example, Node.js can be used to run JavaScript on a server. By far the most common use of JavaScript is still to make web pages interactive. This means we should have a look at what makes a web page.

Three Layers of the Web

Nearly all web pages are made up of three key ingredients—HTML, CSS, and JavaScript. HTML is for the content, CSS is the presentation layer, and JavaScript adds the interactivity. You can think of this as being a bit like a pizza. You start with the base, the HTML. Then you layer the sauce and cheese on top, that's the CSS. And last of all you put the toppings on. Each layer exists separately, but adds something extra to the pizza. In the same way that you can have a perfectly good pizza without any toppings, it isn't essential to have JavaScript on a website. And just as you can also have a pizza without any cheese that won't taste any good, a website without CSS will function perfectly well, but it won't look particularly good.

 Keeping the Layers Separate

It is now widely considered best practice to keep all of these layers separate and separate the concerns of each layer, so each layer is only responsible for one thing. Putting them altogether can lead to very complicated pages where all of the code is mixed up together in one file, causing "tag soup" or "code spaghetti". This used to be the standard way of producing a website and there are still plenty of examples around on the web that do this.

Each layer builds on the last. A web page should be able to function with just the HTML layer—in fact, many websites celebrate "naked day[18]" when they remove the CSS layer from their site. A website using just the HTML layer will be in its purest form and look very old school, but should still be fully functional.

---

[18] http://naked.threepixeldrift.com/

Unobtrusive JavaScript

When JavaScript was initially used, it was designed to be inserted directly into the HTML code as can be seen in this example:

```
<a id="button" href="#" onclick="alert('Hello World')">Click Me</a>
```

This made it difficult to see what was happening as the JavaScript code was mixed up with the HTML. It also meant that the code was tightly coupled to the HTML, so any changes in the HTML required that the JavaScript code would also need changing to stop it breaking.

It's possible to keep the JavaScript code on its own away from the HTML by placing it inside its own `<script>` tags, like so:

```
<script>
  button = document.getElementById('button')
  button.addEventListener("click", function() {
    console.log("Hello World!");
    };
</script>
```

Unobtrusive JavaScript is when the JavaScript code is kept completely separate from the HTML and CSS, preferably in its own file. This can be linked to using the same `script` tag and the `src` attribute to specify the file to link to:

```
<script src="js/scripts.js"></script>
```

The JavaScript code would then be placed in a file called **scripts.js**.

Avoid Using Self-closing Tags

If you've used XML or XHTML, you might have come across self-closing tags such as this script tag:

```
<script src="js/scripts.js" />
```

These will fail to work in HTML5, so should be avoided.

> You may see some legacy code that uses the language attribute:
>
> ```
> <script src="js/scripts.js" language="javascript"></script>
> ```
>
> This is unnecessary in HTML5, but it will still work.

In a similar way, the CSS should also be kept in a separate file, so the only code in a web page is the actual HTML. This is considered best practice and is the approach we'll be using in the book.

Graceful Degradation and Progressive Enhancement

Graceful degradation is the process of building a website so that it works best in a modern browser that uses JavaScript, but still works to a reasonable standard in older browsers or if JavaScript or some of its features are unavailable. An example of this are programs that are broadcast in high definition (HD)—they work best on HD televisions but still work on a standard TV; it's just that the picture quality will be of lesser quality. The programs will even still work on a black-and-white television.

Progressive enhancement is the process of building a web page from the ground up with a base level of functionality and then adding extra enhancements if they are available in the browser. This should feel natural if you follow the principle of three layers, with the JavaScript layer enhancing the web page rather than being an essential element that the page cannot exist without. An example might be the phone companies who offer a basic level of phone calls, but provide extra services such as call-waiting and caller ID if your telephone supports it.

Whenever you add JavaScript to a web page, you should always think about the approach you want to take. Do you want to start with lots of amazing effects that push the boundaries and then make sure the experience degrades gracefully for those people who might not have the latest and greatest browsers? Or do you want to start off building a functional website that works across most browsers and then enhance the experience using JavaScript? The two approaches are similar, but subtly different. This blog post[19] might help you to decide which approach to take.

---

[19] http://www.sitepoint.com/progressive-enhancement-graceful-degradation-choice/

Your Second JavaScript Program

We're going to finish the chapter with a second JavaScript program. This example is much more complicated than the previous one and includes a lot of concepts that will be covered in later chapters in more depth, so don't worry if you fail to understand them at this stage! The idea is to show you what JavaScript is capable of doing and introduce some of the important concepts that will be covered in the upcoming chapters.

We'll follow the practice of unobtrusive JavaScript mentioned earlier and keep our JavaScript code in a separate file. Start by creating a folder called **rainbow**. Inside that folder create a file called **rainbow.htm** and another folder called **js** that contains a file inside it called **scripts.js**.

Let's start with the HTML. Open up **rainbow.htm** and enter the following code:

rainbow.htm

```
<head>
  <meta charset="utf-8">
  <title>I Can Click A Rainbow</title>
</head>
<body>
  <button id="button">click me</button>
<script src="js/scripts.js"></script>
</body>
</html>
```

This file is a fairly standard HTML5 page that contains a button with an ID of `button`. The ID attribute is very useful for JavaScript to use as a hook to access different elements of the page. At the bottom is a `script` tag that links to our JavaScript file inside the **js** folder.

Now for the JavaScript. Open up **scripts.js** and enter the following code:

js/scripts.js

```
var button = document.getElementById("button");

var rainbow = ["red","orange","yellow","green","blue","indigo",
➡"violet"];
```

```
function change() {
    document.body.style.background = rainbow[Math.floor(7*Math.
➥random())];
}
button.addEventListener("click", change);
```

Our first task in the JavaScript code is create a variable called button (we cover variables in Chapter 2).

We then use the document.getElementById function to find the HTML element with the ID of button (covered in Chapter 6). This is then assigned to the button variable.

We now create another variable called rainbow. This is assigned to an array containing a list of strings of different colors (we cover strings and variables in Chapter 2 and arrays in Chapter 3).

Then we create a function called change (we cover functions in Chapter 4). This sets the background color of the body element to one of the colors of the rainbow (changing the style of a page will be covered in Chapter 6). This involves selecting a random number using the built-in Math object (covered in Chapter 5) and selecting the corresponding color from the rainbow array.

Last of all, we create an *event handler*, which checks for when the button is clicked on. When this happens it calls the change function that we just defined (event handlers are covered in Chapter 7).

Open **rainbow.htm** in your favourite browser and try clicking on the button a few times. If everything is working correctly the background should change to every color of the rainbow, such as in the screenshot in Figure 1.2.

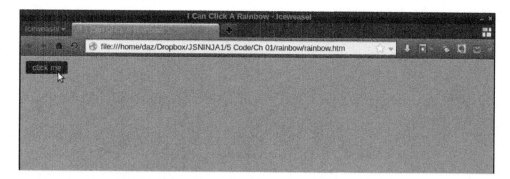

Figure 1.2. I can click a rainbow

The Project: Quiz Ninja

Throughout this book we will be building an example application called "Quiz Ninja". This is a quiz application where the aim is for the player to answer questions the real names of super heroes. The quiz application will run in the browswer and use many of the concepts covered in the book. At the end of each chapter we will use the skills we have covered in that chapter to develop the appliation further.

The application will adhere to the good solid principles of three separate web layers and unobtrusive JavaScript. This means that we need to keep the HTML, CSS, and JavaScript in separate files, so let's create those files now.

Create a folder called **quiz_ninja** and inside create the following files and folders:

- **index.htm**

- **js/scripts.js**

- **css/styles.css**

Add the following code to **index.htm**:

```
                                                            index.htm
<!doctype html>
<html lang="en">
<head>
  <meta charset="utf-8">
  <meta name="description" content="A quiz game for ninjas">
  <meta name="author" content="DAZ">
```

```
  <title>Quiz Ninja</title>
  <link rel="stylesheet" href="css/styles.css">
</head>
<body>
  <header>
    <h1>Quiz Ninja!</h1>
  </header>
<script src="js/scripts.js"></script>
</body>
</html>
```

This is a standard HTML5 layout with a simple heading at the top of the page. We'll add more to the page as the application develops in later chapters.

Now it's time to style the page. Add the following code to the **styles.css** file in the **css** folder:

```
                                                    css/styles.css

*{
  margin: 0;
  padding: 0;
}

header {
  font: bold 36px/120% Arial, Helvetica, sans-serif;
  background: #333;
  color: #c00;
  text-transform: uppercase;
}
```

This resets all the margins and padding to zero and styles the heading in ninja-like red and black colors.

And finally we'll add some interactivity using JavaScript. Place the following code inside the **scripts.js** file in the **js** folder:

js/scripts.js

```
// welcome the user
alert("Welcome to Quiz Ninja!");
```

The first line uses the `alert` function that displays a welcome message to the player in a dialog box in the browser. `alert` isn't actually part of the official ECMAScript specification, but is used by all browsers as a way of showing messages.

To give this a try, open the **index.htm** file in your favorite browser. You should be greeted by the welcome message alert box, such as in the screenshot shown in Figure 1.3.

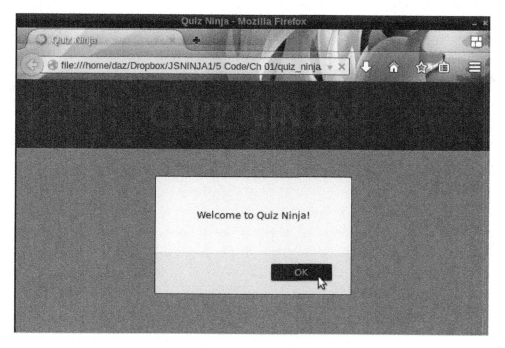

Figure 1.3. Quiz Ninja!

This gives us a good solid start to our project that we can build on over the course of the book as our JavaScript knowledge develops.

Chapter Summary

- JavaScript was created in 1995 by Netscape.

- It became popular very quickly and is now considered the language of the Web.

- The browser wars caused many problems for JavaScript and resulted in lots of fragmented and code that was hard to maintain.

- The advent of Ajax and its use in web apps such as Gmail and Google Maps prompted a resurgence in JavaScript.

- JavaScript's main environment is the browser, but it doesn't have to be used there.

- You only need a text editor and a browser (or other host environment with a JavaScript interpreter) to write JavaScript.

- Graceful degradation and progressive enhancement are the process of ensuring that users receive a decent experience even if they lack some of the requirements.

- Unobtrusive JavaScript is when the JavaScript functionality is separated from the HTML content and CSS styling.

In the next chapter we're going to start looking at some programming fundamentals—let's get to it, ninja!

Programming Basics

In the last chapter, we introduced JavaScript and set up a programming environment where we got our hands dirty with a few JavaScript programs. In this chapter, we're going to delve further to learn how JavaScript works, and start writing some programs.

We'll cover the following topics:

▪ the importance of well-commented code

▪ JavaScript grammar—expressions, statements, semicolons, and whitespace

▪ primitive data types

▪ strings—string literals and string methods such as length

▪ variables—declaring and assigning

▪ numbers—decimal, hexadecimal, octal and exponent form, Infinity, and NaN

▪ arithmetic operations such as +, -, *, /, and %

- undefined and null

- Booleans—truthy and falsy values

- logical operators—AND, OR, and NOT

- our project—where we'll set some question and answer variables and use alert boxes to display them

Comments

Our first task on our journey to becoming a JavaScript ninja is learning how to write comments in JavaScript. This may seem a strange place to start, because in programming a **comment** is a piece of code that is ignored by the language—it doesn't do anything. Despite this, comments are extremely important: well-commented code is the hallmark of a ninja programmer. It makes it easier for anybody reading your code to understand what's going on, and that includes you! Believe me, you'll be thankful you commented your code when you come back to read it after a few weeks. You only need to write enough so that it's clear what the code is supposed to do.

In JavaScript there are two types of comment.

Single line comments start with // and finish at the end of the line:

```
// this is a short comment
```

Multiline comments start with /* and finish with */:

```
/* This is a longer comment
anything here will be ignored
This is a useful place to put notes
*/
```

It's good practice to write comments in your code. There are even utilities that can take your comments and produce documentation from them such as JSDoc Toolkit[1], Docco[2], and YUIDoc[3]. You'll see lots of comments throughout the code in this book.

---

[1] http://code.google.com/p/jsdoc-toolkit/
[2] http://jashkenas.github.io/docco/
[3] http://yui.github.io/yuidoc/

JavaScript Grammar

The syntax used by JavaScript is known as a C-style syntax, which is similar to the one used by Java.

A JavaScript program is made up of a series of **statements**. Each statement ends with a new line or semicolon.

Here is an example of two statements, one on each line:

```
a = "Hello World!"
alert(a)
```

This example could also be written as follows, using semicolons at the end of each statement:

```
a = "Hello World!";alert(a);
```

There's no need to actually use a semicolon to terminate a statement because JavaScript interpreters use a process called **Automatic Semicolon Insertion (ASI)**. This will attempt to place semicolons at the end of lines for you; however, it can be error-prone and cause a number of automated services such as code minifiers and validators to not work properly.

For this reason, it's considered best practice to combine the two and write each statement on a new line, terminated by a semi-colon, like so:

```
a = "Hello World!";
alert(a);
```

A **block** is a series of statements that are collected together inside curly braces:

```
{
  // this is a block containing 2 statements
  var a = "Hello!";
  alert(a);
}
```

Blocks do not need to be terminated by a semicolon.

Whitespace (such as spaces, tabs, and new lines) is used to separate the different values in each statement You can use as much whitespace as required to format your code so that it is neat and easy to read. Examples of this include using spaces to indent nested code and multiple lines to separate blocks of code.

Data Types

JavaScript has six different types of value. There are five primitive **data types**:

- string

- number

- Boolean

- undefined

- null

Any value that isn't one of the primitive data types listed is an **object** (these are covered in Chapter 5). We'll discuss each primitive value over the next few pages.

JavaScript has a special **operator** called `typeof` for finding out the type of a value.

Here are some examples of the different value types:

```
typeof "hello"
<< "string"

typeof 10
<< "number"

typeof true
<< "boolean"
```

```
typeof { ninja: "turtle" }
<< "object"
```

 Operators

An operator applies an operation to a value, which is known as the *operand*. A **unary operator** only requires one operand; for example:

```
typeof "hello"
```

The operator is `typeof` and the string `"hello"` is the operand.

A **binary operator** requires two operands; for instance:

```
3 + 5
```

The operator is + and the numbers **3** and **5** are the operands. There is also a **ternary operator** that requires three operands, which is covered in the next chapter.

Strings

A **string** is a collection of letters (or characters, to be more precise). We can create a string literal by writing a group of characters inside quote marks like this:

```
"hello"
```

 String Constructor Function

You can also create a string object using the following constructor function:

```
new String("hello")
```

This will create a new string that is the same as the string literal "`hello`", although it will be classed as an object rather than a primitive value. For this reason it is preferable to use the string literal notation ... not to mention it requires less typing to use literals!

We can also use single quote marks if we prefer:

```
'hello'
```

If you want to use double quote marks inside a string literal, you need to use single quote marks to enclose the string. And if you want to use an apostrophe in your string, you need to employ double quote marks to enclose the string:

```
"It's me"
```

Another option is to do what's called **escaping** the quotation mark. You place a backslash before the apostrophe so that it appears as an apostrophe inside the string instead of terminating the string:

```
'It\'s me'
```

 Escaping Characters

The backslash is used to escape special characters in strings such as:

- single quote marks \ '

- double quote marks \ "

- end of line \n

- carriage return \r

- tab \t

If you want to actually write a backslash, you need to escape it with another backslash:

```
"This is a backslash \\"
<< "This is a backslash \"
```

Variables

Variables are common in programming languages. They are a way of storing a value in memory for later use. In JavaScript, we start by declaring a variable. This is done using the keyword var:

```
var a; // declare a variable called a
<< undefined

var message;
<< undefined
```

Notice that the console outputs undefined. This is a special JavaScript primitive value that is covered later in the chapter, but it's basically saying that the variable has been created but is yet to be assigned a value.

You don't actually have to declare variables before using them, but as we'll see later, bad things can happen if you choose not to. So remember, a ninja will always declare variables.

You can even declare multiple variables at once:

```
var a,b,c; // 3 variables declared at once
<< undefined
```

Rules for Naming Variables

When naming variables, you should try to give them sensible names that describe what the variable represents; hence, answer is a better variable name than x.

A variable name can start with any upper or lower case letter, an underscore (_), or dollar symbol ($). It can also contain numbers but cannot start with them. Here are some examples:

```
$name
_answer
firstName
last_name
address_line1
```

Variable names are case sensitive, so ANSWER is different to Answer and answer.

When using multiple words for variable names there are two conventions that can be used. Camel case starts with a lowercase letter and then each new word is capitalized:

```
firstNameAndLastName
```

Underscore separates each new word with an underscore:

```
first_name_and_last_name
```

JavaScript's built-in functions use the camel-case notation, but you can choose to use one or the other or a combination of the two when naming variables. What's important for a ninja is to *be consistent*.

Reserved Words

The following words are *reserved* for use by the language and cannot be used to name variables (or the function parameters and object properties that appear in later chapters):

```
abstract, boolean, break, byte, case, catch, char, class, const,
continue, debugger, default, delete, do, double, else, enum,
export, extends, false, final, finally, float, for, function,
goto, if, implements, import, in instanceof, int, inteface,
long, native, new, null, package, private, protected, public,
return, short, static, super, switch, synchronized, this, throw,
throws, transient, true, try, typeof, var, volatile, void, while,
with
```

These words are reserved because many of them are used by the language itself, and you will come across them later in this book.

Many are not used by the language, however; one can only assume they were planned to be used at some point, but never were. There are also a few words *not* reserved that should have been as they are an important part of the language:

```
undefined, NaN, Infinity
```

These are covered later in this chapter. You should also avoid using these words for variable names.

Assignment

To assign a value to a variable, we use the = operator. This example shows how we would set the variable name to point to the string literal "Walter":

```
var name; // declare the variable first
<< undefined

name = "Walter"; // assign the variable to a string
<< "Walter"
```

Once the variable has been assigned a value, it is displayed in the console output.

To see the value of a variable, simply enter it in the console. The variable name now refers to the string "Walter", so it will behave exactly the same as that string:

```
name;
<< "Walter"

typeof name;
<< "string"
```

This is a useful way of dealing with long strings as it saves us from typing them over and over again. It's also useful if the value stored in the variable is likely to change (hence the name, variable).

You can declare and initialize a variable at the same time:

```
var name = "Jesse";
<< "Jesse"
```

You can also declare and assign values to multiple variables in a single statement:

```
var x = 2, y, z = "Hi!"; // y has only been declared, it's undefined
<< undefined
```

String Properties and Methods

Primitive values and objects have properties and methods. Properties are information about the object or value, while methods perform an action on the object or value—either to change it or to tell us something about it.

Object Wrappers

Technically, only objects have properties and methods. JavaScript overcomes this by creating *wrapper objects* for primitive values. This all happens in the background, so for all intents and purposes it appears that primitive values also have properties and methods.

We can access the properties of a string using dot notation. This involves writing a dot followed by the property we are interested in. For example, every string has a `length` property that tells us how many characters are in the string:

```
name = "Heisenberg"; // declare and assign a variable
<< "Heisenberg"

name.length; // call the length method on name
<< 10
```

As you can see, this tells us that there are ten characters in the string stored in the `name` variable.

Bracket Notation

Another notation you can use to access a primitive value's properties are square brackets:

```
name['length']; // note the property name is in quote marks
<< 10
```

All properties of primitive values are **immutable**, which means that they're unable to be changed. You can try, but your efforts will be futile:

```
name.length;
<< 10

name.length = 7; // try to change the length
<< 7
```

```
name.length; // check to see if it's changed
<< 10
```

A method is an action that a primitive value or object can perform. To call a method, we use the dot operator [.] followed by the name of the method, followed by parentheses (this is a useful way to distinguish between a property and a method—methods end with parentheses). For example, we can write a string in all capital letters using the toUpperCase() method:

```
name.toUpperCase();
<< "HEISENBERG"
```

Or the toLowerCase() method, which will write my name in all lower-case letters:

```
name.toLowerCase();
<< "heisenberg"
```

If you want to know which character is at a certain position, you can use the charAt() method:

```
name.charAt(1);
<< "e"
```

This tells us that the character "e" is at position 1. If you were thinking that it should be "H", this is because the first letter is classed as being at position 0 (you'll find that counting usually starts at zero in programming!).

If you want to find where a certain character or substring appears in a string, we can use the indexOf() method:

```
name.indexOf("H");
<< 0
```

If a character doesn't appear in the string, -1 will be returned:

```
name.indexOf("a");
<< -1
```

If we want the last occurrence of a character or substring, we can use the `lastIndex-Of()` method:

```
name.lastIndexOf("e");
<< 7
```

The `concat()` method can be used to concatenate two or more strings together:

```
"JavaScript".concat("Ninja");
<< "JavaScriptNinja"

"Hello".concat(" ","World","!");
<< "Hello World!"
```

A shortcut for string concatenation is to use the + symbol to add the two strings together:

```
"Java" + "Script" + " " + "Ninja";
<< "JavaScript Ninja"
```

The `trim()` method will remove any whitespace from the beginning and end of a string:

```
"    Hello World    ".trim();
➥// the space in the middle will be preserved
<< "Hello World"

"   \t\t JavaScript Ninja! \r".trim();
➥// escaped tabs and carriage returns are also removed
<< "JavaScript Ninja!"
```

 Support for `trim()`

The `trim()` method was a relatively recent addition to the collection of string methods so is not supported in older browsers.

Numbers

Number can be *integers* (whole numbers, such as 3) or *floating point decimals* (often referred to as just "decimals" or "floats", such as 3.14159). For example:

```
typeof 3;
<< "number"

typeof 3.14159;
<< "number"
```

As you can see in the examples above, JavaScript doesn't distinguish between integers and floating point decimals—they are both given the type of "number", which is a different approach to most other programming languages. This is set out in the ECMAScript specification, although most JavaScript engines will treat integers and floats differently in the background in order to improve efficiency.

 Number Constructor Function

Just like strings, numbers also have a constructor function:

```
new Number(3)
```

This is much more verbose than simply writing the number **3**, which is known as a **number literal**, so it is recommended that you stick to using number literals.

Octal and Hexadecimal Numbers

If a number starts with a 0x, it is considered to be in hexadecimal (base 16) notation:

```
0xAF; // A represents 10, F represents 15
<< 175
```

Hexadecimal or "hex" numbers are often used for color codes on the Web. You can read more about them on Wikipedia[4].

If a number starts with a zero, it is *usually* considered to be in octal (base 8) notation:

---

[4] http://en.wikipedia.org/wiki/Hexadecimal

```
047; // 4 eights and 7 units
<< 39
```

Octal numbers are not actually part of the ECMAScript standard, but many JavaScript engines implement this convention.

Exponential Notation

Numbers can also be represented in exponential notation, which is shorthand for "multiply by 10 to the power of" (you may have heard this referred to as "scientific notation" or "standard form"). Here are some examples:

```
1e6; // means 1 multiplied by 10 to the power 6 (a million)
<< 1000000

2E3; // can also be written as 2E3, 2E+3 and 2e+3
<< 2000
```

Fractional values can be created by using a negative index value:

```
2.5e-3; // means 2.5 multiplied by 10 to the power -3 (0.001)
<< 0.0025
```

Number Methods

Numbers also have some built-in methods, although you need to be careful when using the dot notation with number literals that are integers because the dot can be confused for a decimal point. There are a few ways to deal with this, which we'll demonstrate with the `toExponential()` method; this returns the number as a string in exponential notation.

Use two dots:

```
5..toExponential(); >> "5e+0"
```

Put a space before the dot:

```
5 .toExponential(); >> "5e+0"
```

Always write integers as a decimal:

```
5.0.toExponential(); >> "5e+0"
```

Place the integer in parentheses:

```
(5).toExponential(); >> "5e+0"
```

Assign the number to a variable:

```
var number = 5;
>> 5

number.toExponential();
>> "5e+0"
```

The toFixed() method rounds a number to a fixed number of decimal places:

```
var pi = 3.1415926;
<< undefined

pi.toFixed(3); // only one dot needed when using variables
<< "3.142"
```

Note that the value is returned as a string.

The toPrecision() method rounds a number to a fixed number of significant figures that is once again returned as a string (and often using exponential notation):

```
325678..toPrecision(2);
<< "3.3e+5"

2.459.toPrecision(2);
<< "2.5"
```

Arithmetic Operations

All the usual arithmetic operations can be carried out in JavaScript.

Addition:

```
5 + 4.3;
<< 9.3
```

Subtraction:

```
6 - 11;
>> -5
```

Multiplication:

```
6 * 7;
<< 42
```

Division:

```
3/7;
<<0.42857142857142855
```

You can also calculate the remainder of a division using the % operator:

```
23%6; // the same as asking 'what is the remainder
➥when 13 is divided by 6'
<< 5
```

This is similar to, but not quite the same as, modulo arithmetic. That's because the result always has the same sign as the first number:

```
-4%3; // -4 modulo 3 would be 2
<< -1
```

Changing Variables

If a variable has been assigned a numerical value, it can be increased using the following operation:

```
points = 0; // initialize points score to zero
<< 0

points = points + 10;
<< 10
```

This will increase the value held in the points variable by 10. You can also use the compound assignment operator, +=, which is a shortcut for performing the same task, but helps you avoid writing the variable name twice:

```
points += 10;
<< 20
```

There are equivalent compound assignment operators for all the operators in the previous section:

```
points -= 5; // decreases points by 5
<< 15

points *= 2; // doubles points
<< 30

points /= 3; // divides value of points by 3
<< 10

points %= 7; // changes the value of points to the remainder
➥if its current value is divided by 7
<< 3
```

Incrementing Values

If you only want to increment a value by 1, you can use the ++ operator. This goes either directly before or after the variable.

So what's the difference between putting the ++ operator before or after the variable? The main difference is the value that is returned by the operation. Both operations increase the value of the points variable by 1, but points++ will return the original value *then* increase it by 1, whereas ++points will increase the value by 1, then return the new value:

```
points++; // will return 3, then increase points to 4
<< 3

++points; // will increase points to 5, then return it
<< 5
```

There is also a -- operator that works in the same way:

```
points--;
<< 5

--points;
<< 3
```

Infinity

Infinity is a special error value in JavaScript that is used to represent any number that is too big for JavaScript to deal with. The biggest number that JavaScript can handle is 1.7976931348623157e+308:

```
1e308; // 1 with 308 zeroes!
<< 1e308

2e308; // too big!
<< Infinity
```

There is also a value -Infinity, which is used for negative numbers that go below -1.7976931348623157e+308:

```
-1e309;
<< -Infinity
```

The value of Infinity can also be obtained by dividing by zero:

```
1/0;
<< Infinity
```

The smallest number that JavaScript can deal with is 5e-324. Anything below this evaluates to either 5e-324 or zero:

```
5e-324;
<< 5e-324

3e-325;
<< 5e-324

2e-325;
<< 0
```

NaN

NaN is an error value that is short for "Not a Number". It is used when an operation is attempted and the result isn't numerical:

```
"hello" * 5;
<< NaN
```

The result returned by the `typeof` operator is rather ironic, however:

```
typeof Nan;
<< 'number'
```

Type Coercion

Type coercion is the process of converting the type of a value in the background to try and make an operation work. For example, if you try to multiply a string and a number together, JavaScript will attempt to coerce the string into a number:

```
"2" * 8;
<< 16
```

This may seem useful, but the process is not always logical or consistent, causing a lot of confusion. For example, if you try to *add* a string and a number together, JavaScript will convert the number to a string and then concatenate the two strings together:

```
"2" + 8;
<< "28"
```

This can make it difficult to spot type errors in your code, so you should always try to be very explicit about the types of values you are working with.

Converting Between Strings and Numbers

We can convert numbers to strings and vice versa using a variety of methods.

Converting Strings to Numbers

To covert a string into a number we can multiply a numerical string by 1, which will convert it into a number because of type coercion:

```
answer = "5" * 1;
<< 5

typeof answer;
<< "number"
```

Another neat way of converting a string to an integer is to simply place a + symbol in front of it:

```
answer = +"5";
<< 5

typeof answer;
<< "number"
```

Yet another way to convert a string into a number is to use the Number function:

```
Number("23");
<< 23
```

This is the preferred way to convert strings to numbers as it avoids type coercion in the background. The conversion is explicit, making it obvious what is being done.

Converting Numbers to Strings

To change numbers into strings you can add an empty string, which will use type coercion to silently convert the number into a string in the background:

```
3 +'';
<< "3"
```

The preferred way, however, is to use the String function:

```
String(3);
<< "3"
```

There is also the very similar toString() method, but this may change the base of the number. For example, if you want to write the number 10 in binary (base two), you could write:

```
> 10..toString(2):
<< "1010"
```

You can go up to base 36, although after base ten, letters are used to represent the digits:

```
> 1000000..toString(36) // a million in base 36
<< "1fls"
```

Parsing Numbers

There is also a useful function called parseInt() that can be used to convert a string representation of a numerical value back into an integer. You can specify the base of the number you are trying to convert, for example:

```
parseInt("1010",2); // converts from binary, back to decimal
<< 10

parseInt("omg",36);
<< 31912
```

```
parseInt("23",10);
<< 23
```

If a string starts with a number, the `parseInt` function will use this number and ignore any letters that come afterwards:

```
var address = "221B Baker Street"
<< undefined

parseInt(address, 10)
<< 221
```

If you try to do this with the `Number` function, it returns NaN:

```
Number(address)
<< NaN
```

And if you use `parseInt` with a decimal, it will remove anything after the decimal point:

```
parseInt("2.4",10)
<< 2
```

Be careful not to think that this is rounding the number to the nearest integer; it simply removes the part after the decimal point, as seen in this example:

```
parseInt("2.9",10)
<< 2
```

There is also a similar function called `parseFloat()` that converts strings into floating point decimal numbers:

```
parseFloat("2.9",10)
<< 2.9
```

Undefined

`undefined` is the value given to variables that have not been assigned a value. It can also occur if an object's property doesn't exist or a function has a missing parameter. It is basically JavaScript's way of saying "I can't find a value for this."

Null

`null` means "no value". It can be thought of as a placeholder that JavaScript uses to say "there should be an value here, but there isn't at the moment."

`undefined` and `null` are both "non-value" values. They are similar, although they behave slightly differently. For example, if you try to do sums with them:

```
10 + null // null behaves like zero
<< 10

10 + undefined // undefined is not a number
<< NaN
```

`null` is coerced to be 0, making the sum possible whereas `undefined` is coerced to NaN, making the sum impossible to perform.

Values tend to be set to `undefined` by JavaScript, whereas values are usually set to `null` manually by the programmer.

Booleans

There are only two Boolean values: `true` and `false`. They are named after George Boole, an English mathematician who worked in the field of algebraic logic. Boolean values are fundamental in the logical statements that make up a computer program. Every value in JavaScript has a Boolean value and most of them are `true` (these are known as 'truthy' values).

To find the Boolean value of something, you can use the `Boolean` function like so:

```
Boolean("hello");
<< true

Boolean(42);
<< true

Boolean(0);
<< false
```

Only seven values are always `false` and these are known as falsy values:

```
* "" // double quoted empty string
* '' // single quoted empty string
* 0
* NaN
* false
* null
* undefined
```

 Truthy and Falsy Values

The fact that empty strings and zero are considered falsy can cause confusion at times, especially since other programming languages don't behave similarly. A ninja needs to be especially careful when dealing with numbers that might be zero, or strings that are empty.

For more on truthy and falsy values, see this article on SitePoint.[5]

Logical Operators

A logical operator can be used with any primitive value or object. The results are based on whether the values are considered to be truthy or falsy.

! (Logical NOT)

Placing the ! operator in front of a value will convert it to a Boolean and return the opposite value. So truthy values will return `false`, and falsy values will return `true`. This is known as *negation*:

---

[5] http://www.sitepoint.com/javascript-truthy-falsy/

```
!true;
<< false

!0;
<< true
```

You can use double negation (!!) to find out if a value is truthy or falsy (it is a shortcut to using the `Boolean` function we employed earlier because you are effectively negating the negation):

```
!!'';
<< false

!!"hello";
<< true

!!3;
<< true

!!NaN;
<< false

!!"false";
<< true

!!'0';
<< true
```

&& (Logical AND)

Imagine that you are having a party and want to have some rules about who is allowed in. You might want to only allow people who are wearing glasses AND who are over 18 to be allowed in. This is an example of a logical AND condition: anybody coming to the party must satisfy *both* conditions before they are let in.

The logical AND operator works on two or more values (the operands) and only evaluates to `true` if *all* the operands are truthy. The value that is returned is the *last* truthy value if they are all true, or the *first* falsy value if at least one of them is false:

```
true && true;
<< true

3 && 0; // returns 0 because it is falsy
<< 0
```

|| (Logical OR)

Now imagine that you relax the rules for your party and allow people in if they wear glasses OR are over 18. This means that they only have to satisfy one of the rules to be allowed in—an example of a logical OR condition.

The logical OR operator also works on two or more operands, but evaluates to true if *any* of the operands are true, so it only evaluates to false if both operands are falsy. The value that is returned is the *first* truthy value if any of them are true, or the *last* falsy value if all of them are false:

```
true || false;
<< true

NaN || undefined;
➥// both NaN and undefined are falsy, so undefined will be returned
<< undefined
```

Lazy Evaluation

Remember the party example when the condition for entry was that attendees had to wear glasses *and* be over 18? If you saw somebody without glasses, would you bother asking them to prove that they were over 18? There'd be no point because by not wearing glasses, they wouldn't be allowed in anyway.

When the rules were relaxed, people were allowed in if they were wearing glasses *or* if over 18. If somebody arrived wearing glasses, there would be no need to check their age.

These are examples of **lazy evaluation**—you only check as many conditions as you have to for somebody to be allowed in. JavaScript performs a similar task and uses lazy evaluation when processing the logical AND and OR operators. This means that it stops evaluating any further operands once the result is clear.

For example, for a logical AND expression to be true, all the operands have to be true; if any of them are false, there is no point checking any subsequent operands as the result will still be false. Similarly, for a logical OR to be true, only one of the operands has to be true; hence, as soon as an operand is evaluated to true, the result is returned as true and any subsequent operands won't be checked as the result is of no consequence.

This is demonstrated in the examples below:

```
a = 0; // declare the variable a and assign the value of 0
<< 0

false && (a = 1); // (a = 1) is truthy, but it won't be evaluated,
➥ since the first operand is false
<< false

a; // the value of a is still 0
<< 0

false || (a = 1); // this will evaluate both operands, so a will be
➥ assigned the value of 1, which is returned
<< 1
```

Bitwise Operators

Bitwise operators work with operands that are 32-bit integers. These are numbers written in binary (base two) that have 32 digits made up of just 0s and 1s. Here are some examples:

```
5 is written as   00000000000000000000000000000101
100 is written as 00000000000000000000000001100100
15 is written as  00000000000000000000000000001111
```

JavaScript will convert any values used with bitwise operators into a 32-bit integer and then carry out the operation.

Bitwise NOT

The bitwise NOT operator [~] will convert the number to a 32-bit integer, then change all the 1s to 0 and all the 0s to 1s. For example, 2476 can be represented as:

```
0000000000000000001011010101100
```

Which will change to:

```
11111111111111110100101010011
```

This is 1073736019, but the result actually uses negative values, as you can see in the code:

```
~44;
<< -45
```

In most cases, this operator will return an integer that adds to the original operand to make -1.

Bitwise AND

You can also use the bitwise AND operator, [&], which will convert both numbers into binary and returns a number that in binary has a 1 in each position for which the corresponding bits of both operands are 1s. Here's an example:

```
12 & 10; // in binary this is 1100 & 1010, so only the first digit
➡is 1 in both cases
<< 8
```

It can also be used with non-integers, where it returns 1 for true and 0 for false.

```
5 & "hello"; // both are true
<< 1
```

Bitwise OR

There is also the bitwise OR operator, [|], which will convert both numbers into binary and return a number that in binary has a 1 in each position for which the corresponding bits of either operands are 1s. Here's an example:

```
12 | 10; // in binary this is 1100 & 1010, so the first 3 digits
➥contain a 1
<< 14
```

This can also be used with non-integers, and returns 1 for true and 0 for false.

```
' ' | "";
<< 0 // both are falsy
```

Bitwise XOR

Another operation is the bitwise XOR operator, [^], which stands for "eXclusive OR". This will convert both numbers into binary and return a number that in binary has a 1 in each position for which the corresponding bits of either operands are 1s, but not both 1s. Here's an example:

```
12 ^ 10; // in binary this is 1100 & 1010, so only the second and
➥third digits are exclusively 1s
<< 6
```

When using non-integer values, this evaluates to 1 if *either* operands are truthy and evaluates to 0 if both operands are truthy or both are falsy:

```
1 ^ 0; // The first operand is truthy
<< 1

true ^ true; // if both operands are true then the result is false
<< 0
```

Bitwise Shift Operators

The bitwise shift operators, << and >>, will move the binary representation a given number of places to the right or left, which effectively multiplies or divides the number by powers of two:

```
3 << 1; // multiply by 2
<< 6

16 >> 1; // divide by 2
<< 8
```

```
5 << 3; multiply by 2 cubed (8)
<< 40
```

Comparison

We often need to compare values when we are programming. JavaScript has several ways to compare two values.

Equality

Remember earlier, when we assigned a value to a variable? We used the = operator to do this, which would be the logical choice for testing if two values are equal.

Unfortunately, we can't use it because it is used for assigning values to variables. For example, say we had a variable called answer and we wanted to check if it was equal to 5, we might try doing this:

```
answer = 5;
<< 5
```

What we've actually done is *assign* the value of 5 to the variable answer, effectively overwriting the previous value!

The correct way to check for equality is to use either a double equals operator, ==, known as "soft equality" or the triple equals operator, ===, known as "hard equality".

Soft Equality

We can check if answer is in fact equal to 5 using soft equality, like so:

```
answer == 5;
<< true
```

This seems to work fine, but unfortunately there are some slight problems when using soft equality:

```
answer == "5";
<< true
```

As you can see, JavaScript is returning true when we are checking if the variable answer is equal to the *string* "5", when in fact answer is equal to the *number* 5. This is an important difference, but when a soft inequality is used, JavaScript will attempt to coerce the two values to the same type when doing the comparison. This can lead to some very strange results:

```
"  " == 0;
<< true

"  " == "0";
<< false

false == "0";
<< true

"1" == true;
<< true

"2" == true;
<< false

"true" == true;
<< false

null == undefined;
<< true
```

As you can see, values that are not actually equal have a tendency to be reported as being equal to each other when using the soft equality operator.

Hard Equality

Hard equality also tests that the two values are the same type:

```
answer === 5;
<< true

answer === "5";
<< false
```

```
null === undefined;
<< false
```

As you can see, hard equality reports that the variable answer is the number 5, but not the string "5". It also correctly reports that null and undefined are two different values.

 When is Not a Number not Not a Number?

The only strange result produced by hard equality is this:

```
NaN === Nan;
<< false
```

NaN is the only value in JavaScript that is not equal to itself. To deal with this, there is a special function called isNaN to test it:

```
isNaN(NaN);
<< true

isNaN(5);
<< false
```

Unfortunately, this doesn't always work properly, as can be seen in this example:

```
isNaN("hello");
<< true
```

This is because the function first of all tries to convert the string to a number, and strings without numerals are converted to NaN:

```
Number("hello");
<< NaN
```

The only way to accurately check if a value is NaN is to check that its type is a number (because NaN is of type "number") and also check that the isNaN function returns true. These two conditions should be combined using the logical AND (&&) that we saw earlier:

```
isnan = NaN; // set the variable isnan to be NaN
<< NaN

notnan = "hello"; // set the variable notnan to "hello"
<< "hello"

typeof(isnan) === "number" && isNaN(isnan);
<< true

typeof(notnan) === "number" && isNaN(notnan);
<< false
```

So, a JavaScript ninja should always use hard equality when testing if two values are equal. This will avoid the problems caused by JavaScript's type coercion.

If you want to check whether a number represented by a string is equal to a number, you should convert it to a number yourself explicitly:

```
> Number("5") === 5
<< true
```

This can be useful when you're checking values entered in a form as these are always strings.

Inequality

We can check if two values are *not* equal using the inequality operator. There is a soft inequality operator, != and a hard inequality operator, !==. These work in a similar way to the soft and hard equality operators:

```
16 != "16"; // type coercion makes these equal
<< false

16 !== "16";
<< true
```

As with equality, it is much better to use the hard inequality operator as this will give more reliable results unaffected by type coercion.

Greater Than and Less Than

We can check if a value is greater than another using the > operator:

```
8 > 4; << true
```

You can also use the "less than" < operator in a similar way:

```
8 < 4; << false
```

If you want to check if a value is greater than *or equal* to another value, you can use the >= operator, but be careful, the equality test works in the same way as the soft equality operator:

```
8 >= 4;
<< true

8 >= 8;
<< true

8 >= "8";
<< true
```

As you can see, type coercion means that strings can be confused with numbers. Unfortunately, there are no "hard" greater-than or equal-to operators, so an alternative way to avoid type coercion is to use a combination of the greater-than operator, logical OR, and a hard equality:

```
8 > 8 || 8 === 8;
<< true

8 > "8" || 8 === "8";
<< false
```

There is also a similar "less-than or equal-to" operator:

```
-1 <= 1;
<< true

-1 <= -1;
<< true
```

These operators can also be used with strings, which will be alphabetically ordered to check if one string is "less than" the other:

```
"apples" < "bananas";
>> true
```

Be careful, though, as the results are case-sensitive and upper-case letters are considered to be "less than" lower-case letters:

```
"apples" < "Bananas";
>> false
```

Quiz Ninja Project

Now that we have come to the end of the chapter, it's time to put what we've learned into practice in our Quiz Ninja project.

Since we've been learning all about JavaScript in this chapter, we're going to add some code in the **scripts.js** file. Open that file and add the following lines:

scripts.js (excerpt)

```
var question = "What is Superman's real name?"
var answer = prompt(question);
alert("You answered " + answer);
```

Now let's go through this code line by line to see what is happening:

```
var question = "What is Superman's real name?"
```

This declares a variable called name and assigns the string "What is Superman's real name?" to it. Next, we need to ask the question stored in the question variable, using a prompt dialog:

```
var answer = prompt(question);
```

A **prompt dialog** allows the player to type in an answer, which is stored in a variable called answer.

Finally, we use an alert dialog to display the player's answer:

```
alert("You answered " + answer);
```

This shows the player the answer they provided. In the next chapter we'll look at how to check if it's correct.

Have a go at playing the quiz by opening the **index.htm** file in your browser. It should look a little like the screenshot in Figure 2.1.

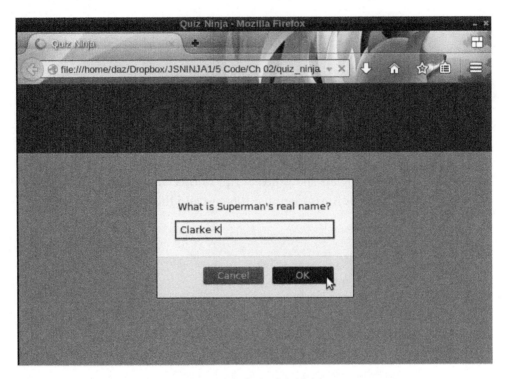

Figure 2.1. Let's play Quiz Ninja!

This is a good example of using the prompt and alert dialogs, along with variables to store the responses in to create some interactivity with the user.

Summary

In this chapter, we've learned about the primitive data types that are the basic building blocks of all JavaScript programs: strings, numbers, Booleans, undefined and null. We've also learned about variables and different methods for strings and numbers, as well as how to convert between the two types. We finished by looking at the different logical operators and ways of comparing values.

In the next chapter, we'll be looking at arrays, logic, and loops.

Chapter

3

Arrays, Logic, and Loops

In the last chapter we were introduced to JavaScript's primitive values, and also did a bit of programming. In this chapter we're going to look at **arrays**, a useful data structure for storing lists of values. We'll also look at **logical statements** that allow us to control the flow of a program, as well as **loops** that allow us to repeat blocks of code over and over again.

We will cover the following topics:

* array literals

* adding and removing values from arrays

* array methods

* `if` and `else` statements

* `switch` statements

* `while` loops

* `do … while` loops

■ `for` loops

■ iterating over an array

■ our project—use arrays, loops, and logic to ask multiple questions in our quiz

Arrays

An **array** is an ordered list of values. To create an array literal, simply write a pair of square brackets:

```
var myArray = [];
<< []
```

You can also use an array constructor function:

```
var myArray = new Array();
<< []
```

Both of these produce an empty array object, but it is preferable to stick to using array literals as they take less typing.

Arrays are not primitive values but a special built-in object, as we can see when we use the `typeof` operator:

```
typeof []
<< "object"
```

Stacks of Pizza

Donatello works at the Ninja Pizzeria where he cooks pizzas and then boxes them ready for delivery. He has a large pile of empty boxes ready to be filled up with pizza. Each box has a number on the side and since Donatello is also a programming ninja, he always starts counting from zero! Donatello's stack of boxes can be seen in Figure 3.1.

Figure 3.1. A stack of pizza boxes

We can create an array to represent Donatello's pile of pizza boxes in JavaScript by creating an empty array literal called `pizzas`:

```
var pizzas = [];
```

Each empty box can be thought of as representing an empty *element* in this array.

To find out what is in box 0, Donatello can open it up and peek inside. In JavaScript, we can find out the value of element 0 in the `pizzas` array using the following code:

```
pizzas[0];
<< undefined
```

To access a specific value in an array, we write its position in the array in square brackets (this is known as its **index**). If an element in an array is empty, `undefined` is returned.

Adding Values to Arrays

If Donatello wants to put a Margherita pizza in box 0, he just needs to open the box and put it inside. To place the string "Margherita" inside the first element of our `pizzas` array, we need to assign it to element 0, like so:

```
pizzas[0] = "Margherita";
```

Each item in an array can be treated like a variable. You can change the value using the assignment operator =. For example, we can change the value of the first item in the `pizzas` array to "Ham & Pineapple":

```
pizzas[0] = "Ham & Pineapple";
```

If Donatello receives a few more pizza orders, he can fill up the boxes up with pizzas one by one. We can also do this to our array by assigning more values:

```
pizza[1] = "Mushroom";
pizza[2] = "Spinach & Rocket"
```

Just as Donatello can put a pizza in any of the boxes in the pile, we can also use the index notation to add new items to any element in the `pizzas` array:

```
pizzas[5] = "Pineapple & Sweetcorn";
<< "Pineapple & Sweetcorn"
```

We can look at the `pizzas` array by simply typing its name into the console:

```
pizzas;
<< ["Ham & Pineapple", "Mushroom", "Spinach & Rocket", undefined,
➥ undefined, "Pineapple & Sweetcorn"]
```

Here we can see that the sixth item (with an index of 5) has been filled with the string "Pineapple & Sweetcorn". This has made the array longer than it was before, so all the other unused slots in the array are filled by the value `undefined`, just as if Donatello had put a pizza in the sixth box and left the other boxes empty.

Creating Array Literals

We can create an array literal using square brackets that already contain some initial values, so there's no need to add each value one by one. So we could create another pile of pizza boxes as the following array literal:

```
var pizzas = ["Margherita", "Mushroom", "Spinach & Rocket",
➥"Pineapple & Sweetcorn"];
<< ["Margherita", "Mushroom", "Spinach & Rocket", "Pineapple &
➥Sweetcorn"];
```

You don't even have to use the same types of items inside an array. This array contains each of the five different types of primitive values, as well as an empty object:

```
mixedArray = [null, 1, "two", true, undefined, {} ];
<< [null, 1, "two", true, undefined, {}]
```

Removing Values from Arrays

Donatello can remove a pizza from a box, by opening it and taking the pizza out, leaving the box empty. The `delete` operator does the same task and will remove an item from an array:

```
delete pizzas[3];
<< true
```

If we look at the pizzas array, we can see that the fourth entry (with an index of 3) has indeed been removed ... but it has been replaced by a value of `undefined` (as if the box was empty):

```
pizzas;
<< ["Margherita", "Mushroom", "Spinach & Rocket", undefined]
```

Watch out for this as it can even trip up experienced programmers. The *value* that was in position 3 ("`Pineapple & Sweetcorn`") has been deleted from the array, but the space that it occupied is still there and contains a value of `undefined`. Remember that Donatello only removed the pizza from the box and didn't remove the box completely. This means that the array still has the same number of elements and the position can still be referenced as an index, but it will just return `undefined`:

```
pizzas[3]
<< undefined
```

Array Properties and Methods

Arrays are a powerful weapon in a JavaScript ninja's toolkit and have some useful methods. To demonstrate these, we're going to use the following `pizzas` array that is similar to the one we produced earlier. You'll need to create a reference to it by entering the following into the console:

```
pizzas = ["Margherita", "Mushroom", "Spinach & Rocket", "Ham &
➡Pinapple", "Pineapple & Sweetcorn"]
```

To find the length of an array, we can use the `length` property. This is the equivalent to Donatello counting how many boxes are in his pile of pizza boxes:

```
> pizzas.length
<< 5
```

We can use the `length` to find the last item in an array:

```
> pizzas[pizzas.length - 1]
<< "Pineapple & Sweetcorn"
```

Notice that we have to subtract 1 from the `length` value. This is because the index starts at 0, so the last item in the array will have an index of 1 less than the array's length.

The `length` property is **mutable**, meaning you can manually change it:

```
> pizzas.length = 8
<< 8
> pizzas
<< ["Margherita", "Mushroom", "Spinach & Rocket", "Ham & Pinapple",
➡"Pineapple & Sweetcorn", undefined, undefined, undefined]
```

As you can see, if you make the array longer, the extra slots will be filled in with `undefined`:

```
> pizzas.length = 3
<< 3
> pizzas
<< ["Margherita", "Mushroom", "Spinach & Rocket"]
```

If you make the array shorter than it already is, all the extra elements will be removed completely.

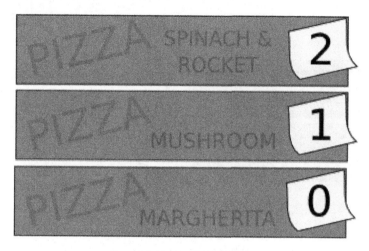

Figure 3.2. Making the array shorter

Figure 3.2 shows the effect of making the array shorter.

Pop, Push, Shift, and Unshift

To remove the last item from an array, we can use the pop() method. This is just as if Donatello removed a pizza box from the top of his pile:

```
pizzas.pop();
<< "Spinach & Rocket"
```

Figure 3.3. Popping a pizza box from the array

Figure 3.3 shows the effect of using pop on the array. The `pizzas` array no longer contains the string "`Spinach & Rocket`".

The `push()` method appends a new value to the end of the array. This is like Donatello putting a new pizza box on top of the pile, as shown in Figure 3.4. The method returns the new length of the array:

```
pizzas.push("Pepperoni");
<< 3
```

Figure 3.4. Pushing a pizza box onto our array

The shift() method works in a similar way to the pop() method, but this removes the *first* item in the array. This is like Donatello removing a pizza box from the bottom of his stack of boxes, as shown in Figure 3.5:

```
pizzas.shift();
<< "Margherita"
```

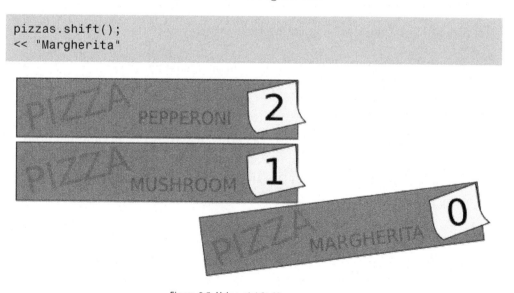

Figure 3.5. Using shift() on our array

The unshift() method is similar to the push() method, but this appends a new item to the *beginning* of the array. This is the equivalent of Donatello adding a new pizza box to the bottom of the pile, as shown in Figure 3.6:

```
pizzas.unshift("Chicken & Bacon");
<< 3
```

Figure 3.6. Using unshift() on our array

Merging Arrays

The concat() method can be used to merge an array with one or more arrays:

```
pizzas.concat(["Spicy Beef", "Chicken and Mushroom"]);
<< ["Chicken & Bacon", "Mushroom", "Pepperoni","Spicy Beef",
➥ "Chicken and Mushroom"]
```

Note that this does not change the pizzas array, it simply creates another array combining the two arrays. You can use assignment to change the pizzas array to this new array. This would be like Donatello adding a whole new pile of boxes on top of the pile he already has:

```
pizzas = pizzas.concat(["Spicy Beef", "Chicken and Mushroom"]);
<< ["Chicken & Bacon", "Mushroom", "Pepperoni","Spicy Beef",
➥ "Chicken and Mushroom"]
```

Now the pizzas array contains these two new strings.

The `join()` Method

The `join()` method can be used to turn the array into a string that comprises all the items in the array, separated by commas. This is as if Donatello was asked to write down a list of all the pizzas in his pile of boxes:

```
pizzas.join();
<< "Chicken & Bacon,Mushroom,Pepperoni,Spicy Beef,Chicken
➥and Mushroom"
```

You can choose a separator other than a comma by placing it inside the parentheses. Let's try using an ampersand:

```
pizzas.join(" & ");
<< "Chicken & Bacon & Mushroom & Pepperoni & Spicy Beef & Chicken
➥and Mushroom"
```

Slicing and Splicing

Be careful not to get confused with the pizza analogy here—we're slicing the array, not the actual pizzas! The `slice()` method creates a subarray, effectively chopping out a slice of an original array starting at one index and finishing at the next. This would be the same as Donatello taking a selection of the pizza boxes from the whole pile, from the second pizza up to but not including the fourth:

```
pizzas.slice(2,4) // starts at the third item (index of 2) and
➥finishes at the fourth (the item with index 4 is not included)
<< ["Pepperoni", "Spicy Beef"]
```

Note that this operation is **non-destructive**—no items are actually removed from the array, as we can see if we look at the `pizzas` array:

```
pizzas;
<< ["Chicken & Bacon", "Mushroom", "Pepperoni", "Spicy Beef",
➥"Chicken and Mushroom"]
```

The `splice()` method removes items from an array and then inserts new items in their place. Say Donatello wanted to remove the Pepperoni pizza from the pile and replace it with some other boxes containing Chicken and Pepper, and Veggie Deluxe:

```
> pizzas.splice(2, 1, "Chicken and Pepper", "Veggie Deluxe")
<< ["Pepperoni"]

> pizzas
<< ["Chicken & Bacon", "Mushroom", "Chicken and Pepper", "Veggie
➥Deluxe", "Spicy Beef", "Chicken and Mushroom"]
```

The first number tells us the index at which to start the splice. In the example we started at index 2, which is the third item in the array ("Pepperoni"). The second number tells us how many items to remove from the array. In the example, this was just the one item. Every value after this is then inserted into the array at the same place the other items were removed. The strings "Chicken and Pepper", "Veggie Deluxe" are inserted in our example, starting at the third item. Notice that the `splice()` method returns the items removed from the array as a subarray, so in the example, it returned the array `["Pepperoni"]`.

The `splice()` method can also be used to insert values into an array at a specific index without removing any items, by indicating that zero items are to be removed:

```
pizzas.splice(4,0,"Ham & Mushroom"); // inserts "Ham & Mushroom as
➥the fifth item in the pizzas array
<< []
```

Notice that an empty array is returned, but the new value of "Ham & Mushroom" has been inserted, which we can see if we look at the `pizzas` array:

```
pizzas;
<< ["Chicken & Bacon", "Mushroom", "Chicken and Pepper", "Veggie
➥Deluxe", "Ham & Mushroom", "Spicy Beef", "Chicken and Mushroom"]
```

We saw earlier that we can use the `delete` operator to remove an item from an array. Unfortunately, this leaves a value of `undefined` in its place. If you want to remove a value completely, you can use the `splice()` method with a length of 1 and without specifying any values to add:

```
pizzas.splice(2,1); // will remove the item at index 2 (i.e. the
⮑third item in the array)
<< ["Chicken and Pepper"];
```

The value that has been removed will be returned as an array containing that value.

If we now look at the `pizzas` array, we can see that "Chicken and Pepper" has been removed completely:

```
pizzas;
<< ["Chicken & Bacon", "Mushroom", "Veggie Deluxe", "Ham & Mushroom"
⮑, "Spicy Beef", "Chicken and Mushroom"]
```

Reverse

We can reverse the order of an array using the `reverse()` method:

```
pizzas.reverse();
<< ["Chicken and Mushroom", "Spicy Beef", "Ham & Mushroom",
⮑"Veggie Deluxe", "Mushroom", "Chicken & Bacon"]
```

Note that this changes the order of the array permanently.

Sort

We can sort the order of an array using the `sort()` method:

```
pizzas.sort();
<< ["Chicken & Bacon", "Chicken and Mushroom", "Ham & Mushroom"
⮑, "Mushroom", "Spicy Beef", "Veggie Deluxe"]
```

It is alphabetical order by default for String objects. Note that this also changes the order of the array permanently.

 Numbers Are Sorted Alphabetically

Numbers are also sorted alphabetically, so 9 will come after 10 when you try to sort an array of numbers:

```
[5, 9, 10].sort();
<< [10, 5, 9]
```

This can be fixed using a special type of function called a **callback**. We'll cover how to do this in Chapter 4.

Finding if a Value is in an Array

We can find out if an array contains an object using the `indexOf()` method to find the first occurrence of a value in an array. If the item is in the array, it will return the index of the first occurrence of that item:

```
pizzas.indexOf("Spicy Beef");
<< 4
```

If the item is not in the array, it will return `-1`:

```
pizzas.indexOf("Margherita");
<< -1
```

Multidimensional Arrays

You can even have an array of arrays, known as a **multidimensional array**, for example:

```
multiDimensional = [[0,1],["one","two","three"],[],[true,false]];
<< [[0,1],["one","two","three"],[],[true,false]]
```

This could be used to create a coordinate system:

```
coordinates = [[1,3],[4,2]];
<< [[1,3],[4,2]]
```

To access the values in a multidimensional array, we use two indices: one to refer to the item's place in the outer array, and one to refer to its place in the inner array:

```
x1 = coordinates[0][0]; // The first value of the first array
<< 1
```

```
x2 = coordinates[1][0]; // The first value of the second array
<< 4

y1 = coordinates[0][1]; // The second value of the first array
<< 3

y2 = coordinates[1][1]; // The second value of the second array
<< 2
```

Logic

In this section we will begin to look at logical conditions that allow you to control the flow of a program.

if Statements

An if looks like the following:

```
if (condition) {
    code to run if condition is true
}
```

The code inside the block will only run if the condition is true. If the condition is not a Boolean value, it will be converted to a Boolean, depending on whether or not it is truthy or falsy (see Chapter 2).

Here is an example that will only display the alert message if the value of the age variable is less than 18:

```
var age = 23;
if (age<18) {
    alert("Sorry, you are not old enough to play this game");
}
```

Try changing the value of the age variable to a value below 18 as it does in this code, and the alert box will show as in Figure 3.7:

```
var age = 12;
if (age < 18) {
  alert("Sorry, you are not old enough to play this game");
}
```

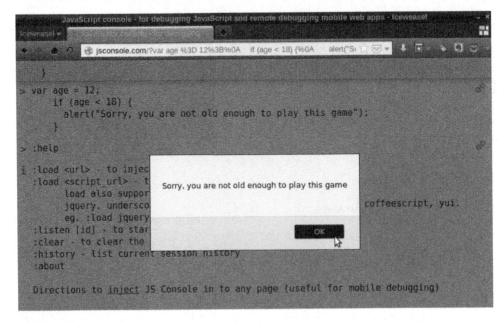

Figure 3.7. Adding age verification

`else` Statements

The `else` keyword can be used to add an extra block of code to run if the condition is false. An `if ... else` statement looks like this:

```
if (condition) {
  code to run if condition is true
} else {
  code to run if condition isn't true
}
```

As an example, we can test if a number is even or odd using the following code:

```
n = 12;
if (n%2 === 0) {
  console.log("n is an even number");
```

```
} else {
  console.log("n is an odd number");
}
```

This uses the % operator that we met in the last chapter to check the remainder when dividing the variable n by 2. All even numbers leave no remainder when divided by 2, so we can test to see if n%2 is equal to zero; if it is, n must be even. If n is not even, then it must be odd.

Try running the code with different values of n, to check that it works.

Ternary Operator

A shorthand way of writing an `if ... else` statement is to use the ternary operator, ?, which takes three operands in the following format:

```
condition ? (code to run if condition is true) : (code to run if
➥condition isn't true)
```

Here's the example for testing if the variable n is odd or even, rewritten to use the ternary operator:

```
n = 5;
n%2 === 0 ? console.log("n is an even number") : console.log("n is
➥an odd number");
<< n is an odd number
```

The ternary operator can make your code more succinct, but can also make it difficult to read, so be careful when you use it.

`switch` Statements

You can actually string lots of `if` and `else` statements together to make a logical decision tree:

```
if (number === 4) {
  alert("You rolled a four");
} else if (number === 5) {
  alert("You rolled a five");
} else if(number === 6){
```

```
    alert("You rolled a six");
} else {
    alert("You rolled a number less than four");
}
```

The `switch` operator can be used instead, like so:

```
switch (number) {
case 4:
    alert("You rolled a four");
    break;
case 5:
    alert("You rolled a five");
    break;
case 6:
    alert("You rolled a six");
    break;
default:
    alert("You rolled a number less than four");
    break;
}
```

The value that you are comparing goes in parentheses after the `switch` operator. A `case` keyword is then used for each possible value that can occur (4, 5, and 6 in the example above). After each `case` statement is the code that that needs to be run if that case occurs.

It is important to finish each `case` block with the `break` keyword, as this stops any more of the case blocks being executed. Without a `break` statement, the program will "fall through" and continue to evaluate subsequent case blocks. This is sometimes implemented on purpose, but it is confusing and should be avoided—a ninja always finishes a `case` block with a `break`!

The `default` keyword is used at the end for any code than needs to be run if none of the cases are true.

Loops

Loops will repeat a piece of code over and over again according to certain conditions.

`while` Loops

We'll start by looking at a `while` loop. This will repeatedly run a block of code while a certain condition is true and takes the following structure:

```
while (condition) {
  do something
}
```

Here's an example that will count down from ten, alerting us with a line from the famous song:

```
var bottles = 10;
while (bottles > 0){
  alert("There were " + bottles + " green bottles, hanging on the
➥wall. And if one green bottle should accidently fall, there'd be
➥ " + (bottles-1) + " green bottles hanging on the wall");
  bottles--;
}
```

We start by declaring a variable called `bottles`. Any variables that are used in the loop must be initialized before the loop is run, otherwise there will be an error when they are mentioned.

The loop starts here with the `while` keyword and is followed by a condition and a block of code. The condition in the example is that the number of bottles has to be greater than zero. This basically means "keep repeating the block of code, as long as the number of bottles is greater than zero".

The block of code uses the `alert` function to display a message about the number of bottles, and then uses the decrement operator to decrease the `bottles` variable by one.

Here's a more concise way of writing the same loop that moves the increment into the condition:

```
var bottles = 11;
while (--bottles){
  alert("There were " + bottles + " green bottles, hanging on the
```

```
➥wall. And if one green bottle should accidently fall, there'd be
➥" + (bottles-1) + " green bottles hanging on the wall");
}
```

The reason that this code works is because the loop will continue while the `bottles` variable is true, and after each loop, the value of the `bottles` variable decreases by 1. When the `bottles` variable reaches 0, it is not true anymore (remember that 0 is a falsy value) so the loop will stop. Notice that you have to start with one more bottle (11) as it will be decreased by one even before the first block is run.

Infinite Loops

It is important that the condition in a `while` loop will be met at some point, otherwise you'll be stuck in an infinite loop that can crash your program.

Consider the following loop:

```
var n = 1;
while(n>0){
    alert("Hello");
    n++;
}
```

This loop will keep running, as the variable n will *always* be above zero. Most browsers will warn you that there is a slow running script when this happens and give you the option to stop it. If not, you can usually kill the process by closing the tab or restarting the browser.

do ... while Loops

A do ... while loop is similar to a `while` loop. The only difference is that the condition comes *after* the block of code:

```
do {
    do something
} while(condition)
```

This means that the block of code will always be run at least once, regardless of the condition being true or not.

Here's the same example we saw before, rewritten as a do ... while loop:

```
var bottles = 10;
do {
  alert("There were " + bottles + " green bottles, hanging on the
➥wall. And if one green bottle should accidently fall, there'd be
➥ " + (bottles-1) + " green bottles hanging on the wall");
  bottles--;
} while (bottles > 0)
```

for Loops

for loops are by far the most common in JavaScript and take the following form:

```
for (initialization ; condition ; after) { do something }
```

The *initialization* code is run *before* the loop starts and is usually employed to initialize any variables used in the loop. The *condition* has to be satisfied for the loop to continue. The *after* code is what to do after *each iteration* of the loop, and it is typically used to increment a counter of some sort.

Here's the green bottles example written as a for loop:

```
for (var bottles = 10 ; bottles > 0 ; bottles--) {
  alert("There were " + bottles + " green bottles, hanging on the
➥wall. And if one green bottle should accidently fall, there'd be
➥ " + (bottles-1) + " green bottles hanging on the wall");
}
```

Each of the three parts are optional, and the code could be written as:

```
var bottles = 10; // bottles is initialized here instead
for ( ; bottles > 0 ; ) { // empty initialization and increment
  alert("There were " + bottles + " green bottles, hanging on the
➥wall. And if one green bottle should accidently fall, there'd be
➥ " + (bottles-1) + " green bottles hanging on the wall");
  bottles--; // increment moved into code block
}
```

As you can see, it's possible to use a while loop, a do ... while loop, or a for loop to achieve the same results. A for loop is the most common as it keeps all the details of the loop (the initialization, condition, and increment) in one place and separate from the code block.

Nested for Loops

You can place a loop inside another loop to create a nested loop. It will have an inner loop that will run all the way through before the next step of the outer loop occurs.

Here's an example that produces a multiplication table up to 12 x 12:

```
for(var n=1 ; n<13 ; n++){
  for(var m=1 ; m<13 ; m++){
    console.log(m + " multiplied by " + n + " is " + n*m);
    }
  }
```

The outer loop counts up from n=1 to n=12. For every iteration of the outer loop, the inner loop counts up from m=1 to m=12. This means that it starts in the first iteration with n = 1 and m = 1, producing the following output that is logged to the console:

```
<< 1 multiplied by 1 is 1
```

In the next iteration, we are still inside the inner loop, so n remains as 1, but m is incremented to 2, giving:

```
<< 1 multiplied by 2 is 2
```

m continues to increase until it reaches 12. After this, we leave the inner loop and return to the outer loop, where n increases to 2. We then re-enter the inner loop and m is reset back to 1 and begins counting up to 12 again. This continues until the last iteration produces the line:

```
<< 12 multiplied by 12 is 144
```

Looping over Arrays

A `for` loop can be used to iterate over each value in an array. If we take our `pizzas` array example from earlier, we can create a `for` loop that outputs each item in the array to the console using the following loop:

```
for(var i=0, max=pizzas.length; i < max; i++){
  console.log(pizzas[i]);
}
<< "Chicken & Bacon"
<< "Chicken and Mushroom"
<< ""Ham & Mushroom""
<< "Mushroom"
<< "Spicy Beef"
<< "Veggie Deluxe"
```

There are a few points to note in this example. Array indices start their numbering at zero, so make sure that the value in the `for` loop also starts at zero. We want the loop to continue until it reaches the length of the array; this can be set as the variable `max` in the initialization part of the `for` loop, then the condition becomes `i < max`. This is preferable to using `i < pizzas.length` because then the length of the pizzas array would have to be calculated after every pass through the loop. This might not sound all that important, but it can make a big difference to the speed of the program when using large arrays.

Quiz Ninja Project

Now we've reached the end of the chapter, so it's time to use what we have learned to add some features to our Quiz Ninja project. Open up **scripts.js** in the **js** folder.

We'll start by creating a nested array called `quiz` that contains all the questions and answers. Each item will be another array that contains the question as its first item and the answer as its second item:

```
                                                    scripts.js (excerpt)

var quiz = [
    ["What is Superman's real name?","Clarke Kent"],
    ["What is Wonderwoman's real name?","Dianna Prince"],
    ["What is Batman's real name?","Bruce Wayne"]
    ];
```

Next, we create and initialize a variable called score to keep track of how many correct answers the player has given:

```
                                                    scripts.js (excerpt)

var score = 0 // initialize score
```

Then we loop through the quiz array, asking each question using a prompt dialog that allows the player to enter an answer which is stored in a variable called answer. We can then compare this to the actual answer stored in the quiz array:

```
                                                    scripts.js (excerpt)

for(var i=0,max=quiz.length;i<max;i++){

    // get answer from user
    var answer = prompt(quiz[i][0]); // quiz[i][0] is the ith question

    // check if answer is correct
    if(answer === quiz[i][1]){ // quiz[i][1] is the ith answer
        alert("Correct!");
        // increase score by 1
        score++;
    } else {
        alert("Wrong!");
    }
}
```

An if ... else block is then used, depending on whether the answer is right or wrong. If it is right, then an alert dialog is shown saying that it is correct and the score is incremented by 1, using score++. Otherwise, if the answer is wrong, an alert dialog informs the player.

When the loop has finished iterating through each question in the `questions` array, we finish by using another alert dialog to inform the player that the game is over and tell them how many questions they answered correctly:

scripts.js (excerpt)

```
alert("Game Over, you scored " + score + " points");
```

Have a go at playing the quiz in your browser by opening the **index.htm** file. It should look like the screenshot shown in Figure 3.8.

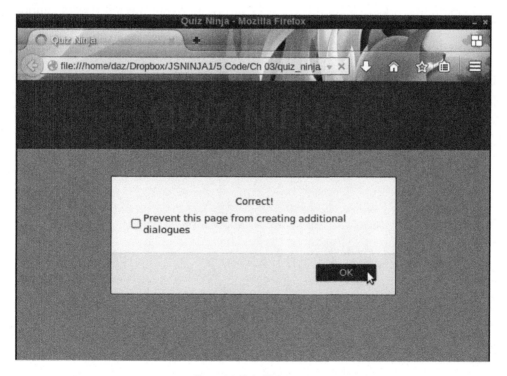

Figure 3.8. Quiz Ninja scores

Our quiz now feels much more like an actual program, and demonstrates the power of concepts such as arrays, logic, and loops that we've learned about in this chapter.

Summary

In this chapter we have learned the following:

- arrays are an ordered list of values

- multidimensional arrays contain arrays

- arrays have lots of methods that can be used to manipulate items in the array

- we can use an `if` and `else` statement to control the flow of code

- the `switch` statement can be used instead of multiple `if` and `else` statements

- a `while` loop and `do ... while` loop can be used to repeat a block of code while a condition is still true

- a `for` loop works in a similar way to a `while` loop, but has a different syntax

- a `for` loop can be used to iterate over an array

In the next chapter we'll be learning all about functions, a fundamental part of the JavaScript language.

Chapter **4**

Functions

In the last chapter, we covered arrays, logic, and loops. In this chapter, we're going to look at functions. A function is a chunk of code that is almost like a small, self-contained mini program that can be referenced by a name. They can help to reduce repetition and make code easier to follow.

In this chapter, we'll be covering these topics:

■ defining functions—function declarations, function expressions, and `Function()` constructors

■ invoking a function

■ return values

■ parameters and arguments

■ scope—global and local

■ hoisting—variables and functions

■ callbacks—functions as a parameter

■ project—we'll be using functions to make it simpler to understand the Quiz Ninja code

In JavaScript, functions are considered to be just another value. This means that they do all the same tasks that other values and objects can do, such as be assigned to variables, changed and stored in arrays. You can even define a function inside another function. In technical terms, this means that functions are considered to be **first-class objects** in JavaScript.

This makes functions a very important and powerful part of the JavaScript language with many of its features relying on them. Hence, fully understanding functions is an essential skill of the JavaScript ninja.

Defining a Function

There are three ways to define a function.

Function Declarations

To define a function literal we can use a `function` declaration:

```
function hello(){
  alert("Hello World!");
}
```

This starts with the `function` keyword and is followed by the name of the function, which in this case is called 'hello', followed by parentheses. After this is a block that contains the code for the function.

This is known as a **named function** as the function has a name: 'hello'.

Function Expressions

Another way of defining a function literal is to create a **function expression**. This assigns an *anonymous function* to a variable:

```
var goodbye = function(){
  alert("Goodbye World!");
};
```

The function in this example is known as an anonymous function because it does not have a name; it is simply created, then assigned to the variable goodbye. Alternatively we can create a named function expression instead:

```
var goodbye = function bye(){
  alert("Goodbye World!");
};
```

The name of this function is bye, and it has been assigned to the variable goodbye.

Notice also that the example ends with a semicolon. This finishes the assignment statement, whereas a normal function declaration ends in a block (no need for semicolons at the end of blocks).

 A Function's name Property

Functions are just objects, and objects have properties (more about this in the Chapter 5). All functions haves a read-only property called name, which can be accessed like so:

```
hello.name
<< "hello"
```

The name property is not actually part of the ECMAScript standard, although most JavaScript engines support it and use it internally.

Anonymous functions have an empty string as their name property in most browsers, although some versions of Internet Explorer use undefined.

The name property can be useful when debugging code, as the name of a function will be used to indicate which functions are causing a problem.

Function() Constructors

A function can also be declared using the constructor Function(). The body of the function is entered as a string, as shown in this example:

```
hi = new Function('alert("Hi World!");');
```

We'd avoid recommending this way of declaring functions as it is slower and there are problems with placing the function's code inside a string. Even in this simple example, we had to use different quotation marks for the `alert` function as those used for defining the function body itself.

A ninja should always declare functions using function literals—function declarations or function expressions. These two ways of creating functions are similar, although there are some subtle differences that will be covered later in the chapter. Some people prefer function declarations as they are akin to how functions are declared in other languages. Others prefer function expressions because it is clear that functions are just another value assigned to a variable, rather than a special feature of the language. Whether you use function declarations or function expressions is often a matter of personal taste, but whatever you choose to do—be consistent!

Invoking a Function

Invoking a function is to run the code inside the function's body. To invoke a function, simply enter its name, followed by parentheses. This is how we'd invoke the `hello` function, for example:

```
hello();
<< "Hello world!"
```

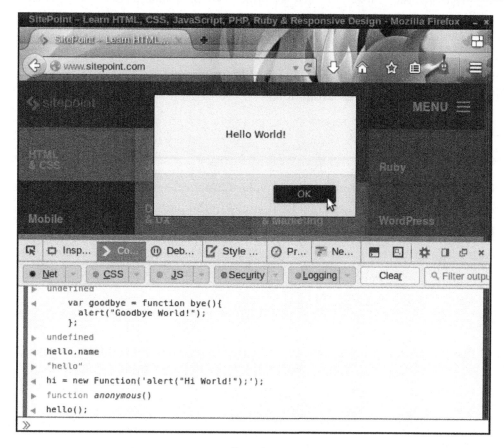

Figure 4.1.

As you can see in Figure 4.1, we get an alert box saying "Hello World!".

The function can be invoked over and over again just by typing its name followed by parentheses. This is one of the advantages of using functions—there's no need to write repetitive blocks of code. Another advantage is that all the functionality is kept in one place. So if you want to change part of it, you only need to update the code in one place. This is known as the DRY principle, which stands for **Don't Repeat Yourself**, and it's important to keep in mind when programming.

Don't Repeat Yourself

Don't Repeat Yourself,[1] or DRY, is a principle of programming that specifies that every part of a program should only be written once. This avoids duplication and means that there's no need to keep multiple pieces of code up to date and in sync.

If you have assigned a function to a variable, you need to place parentheses after the variable to invoke it as a function:

```
goodbye();
<< "Goodbye World!"
```

Remember: you need parentheses to invoke a function—either by name or by reference to the variable it is assigned to. If you skip the parentheses, you are simply referencing the function itself rather than invoking it, as you can see here:

```
goodbye;
<< function bye(){
   alert("Goodbye World!");
}
```

All that has been returned is the function definition that the variable goodbye is pointing to, rather than running the code. This can be useful if you want to assign the function to another variable, like so:

```
seeya = goodbye;
<< function bye(){
   alert("Goodbye World!");
}
```

Now the variable seeya also points to the function called bye and can be used to invoke it:

```
seeya();
<< "Goodbye World!"
```

The result can be seen in Figure 4.2.

---

[1] http://en.wikipedia.org/wiki/Don%27t_repeat_yourself

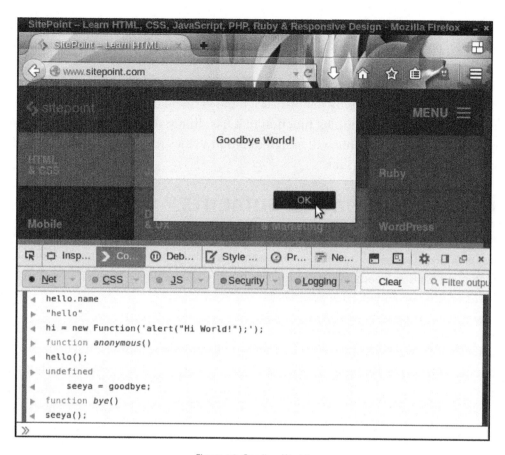

Figure 4.2. Goodbye World!

Return Values

All functions **return** a value, which can be specified using the `return` operator. A function that doesn't explicitly return anything (such as all the examples we have seen so far) will return `undefined` by default.

The function in this example will return the string "Yo World!":

```
function yo(){
  return "Yo World!";
}
```

This means that we can assign a variable to a function invocation and the value of that variable will be set to the return value of that function:

```
> message = hi();
<< "Yo World!"
```

The variable `message` now points to the string "Yo World!". This may seem trivial in this instance (that is, why not just assign the variable to the string directly?), but we can create a more complex function that has different return values depending on certain conditions. This will assign different values to the `message` variable depending on those conditions.

Parameters and Arguments

Parameters and **arguments** are often used interchangeably to represent values that are provided for the function to use. There is a subtle difference though: any parameters a function needs are set when the function is *defined*. When a function is *invoked*, it is provided with arguments.

JavaScript does not have a built-in function to square numbers, so we can create one to demonstrate using parameters. In the example that follows, the `square` function takes one parameter, `x`, which is the number to be squared. In the body of the function, the name of the parameter acts like a variable equal to the value that is entered when the function is invoked. As you can see, it is multiplied by itself and the result is returned by the function:

```
function square(x){
    return x*x;
}
```

When we invoke this function, we need to provide an argument, which is the number to be squared:

```
square(4.5);
<< 20.25
```

You can use as many parameters as you like when defining functions. For example, the following function finds the mean of any three numbers:

```
function mean(a,b,c){
  return (a+b+c)/3;
}
<< undefined

mean(2, 6, 19);
<< 9
```

If a parameter is not provided as an argument when the function is invoked, the function will still be invoked, but the parameter will be given a value of undefined. If we try to invoke the mean function with only two arguments, we can see that it returns NaN because the function cannot do the required operation with undefined:

```
mean(1,2)
<< NaN
```

If too many arguments are provided when a function is invoked, the function will work as normal and the extra arguments will be ignored (although they can be accessed using the arguments object that is discussed in the next section):

```
mean(1,2,3,4,5); // will only find the mean of 1,2 and 3
<< 2
```

The arguments Variable

Every function has a special variable called arguments. This is an array-like object that contains every argument of the function when it is invoked:

```
function arguments(){
  return arguments;
}
```

 arguments is not an Array!

Be careful: arguments is not an array. It has a length property and you can read and write each element using index notation, but it doesn't have array methods such as slice(), join(), and forEach(). (However, there is a way of "borrowing" these methods from arrays that we will look at in a later chapter.)

Rounding Errors

The last example highlights a problem when doing division in JavaScript. Because it uses base 2 in the background, it can struggle with some division calculations and often has slight rounding errors. This usually doesn't cause a problem, but you should be aware of it.

Default Arguments

We can use the fact that `undefined` is used when arguments are not supplied to provide default values for a function. For example, we can improve the `hello` function that we created earlier by adding a `name` parameter so that it says "hello" to the value provided as an argument:

```
function hello(name){
    console.log("Hello " + name + "!");
}
```

This works as expected, but says "hello" to `undefined` if no argument is provided:

```
hello("DAZ");
<< "Hello DAZ!"

hello();
<< "Hello undefined!"
```

We can improve the function by checking if the `name` parameter has a value of un-`defined` and providing a default value of "World" if so:

```
function hello(name){
    if (name === undefined) name = "World";
    console.log("Hello " + name + "!");
}
```

Now we can invoke the `hello` function with or without arguments:

```
hello();
<< "Hello World!"

hello("DAZ");
<< "Hello DAZ!"
```

Another way of assigning default values is to use the following line:

```
name = name || "World";
```

This is using the logical OR operator to check if the name parameter has a truthy value. If it does, then name will stay the same. If name is falsy (such as undefined), it will take the value of "World". Be careful using this method, however; if the name argument is a falsy value it will be set to the default value of "World", and in some cases you might want it to be the falsy value instead (0, for example).

Default parameters should always come after non-default parameters, otherwise default values will always have to be entered anyway. Consider the following function for calculating a discounted price in a store:

```
function discount(price, amount) {
  if(amount === undefined) amount = 10;
  return price*(100-amount)/100;
}
```

It takes two arguments: the price of an item and the percentage discount. The store's most common discount is 10%, so this is provided as a default value. This means that the amount argument can be omitted in most cases and a 10% discount will still be applied:

```
discount(20) // standard discount of 10%
<< 18
```

If a different discount is applied, the amount argument can be provided:

```
discount(15, 20) // discount of 20%
<< 12
```

This will fail to work, however, if the parameters are reversed:

```
function discount(amount, price) {
  if (amount===undefined) amount = 10;
  return price*(100-amount)/100;
}
```

Now if we try to use the function with just one argument, the function won't work, because `price` has not been set:

```
discount(20);
<< NaN
```

It will work, though, if both values are entered:

```
discount(10,20);
<< 18
```

And it will also work if `undefined` is supplied as the first argument, since `amount` will then default to 10:

```
discount(undefined,20);
<< 18
```

This somewhat defeats the object of having default parameters! The golden rule to remember here is that a ninja always put default parameters *after* all the other parameters.

Scope

Scope is an important concept in programming. It refers to where a variable is visible and accessible.

In JavaScript, a function creates its own **local scope**. This means that any local variables defined inside a function using the `var` keyword are not accessible outside the function.

Global Scope

Any variable declared outside of any function is said to have **global scope**. That means that it is accessible everywhere in the program. While this may seem to be a good idea at first, it is not considered good practice. A ninja will try to limit the number of global variables to a minimum, because any variable that shares the same name will clash and potentially overwrite each other's values. It might seem unlikely that this would happen, but it is all too common in large programs when you forget which variables you have used—think how often we have used the variable i in for loops already! It can also be a problem when you are writing code in teams or if you're using code libraries that may use the same variable names as some of your code.

Local Scope

Any variable that is declared inside a function using the var statement will only be available inside that function. This is known as having **local scope**, as the variable is only visible in the locality of the function (in other words, inside the function block).

If the var statement is not used, the variable will have global scope and be available outside the function. This can be demonstrated in the following example, where the variable a can have two different values depending on whether it is defined inside or outside a function:

```
var a = 1;

function locala() {
  var a = 3; // local variable
  console.log("a inside function: " + a);
}

locala(); // invoke the locala function

console.log("a outside function: " + a);
```

This results in the subsequent console log:

```
"a inside function: 3"
"a outside function: 1"
```

In the example, a is defined globally outside the function and is given the value of 1. This means it has global scope and is available inside and outside the function. But then a is defined inside the local function using var. This gives it local scope inside the function where it has a value of 3, but it retains the value of 1 outside the function. For all intents and purposes, the two a variables are different variables.

Here's another example where we define a global variable and then overwrite it from within the function:

```
b = 2;

function localb() {
    b = 4; // overwrites the global variable
    console.log("b inside function: " + b);
}

localb(); // invoke the localb function

console.log("b outside function: " + b);
```

Here's the resultant console log:

```
"b inside function: 4"
"b outside function: 4"
```

In this example, b is defined globally outside the function and given the value of 2. Yet b is not declared using var inside the function, so it still refers to the global variable *outside* the function. This means that b is the same variable both inside and outside the function and the value of b is overwritten globally to be 4.

Here's another example that creates a global variable from within a function that is then still accessible from outside of function:

```
function localc() {
    c = 5; // creates a new global variable
    console.log("c inside function: " + c);
}

localc(); // invoke the localc function

console.log("c outside function: " + c);
```

This results in the following console log:

```
"c inside function: 5"
"c outside function: 5"
```

In the example, c is only defined inside the function, but because this is done without using var, it has global scope and is also available outside the function.

Here's another function that creates a local variable inside the function that is not accessible outside the function:

```
function locald() {
  var d = 6; // creates a new local variable
  console.log("d inside function: " + d);
}

locald(); // invoke the locald function

console.log("d outside function: " + d);
```

Here's the console log result:

```
"d inside function: 6"
"d is not defined"
```

In this example, d is also only defined inside the function, but by using var it has local scope and is only accessible inside the function. When we try to log the value of d outside the function, it causes an error because d is not defined outside its scope.

Hoisting

Hoisting is the process of moving a value to the top of the code block where it is used, regardless of where it is defined.

Variable Hoisting

All variable declarations are automatically moved to the top of a function's scope, as if they were defined at the start of the function. Variable assignment is not hoisted, however. This means that a variable assigned at the end of the function will have a value of undefined until the assignment is made. The following example shows how this works:

```
function hoist(){
  console.log(a); // at this point a is undefined
  //
  // imagine lots more code here
  //
  var a = "Hoist Me!";
  console.log(a); // now is a string
}
```

At the beginning of the function, the variable a has not been declared or assigned a value, so in theory, trying to write its value using `console.log(a)` should result in an error. Yet the declaration of a is hoisted to the top of the function, so the function knows that a variable called a exists. The value that it is assigned to is not hoisted, however, so until the assignment is made, the value of a is `undefined`.

Hoisting can cause some confusion, so a ninja should declare, and assign if required, all local variables at the beginning of a function so that hoisting is unnecessary.

Function Hoisting

Functions that are defined inside other functions are also hoisted, but they behave differently depending on how they are defined.

If a function is defined using a function declaration, the whole function is hoisted to the top of the function, meaning that it can be invoked before it has been defined.

A function expression (where an anonymous function is assigned to a variable) is hoisted in a similar way to variables. So the declaration will be hoisted, but not the actual function. This means that the function cannot be invoked until after it appears in the code.

This behaviour also applies to the global scope, as can be seen in the following example:

```
add(2,3); // this will work because the add function is hoisted

function add(x,y){
  console.log(x + y);
}

subtract(5,2); // this won't work because the subtract function
```

```
➥hasn't been defined yet

subtract = function(x,y){
  console.log(x - y);
}
```

This is the major difference between the two ways of defining function literals and it may influence your decision regarding which one to use. Some people like that using function expressions means you're required to define all functions and assign them to variables prior to using them. To avoid any problems, a ninja should either use function declarations or ensure that all function expressions are defined at the top of the scope, along with any variable declarations.

Callbacks

Remember at the start of this chapter when we said that functions in JavaScript are first-class objects, and this means that they behave in just the same way as every other value? Well, they can also be given as a parameter to another function. A function that is passed as an argument to another is known as a **callback**.

Here's a basic example of a function called `pizza`, which accepts an argument for the type of topping that goes on the pizza, as well as a callback function saying what to do with the pizza:

```
function pizza(topping, callback) {
  console.log("This is a " + topping + " pizza");
  callback();
}
```

Now we can create some utility functions for what we do with pizzas, such as cook them and eat them:

```
function cook() {
  console.log("The pizza is cooking");
}
```

```
function eat() {
  console.log("I've eaten the pizza!");
}
```

We're just logging some simple messages to the console in these examples, but these functions could be used to do anything in a practical sense.

Let's have a go at using these utility functions as callbacks in our `pizza` function:

```
> pizza("Ham & Pineapple", cook);
<< "This is a Ham & Pineapple pizza"
<< "The pizza is cooking"


> pizza("Ham & Pineapple", eat);
<< "This is a Ham & Pineapple pizza"
<< "I've eaten the pizza!"
```

Okay, so in these examples, the `cook()` and `eat()` functions were quite similar, but they should demonstrate that you could do something very different in the `pizza` function depending on the callback function that is provided as an argument. This can make your functions much more flexible.

Note that the callbacks `cook` and `eat` are passed as arguments without parentheses. This is because the argument is only a reference to the function. The actual callback is invoked in the body of the function, where parentheses are used.

A function can also take an anonymous function as a callback. For example, say we want to deliver a pizza, but we have no `deliver` function. We can write an anonymous function that does what we want:

```
pizza("Ham & Pineapple",function(){
  console.log("The pizza has been delivered.");
});
```

This is only really useful for one-off tasks. It is often a much better idea to keep functions separate and named so that they can be reused again. It's also a bad idea to use this method for long function definitions as it can be confusing where the callback starts and ends.

Callbacks are used extensively in many JavaScript functions and we'll see much more of them throughout the book.

Sorting Arrays

In the last chapter we saw that arrays have a `sort()` method that sorted the items in the array into alphabetical order. This is fine for strings, but it doesn't work so well for numbers:

```
> [1,3,12,5,23,18,7].sort();
<< [1, 12, 18, 23, 3, 5, 7]
```

The reason for this is that the numbers are converted into strings and then placed in alphabetical order.

So how do you sort an array of numerical values? The answer is to provide a callback function to the `sort()` method that tells the `sort()` method how to compare two values, a and b. The callback function should return the following:

- a negative value if a comes before b
- 0 if a and b are in the same position
- a positive value if a comes after b

Here is an example of a `compareNumbers` function that can be used as a callback to sort numbers:

```
function compareNumbers(a,b){
    return a-b;
}
```

This simply subtracts the two numbers that are being compared, giving a result that is either negative (if b is bigger than a), zero (if a and b are the same value), or positive (if a is bigger than b). This means that it can be used as a callback to sort the array of numbers correctly:

```
> [1,3,12,5,23,18,7].sort(compareNumbers);
<< [1, 3, 5, 7, 12, 18, 23]
```

Much better!

Watch Out For Overflows

In some rare instances where an array includes some very large and negative numbers, an overflow error can occur and the result of **a-b** becomes smaller than the smallest number that JavaScript is able to cope with. If this is the case, the following function can be used as a callback instead:

```
function compareNumbers (a,b) {
  if (a < b) {
    return -1;
  } else if (a> b) {
    return 1;
  } else {
    return 0;
  }
}
```

Improving the `mean()` Function

Earlier in the chapter we created a `mean()` function that would calculate the mean of any number of arguments. We can improve on this, allowing a callback to be added as the last argument that specifies a function to be applied to all the numbers before the mean is calculated. This will allow us to work out things such as the mean of all numbers if they were doubled or squared.

Here is the code for the improved function that accepts a callback:

```
function mean(values, callback) {
  var total = 0;
  for(var i=0, max = values.length; i < max; i++) {
    if (typeof callback === "function") {
      total += callback(values[i]);
    } else {
      total += values[i];
    }
  }
  return total/max;
}
```

The next part of the code is similar to our previous `mean()` function. , except in the following `if` block where we check to see if the `callback` argument is a function.

If it is, the callback is applied to each value before being added to the total; otherwise, the total is calculated using just the values from the array given as the first argument:

```
if (typeof callback === "function") {
  total += callback(values[i]);
} else {
  total += values[i];
}
```

Let's have a go at using it:

```
> mean([2,5,7,11,4]); // this should just calculate the mean
<< 5.8
```

Now let's use an anonymous function to double all the numbers before calculating the mean:

```
> mean([2,5,7,11,4],function(x){ return 2*x; });
<< 11.6
```

This is the equivalent of calculating the mean of 2 * 2, 2 * 5, 2 * 7, 2 * 11, and 2 * 4.

Last of all, let's use the `square` function that we wrote earlier in this chapter as a callback to square all the numbers before calculating the mean:

```
> mean([2,5,7,11,4],square);
<< 43
```

This is the equivalent of calculating the mean of 2^2, 5^2, 7^2, 11^2, and 4x^2.

I trust these examples show how using callbacks can make functions much more powerful and flexible.

Array Iterators

ECMAScript 5 introduced a number of methods for arrays that utilize callbacks to make them much more flexible.

forEach()

In the last chapter, we saw that a `for` loop could be used to loop through each value in an array like so:

```
var colors = ["Red", "Green", "Blue"]

for( var i = 0, max = colors.length ; i < max ; i++ ) {
  console.log("Color at position " + i + " is " + colors[i]);
}
<<  "Color at position 0 is Red"
    "Color at position 1 is Green"
    "Color at position 2 is Blue"
```

An alternative is to use the `forEach()` method. This will loop through the array and invoke a callback function using each value as an argument. The callback function takes three parameters, the first represents the value in the array, the second represents the current index and the third represent the array that the callback is being called on. The example above could be written as:

```
colors.forEach(function(color,index){
  console.log("Color at position " + index + " is " + color);
});
<<  "Color at position 0 is Red"
    "Color at position 1 is Green"
    "Color at position 2 is Blue"
```

map()

The `map()` method is very similar to the `forEach()` method. It also iterates over an array and takes a callback function as a parameter that is invoked on each item in the array. This is often used to process data returned from databases in array form, such as adding HTML tags to plain text. The difference is that it returns a new array that replaces each value with the return value of the callback function. For example, we can square every number in an array using the `square` function we wrote previously as a callback to the `map()` method:

```
[1,2,3].map( square )
<< [1, 4, 9]
```

An anonymous function can also be used as a callback. This example will write all items in the array in uppercase and place them inside paragraph tags:

```
["red","green","blue"].map( function(color) { return "<p>" + color.
➡toUpperCase() + "</p>"; } );
<< ["<p>RED</p>", "<p>GREEN</p>", "<p>BLUE</p>"]
```

Notice in this example the anonymous function takes a parameter, `color`, which refers to the item in the array. This callback can also take two more parameters — the second parameter refers to the index number in the array and the third refers to the array itself. All three parameters can be seen in the next example:

```
["red","green","blue"].map( function(color, index, array) { return
➡index + ": " + color + " (length " + array.length + ")"; } );
<< ["0: red (length 3)", "1: green (length 3)", "2: blue (length 3)
➡"]
```

reduce()

The `reduce()` method is another method that iterates over each value in the array, but this time it cumulatively combines each result to return just a single value. The callback function is used to describe how to combine each value of the array with the running total. This is often used to calculate statistics such as averages based on data returned from a database in array form. It usually takes two parameters: The first parameter represents the previous value and the second parameter represents the current item in the array. The following example shows how to sum an array of numbers:

```
[1,2,3,4,5].reduce( function(prev,current){
  return prev + current;
});
<< 15
```

The value of `prev` starts as the first item in the array. The value of `prev` then becomes the result of this operation. Then the next item in the array is added to this running total, and so on, until every item in the array has been added.

The `reduce()` method also takes a second parameter after the callback, which is the inital value of `prev`. For example, we could total the numbers in an array, but starting at 10, instead of zero:

```
[1,2,3,4,5].reduce( function(prev,current){
  return prev + current;
},10); // <---- second parameter of 10 here
<< 25
```

Another example could be to calculate the average word length in a sentence:

```
sentence = "The quick brown fox jumped over the lazy dog"
<< "The quick brown fox jumped over the lazy dog"
```

The sentence can be converted into an array using the `split()` method:

```
words = sentence.split(" ");
<< ["The", "quick", "brown", "fox", "jumped", "over", "the", "lazy",
➡"dog"]
```

Now we can use the `reduce()` function to calculage the total number of letters in the sentence:

```
total = words.reduce( function(prev,word) {
  return prev + word.length;
},0);
<< 36

average = total/words.length;
<< 4
```

Using map() and reduce() Together

The `map()` and `reduce()` methods are often used in combination to create some powerful transformations of data stored in arrays. Because the `map()` function returns the transformed array, the `reduce()` can be chained on the end. For example, we can calculate the sum of square numbers using the `map()` method to square each number in the array and then use the `reduce()` method to add the results together:

```
[1,2,3].map(square).reduce( function(total,x) { return x + total; });
<< 14
```

Another more complex example could be used to take an array of orders, apply a sales tax to them using `map()` and then use `reduce()` to find the total:

```
var sales = [ 100, 230, 55];
totalAfterTaxSales = sales.map( function(amount) {
  return amount * 1.15; // add 15% sales tax
  }).reduce( function(prev,current){
    return prev + current;
  });
<< 442.75
```

filter()

The `filter()` method returns a new array that only contains items from the original array that pass return true when passed to the callback. For example, we can filter an array of numbers to just the even numbers using the following code:

```
var numbers = [2, 7, 6, 5, 11, 23, 12]

numbers.filter( function(number) {
  return number%2 === 0; // this returns true if the number is even
  });

<< [2, 6, 12]
```

There are other array methods that use callbacks that are worth investigating such as `reduceRight()`, `every()`, and `some()`. More information about them can be found at the Mozilla Developer Network[2].

Quiz Ninja Project

Now that we have a good understanding of functions, we're going to have a go at **refactoring** the code for our Quiz Ninja project so that it uses functions to describe the main parts of the program. Refactoring is the process of improving the code's structure and maintainability without changing its behavior.

---

[2] https://developer.mozilla.org/en-US/docs/Web/JavaScript/Reference/Global_Objects/Array

What we're going to do is replace some of the chunks of code with functions. This will make the code easier to follow and maintain because if we want to make a change to the functionality, all we need to do is change the code inside the relevant function.

Open up the **scripts.js** file in the **js** folder and replace all the code with the following:

scripts.js *(incomplete)*

```
var quiz = [
    ["What is Superman's real name?","Clarke Kent"],
    ["What is Wonderwoman's real name?","Dianna Prince"],
    ["What is Batman's real name?","Bruce Wayne"]
  ];

var score = 0 // initialize score

play(quiz);
```

The first part of this code remains the same — we set up an array of questions and answers that is stored in the `quiz` variable and then declare a `score` variable initialized to 0 to keep track of the player's score. The last line contains an important change, though — we invoke a function called `play()` and pass the `quiz` array to it as an argument. This is the main game function that contains all the steps of playing the game. Let's write that function now by adding the following lines of code to the end of our **scripts.js** file (remember that, because of hoisting, function definitions can go after they are invoked):

scripts.js *(excerpt)*

```
function play(quiz){
  // main game loop
  for(var i=0, question, answer, max=quiz.length; i<max; i++) {
    question = quiz[i][0];
    answer = ask(question);
    check(answer);
  }
  // end of main game loop
  gameOver();
}
```

This function also contains a number of functions that help to describe how the game runs, without getting bogged down with too much of the actual logic. It loops through the `quiz` array and selects a question. This is an array containing the question at index 0 and the corresponding answer at index 1 that is stored in the variable `question`. The next step is to ask the question (by invoking the `ask()` function), then checks the answer the player gives (by invoking the `check()` function). After we have looped through every question in the `quiz` array, the game is over, so the `gameOver()` function is invoked. This shows how code can be simplified abstracting it into separate functions that are descriptively named. It is also useful as it allows us to change the content of the functions at a later time; if we decide that the way to check a question will change, for example, all we need to do is edit the `check()` function.

Now we need to write the `ask()` and `check()` functions. These functions need to be placed inside the `play()` function as nested functions. This will give them access to any variables defined inside the `play()` function, which is important as they both require access to the variables that are defined within the scope of the `play()` function. So these functions must also be defined inside the scope of the `play()` function in order to have access to the variables.

First of all, let's write the `ask()` function. This goes at the bottom of the `play()` function block (before the closing curly brace):

scripts.js (excerpt)

```
function ask(question) {
  return prompt(question); // quiz[i][0] is the ith questions
}
```

The `ask()` function accepts a `question` parameter. This combination of function name and parameter name is used to make the code very descriptive — it reads almost like an English sentence: "Ask the question". It uses a prompt dialog and returns the text entered by the player, which is then saved in a variable called `answer`.

The `check()` function is written after the `ask()` function and has an `answer` parameter. This combination of function name and parameter name again make the code read more like an English sentence. Naming functions in this way means that we don't need to use comments to explain what the code does in this case, as it's self-explanatory:

```
                                                    scripts.js (excerpt)

function check(answer) {
  if(answer === quiz[i][1]){ // quiz[i][1] is the ith answer
    alert("Correct!");
    // increase score by 1
    score++;
  } else {
    alert("Wrong!");
  }
}
```

This function uses the same logic that we used in the last chapter to check if the answer entered by the player is the same as the answer stored in the array. If it is, then we increase the score by 1 and if it isn't then we show an alert dialog to say so.

When all the questions have been asked and all the answers have been checked, the program breaks out of the loop and then invokes the gameOver() function. This is also defined at the bottom of the playQuiz function as follows:

```
                                                    scripts.js (excerpt)

function gameOver(){
    // inform the player that the game has finished and tell them
➥how many points they have scored
    alert("Game Over, you scored " + score + " points");
  }
}
```

This uses an alert dialog to give some feedback about how many questions were answered correctly.

Once you've made these changes, have a go at playing the quiz by opening the **index.htm** file in your browser. It should look like the screenshot shown in Figure 4.3.

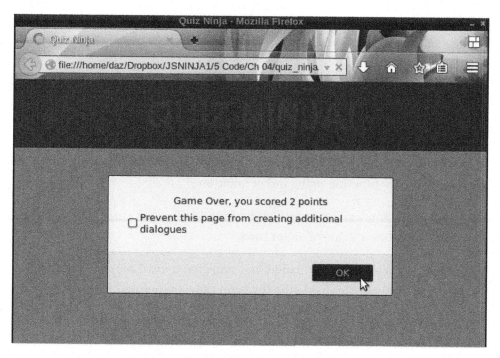

Figure 4.3. Playing Quiz Ninja

While you play, you might notice that there's been no change to the functionality of the quiz. This is the process of refactoring—the functionality of the application remains the same, but the underlying code has become more flexible and easier to maintain, as well as being more readable and descriptive due to the use of functions. We have abstracted much of the internal game logic out into separate functions, which means that we can change the mechanics of different aspects of the quiz by updating the relevant functions.

I hope this helps to demonstrate how functions can make your code more flexible, maintainable, reusable, and easier to read—as long as they are well-named.

Summary

In this chapter we have learned the following:

▤ Functions are first-class objects that behave the same way as all other values.

▤ Function literals can be defined using the `function` declaration, or by creating a *function expression* by assigning an anonymous function to a variable.

■ All functions return a value. If this is not explicitly stated, the function will return `undefined`.

■ A parameter is a value that is written in the parentheses of a function declaration and can be used like a variable inside the function's body.

■ An argument is a value that is provided to a function when it is invoked.

■ The `arguments` variable is an array-like object that allows access to each argument provided to the function using index notation.

■ Default arguments can be supplied to a function by checking if the actual argument entered has a value of `undefined`.

■ Variables defined using `var` inside functions have *local scope*. This means that they are only available inside the function they are defined in.

■ Variables defined without `var` have *global scope*, which means they can be accessed (and overwritten) from anywhere in the program.

■ Variable declarations are *hoisted* to the top of a functions scope, but variable assignments are not.

■ Function declarations can be invoked before they are defined because they are hoisted to the top of the scope, but function expressions cannot be invoked until after they are defined.

■ A *callback* is a function that is provided as an argument to another function.

Everything that isn't a primitive value in JavaScript is an object—the topic of our next chapter.

Chapter 5

Objects

Everything in JavaScript is either one of the five primitive values we met in Chapter 2 (strings, numbers, Booleans, undefined, and null) or an **object**. We've actually met some objects already; arrays in Chapter 3 and functions in Chapter 4 are both objects, although these are built-in objects that are part of the language. In this chapter we're going to look at user-defined objects as well as some other built-in objects.

In this chapter, we'll be covering the following topics:

- object literals

- adding properties to objects

- object methods

- JSON

- the `Math` object

- the `Date` object

- the `RegExp` object

■ our project—create quiz and question objects and ask random questions

Object Literals

An object in JavaScript is a self-contained set of related values and functions. They act as a collection of named properties that map to any JavaScript value such as strings, numbers, Booleans, arrays, and even functions. If a property's value is a function, it is known as a **method**.

One way to think about an object is that it's like a dictionary where you look up a property name and see a value. Another way of is that it is like a database of values; some databases actually use JavaScript objects to store information. This is similar to a hash or associative array in other programming languages; however, JavaScript objects are much more flexible as they can be employed to encapsulate code that can be reused throughout a program. They can also inherit properties from other objects (which we'll cover in Chapter 11).

An **object literal** is an object that is created directly in the language by wrapping all its properties and methods in curly braces {}. Object literals are a distinguishing feature of the JavaScript language, as they allow objects to be created quickly without the need for a class template.

A Super Example

Here is an example of an object literal that describes the Man of Steel:

```
var superman = {
  name: "Superman",
  "real name": "Clark Kent",
  height: 75,
  weight: 235,
  hero: true,
  villain: false,
  allies: ["Batman","Supergirl","Superboy"],
  fly: function(){
```

```
      return "Up, up and away!";
   }
}
```

Each property is a key-value pair, separated by commas. In the example, the first property is called `name` and its value is `"Superman"`, while the property `fly` is a method.

If a property's name doesn't follow the rules for naming variables described in Chapter 2 [14], it needs to be quoted. For example, the property `"real name"` needs to be quoted because it contains a space.

 Property and Method Names in the Real World

> It's very uncommon to use property and method names that don't follow the rules for naming variables. In a real-world app, it is likely that the `"real name"` property would actually be named `real_name` or `realName`.

All objects are mutable at any time when a program is running. This means that its properties and methods can be changed or removed and new properties and methods can be added to the object.

Creating Objects

To create an object literal, simply enter a pair of curly braces. The following example creates an empty object that is assigned to the variable `spiderman`:

```
var spiderman = {};
```

It's also possible to create an object using a constructor function. This example will create an empty object:

```
var spiderman = new Object();
```

This method is not recommended, however, and the object literal notation is the preferred way of creating objects. The obvious reason is because it requires less typing; a constructor takes more steps in the background, which can cause programs to run slower.

Accessing Properties

You can access the properties of an object using the **dot notation** that we've already seen in previous chapters:

```
superman.name
<< "Superman"
```

You can also access an object's properties using **bracket notation**—the property is represented by a string inside square brackets, so needs to be placed inside single or double quotation marks:

```
superman['name']
<< "Superman"
```

Dot notation is much more common, but bracket notation has a few advantages: It is the only way to access nonstandard property and method names that don't follow the variable naming rules. It also lets you evaluate an expression and use it as the object key:

```
superman["real" + " " + "name"] // the property is built using
➥string concatenation
<< "Clarke Kent"
```

If you try to access a property that doesn't exist, `undefined` will be returned:

```
superman.city
<< undefined
```

Calling Methods

To call an object's method we can also use dot or bracket notation. Calling a method is the same as invoking a function, so parentheses need to be placed after the method name:

```
superman.fly()
<< "Up, up and away!"

superman['fly']()
<< "Up, up and away!"
```

Checking if Properties or Methods Exist

The in operator can be used to check whether an object has a particular property. So, for example, we can check if the superman object has a property called city using this code:

```
"city" in superman
<< false
```

Alternatively, you could also check to see if the property or method doesn't return undefined:

```
superman.city !== undefined
<< false
```

As mentioned earlier, objects can inherit properties from other objects, so all objects have a method called hasOwnProperty(). This can be used to check whether an object has a property that is its own, rather than one that has been inherited from another object:

```
superman.hasOwnProperty('city');
<< false

superman.hasOwnProperty('name');
<< true
```

Finding all the Properties of an Object

We can loop through all of an object's properties and methods by using a for in loop. For example, to log all the properties of the superman object to the console, we could use:

```
for(var key in superman) {
  console.log(key + ": " + superman[key]);
}
<< "name: Superman"
<< "real name: Clark Kent"
<< "height: 75"
<< "weight: 235"
<< "hero: true"
<< "villain: false"
<< "allies: Batman,Supergirl,Superboy"
<< "fly: function (){
    console.log(\"Up, up and away!\");
  }"
```

In this example, we create a variable called key. This is then used to represent the name of each property or method in the superman object inside the for loop.

To make sure that only an object's own properties are returned, a quick check can be implemented beforehand:

```
for(var key in superman) {
  if(superman.hasOwnProperty(key)){
    console.log(key + ": " + superman[key]);
  }
}
```

Adding Properties

New properties and methods can be added to objects at any time in a program. This is done by assigning a value to the new property. For example, if we wanted to add a new city property to our superman object, we would do it like so:

```
superman.city = "Metropolis"
<< "Metropolis"
```

Now if we take a look at the superman object, we can see that it has a city property:

```
superman
<< {"city": "Metropolis", "fly": function (){
console.log("Up, up and away!");}, "height": 75, "name": "Superman",
➥"real name": "Clark Kent", "weight": 235}
```

Notice that the properties don't necessarily appear in the order that they were entered. An object is not an ordered list like an array, so you should never rely on the properties being in a certain order.

Changing Properties

You can change the value of an object's properties at any time using assignment. For example, we can change the value of the "real name" property like this:

```
superman['real name'] = "Kal-El"
<< "Kal-El"
```

We can check the update has taken place by taking a look at the object:

```
superman
<< {"allies": ["Batman", "Supergirl", "Superboy"], "city":
➥"Metropolis", "fly": function (){
    console.log("Up, up and away!");
  }, "height": 75, "hero": true, "name": "Superman", "real name":
➥"Kal-El", "villain": false, "weight": 235}
```

Removing Properties

Any property can be removed from an object using the delete operator. For example, if we wanted to remove the fly method from the superman object, we would enter the following:

```
delete superman.fly
<< true
```

Now if we take a look at the superman object, we can see that he has lost his ability to fly:

```
superman
<< {"allies": ["Batman", "Supergirl", "Superboy"], "city":
➥"Metropolis", "height": 75, "hero": true, "name": "Superman",
➥ "real name": "Kal-El", "villain": false, "weight": 235}
```

Nested Objects

It's even possible for an object to contain other objects. These are known as **nested objects**. Here's an example of an object that contains a list of other objects. It has been assigned to the variable `jla`:

```
jla = {
  superman: { realName: "Clarke Kent" },
  batman: { realName: "Bruce Wayne" },
  wonderWoman: { realName: "Diana Prince" },
  flash: { realName: "Barry Allen" },
  greenLantern: { realName: "Hal Jordan" },
  martianManhunter: { realName: "John Jones" }
}
```

The values in nested objects can be accessed by referencing each property name in order using either dot or bracket notation:

```
jla.wonderWoman.realName
<< "Diana Prince"

jla['flash']['realName']
<< "Barry Allen"
```

You can even mix the different notations:

```
jla.martianManhunter['realName']
<< "John Jones"
```

Objects as Parameters to Functions

An object literal can be passed as a parameter to a function. This allows the arguments to be given in any order and for default values to be used.

The following example shows how this can be done:

```
function greet (options) {
  options = options || {};
  greeting = options.greeting || "Hello";
  name = options.name || "Anon";
  age = options.age || 18
  return greeting + "! My name is " + name + " and I am " + age +
➡" years old.";
}
```

It takes an object called `options` as an argument. If no object is provided, we create an empty object instead in this line:

```
options = options || {};
```

This is a common JavaScript pattern used to create default values. It relies on the logical OR statement being lazily evaluated. If `options` already exists, only the first statement will be evaluated, so `options` will remain as its current value. If no arguments are supplied to the function, the value of `options` will be `undefined`, which is falsy. Then the second operand will be evaluated and `options` will be assigned to an empty object literal.

The same method is then used to set default values for the `greeting`, `name`, and `age` properties of the `options` object. At the end of the method, a string is returned that uses the values that were supplied, or the default values.

Here is an example of how the function can be used:

```
greet({ greeting: "Hi", age: 10, name: "Bart" });
<< "Hi! My name is Bart and I am 10 years old."
```

You can enter the parameters in any order and if you don't enter one of the values, its default value will be used:

```
greet({ name: "Lisa", age: 8 });
<< "Hello! My name is Lisa and I am 8 years old."
```

This is a popular pattern used with functions, particularly when there are a lot of options, and it is common to many JavaScript libraries.

Be Careful with Falsy Values

You have to take care when using this method of assigning default values because any falsy value will result in the default value being used.

For example, if an age of 0 is entered, the default value will be used because 0 is falsy:

```
greet({ age: p });
<< "Hello! My name is Anon and I am 18 years old."
```

Built-in Objects

We've already seen the two main built-in objects included in JavaScript: arrays and functions. JavaScript has a number of other built-in *global* objects that can be accessed from anywhere in a program. They provide a number of useful properties and methods that we'll cover in this section.

JSON

JavaScript Object Notation, or **JSON**, was invented by Douglas Crockford in 2001. It is a popular lightweight data-storage format that is used for data serialization and configuration. It is often used to exchange information between web services and is employed by sites such as Twitter, Facebook, and Trello to share information. It manages to hit the sweet spot between being both human- and machine-readable.

JSON is a string representation of the object literal notation that we have just seen. There are a few differences, though, such as property names being quoted and not using functions to create methods.

Here is an example of a JSON object representing the Caped Crusader:

```
var batman = '{"name": "Batman","real name": "Bruce Wayne","height":
➥ 74,"weight": 210,"hero": true,"villain": false,"allies": ["Robin",
➥"Batgirl","Superman"]}'
```

JSON is becoming increasingly popular as a data storage format and many programming languages now have libraries dedicated to parsing and generating it. Since

ECMAScript 5, there has been a global JSON object that can be used to do the same in JavaScript.

The parse method takes a JSON string and returns a JavaScript object:

```
JSON.parse(batman);
<< {"allies": ["Robin", "Batgirl", "Superman"], "height": 74,
➥"hero": true, "name": "Batman", "real name": "Bruce Wayne",
➥"villain": false, "weight": 210}
```

The stringify method does the opposite, taking a JavaScript object and returning a string of JSON data, as can be seen in the example:

```
var wonderWoman = {
    name: "Wonder Woman",
    "real name": "Diana Prince",
    height: 72,
    weight: 165,
    hero: true,
    villain: false,
    allies: ["Wonder Girl","Donna Troy","Superman"],
    lasso: function(){
        console.log("You will tell the truth!");
    }
}

JSON.stringify(wonderWoman);
<< "{\"name\":\"Wonder Woman\",\"real name\":\"Diana Prince\",\
➥"height\":72,\"weight\":165,\"hero\":true,\"villain\":false,\
➥"allies\":[\"Wonder Girl\",\"Donna Troy\",\"Superman\"]}"
```

Note that the quote marks are escaped and any methods an object has (such as the aforementioned lasso method) will simply be ignored by the stringify method.

These methods are useful when passing data to and from a web server using Ajax requests (see Chapter 13) or when using localStorage to store data on a user's machine (see Chapter 14). JSON data is easy to exchange between different services as most languages and protocols are able to interpret data as strings of text.

The Math Object

The Math object has several properties that represent mathematical constants and methods. These are used to carry out a number of useful operations.

All the properties and methods of the Math object are immutable and unable to be changed.

Mathematical Constants

The Math object has eight properties that represent a mix of commonly used math constants. Note that they are all named in capital letters, which is a convention for constant values:

```
> Math.PI // The ratio of the cirumference and diameter of a circle
<< 3.141592653589793

> Math.SQRT2 // The square root of 2
<< 1.4142135623730951

> Math.SQRT1_2 // The reciprocal of the square root of 2
<< 0.7071067811865476

> Math.E // Euler's constant
<< 2.718281828459045

> Math.LN2 // The natural logarithm of 2
<< 0.6931471805599453

> Math.LN10 // The natural logarithm of 10
<< 2.302585092994046

> Math.LOG2E // Log base 2 of Euler's constant
<< 1.4426950408889634

> Math.LOG10E // Log base 10 of Euler's constant
<< 0.4342944819032518
```

Mathematical Operations

The Math object also has several methods to carry out a variety of useful mathematical operations.

The `Math.abs()` method returns the absolute value of a number. So if the number is positive, it will remain the same and if it is negative, it will become positive:

```
> Math.abs(3);
<< 3

> Math.abs(-4.6);
<< 4.6
```

The `Math.ceil()` method will round a number *up* to the next integer, or remain the same if it is already an integer:

```
> Math.ceil(4.2);
<< 5

> Math.ceil(8);
<< 8

> Math.ceil(-4.2);
<< -4
```

The `Math.floor()` method will round a number *down* to the next integer, or remain the same if it is already an integer:

```
> Math.floor(4.2);
<< 4

> Math.floor(8);
<< 8

> Math.floor(-4.2);
<< -5
```

The `Math.round()` method will round a number to the *nearest* integer:

```
> Math.round(4.5);
<< 5

> Math.round(4.499);
<< 4
```

```
> Math.round(-4.2);
<< -4
```

The `Math.exp()` method will raise a number to the power of Euler's constant:

```
> Math.exp(1); // This is Euler's constant
<< 2.718281828459045

> Math.exp(0); // Any number to the power of 0 is 1
<< 1

> Math.exp(-3);
<< 0.04978706836786393
```

The `Math.pow()` method will raise any number (the first argument) to the power of another number (the second argument):

```
> Math.pow(3,2); // 3 squared
<< 9

> Math.pow(4.5,0); // Any number to the power of 0 is 1
<< 1

> Math.pow(27,1/3); // A nice way to do cube roots
<<
```

The `Math.sqrt()` method returns the positive square root of a number:

```
> Math.sqrt(121);
<< 11

> Math.sqrt(2); // same as Math.SQRT2
<< 1.4142135623730951

> Math.sqrt(-1); // No built in imaginary numbers!
<< NaN
```

The `Math.log()` method returns the natural logarithm of a number:

```
> Math.log(Math.E); // Natural logs have a base of Euler's constant
<< 1

> Math.log(1); // log of 1 is zero
<< 0

> Math.log(0); // You can't take the log of zero
<< -Infinity

> Math.log(-2); // You can't take logs of negative numbers
<< NaN
```

The `Math.max()` method returns the maximum number from its arguments:

```
> Math.max(1,2,3);
<< 3

> Math.max(Math.PI,Math.SQRT2, Math.E);
<< 3.141592653589793
```

And the `Math.min()` method unsurprisingly returns the minimum number from the given arguments:

```
> Math.min(1,2,3);
<< 1

> Math.min(Math.PI,Math.SQRT2, Math.E);
<< 1.4142135623730951
```

Trigonometric Functions

The `Math` object also has the standard trigonometric functions, which are very useful when working with geometrical objects. All angles are measured in radians for these functions.

 Remind Me About Radians

Radians[1] are a standard unit of angular measurement, equal to the angle of the circle's center corresponding to the arc that subtends it.

---

[1] http://en.wikipedia.org/wiki/Radian

The `Math.sin()` returns the sine of an angle:

```
> Math.sin(Math.PI/6); // this calculation contains rounding errors,
➥ it should be 0.5
<< 0.49999999999999994
```

The `Math.cos()` returns the cosine of an angle:

```
> Math.cos(Math.PI/6);
<< 0.8660254037844387
```

The `Math.tan()` returns the tangent of an angle:

```
> Math.tan(Math.PI/4); // another rounding error, this should be 1
<< 0.9999999999999999

> Math.tan(Math.PI/2); // this should be NaN or Infinity
<< 16331778728383844
```

The `Math.asin()` returns the arcsine of a number. The result is an angle:

```
> Math.asin(1);
<< 1.5707963267948966
```

The `Math.acos()` returns the arccosine of a number. The result is an angle:

```
> Math.acos(0.5);
<< 1.0471975511965976
```

The `Math.atan()` returns the arctangent of a number. The result is an angle:

```
> Math.atan(Math.sqrt(3)); // Same as Math.PI/3
<< 1.0471975511965976
```

 Rounding Errors

You might have noticed that some of the values in the previous examples were not exactly accurate. For example, sin(π/6) should be 0.5, yet `Math.sin(Math.PI/6)` returns 0.49999999999999994.

This is to be expected when dealing with floating-point decimal numbers. Computers have lots of trouble dealing with decimal fractions (as they work in binary) and the answers can vary from one platform to another.

Another problem is that the value of π using `Math.PI` is only given correct to 16 significant figures, which will affect the overall accuracy.

These rounding errors are no big deal for most web applications. Whenever you perform any calculations, make sure that your program doesn't rely on exact answers, and has some degree of tolerance instead.

Random Numbers

The `Math.random()` method is used to create random numbers, which can be very useful when writing programs. Calling the method will generate a number between 0 and 1, like so:

```
> Math.random();
<< 0.7881970851344265
```

To generate a random number between 0 and another number, we can multiply the value by that number. The following code generates a random number between 0 and 6:

```
> 6 * Math.random();
<< 4.580981240354013
```

If we want to generate a random integer, we can use the `Math.floor()` method that we saw earlier to remove the decimal part of the return value. The following code generates a random integer between 0 and 5 (it will never be 6, because it always rounds down):

```
> Math.floor(6 * Math.random());
<< 4
```

It's a useful exercise to try and write a function that will generate a random number between two values.

Experimental Methods

There are some experimental functions being considered for inclusion in the next version of the ECMAScript specification and are already implemented in some browsers. You can find a full list at the Mozilla Developer Reference.[2]

The Date Object

Date objects hold information about dates and times. Each object represents a single moment in time.

Constructor Function

A constructor function is used to create a new date object using the new operator:

```
> today = new Date();
<< [object Date]{

    }
```

This confirms that the variable today points to a Date object. To see what the date is, we use the toString() method that all objects have:

```
> today.toString();
<< "Sun Jun 08 2014 15:43:03 GMT+0100 (BST)"
```

If an argument is not supplied, the date will default to the current date and time. It's possible to create Date objects for any date by supplying it as an argument to the constructor function. This can be written as a string in a variety of forms:

```
> christmas = new Date('2014 12 25');
<< [object Date]{

    }

> christmas.toString();
<< "Thu Dec 25 2014 00:00:00 GMT+0000 (GMT)"

> chanukah = new Date('16 December 2014');
```

---

[2] https://developer.mozilla.org/en-US/docs/Web/JavaScript/Reference/Global_Objects/Math

```
<< [object Date]{

  }

> chanukah.toString();
<< "Tue Dec 16 2014 00:00:00 GMT+0000 (GMT)"

> eid = new Date('Saturday, July 18, 2015');
<< [object Date]{

  }

> eid.toString();
<< "Sat Jul 18 2015 00:00:00 GMT+0100 (BST)"
```

JavaScript is very flexible in the date format, which can be used in the string that is provided as an argument; however, in order to be more consistent, it is better to provide each bit of information about the date as a separate argument. The parameters that can be provided are as follows:

```
new Date(year,month,day,hour,minutes,seconds,millisecons)
```

Here is an example:

```
> easter = new Date(2015, 3, 05);
<< [object Date]{

  }

> easter.toString();
<< "Sun Apr 05 2015 00:00:00 GMT+0100 (BST)"
```

Notice that the months start counting at zero, so January is 0, February is 1, and so on up to December, which is 11.

An alternative is to use a timestamp, which is a single integer argument that represents the number of milliseconds since the Epoch (1st January 1970):

```
> diwali = new Date(1414018800000);
<< [object Date]{
```

```
    }

> diwali.toString();
<< "Thu Oct 23 2014 00:00:00 GMT+0100 (BST)"
```

 The Epoch

The Epoch is 1st January, 1970. This is an arbitrary date that is used in programming as a reference point in time from which to measure dates. This allows dates to be expressed as an integer that represents the number of seconds since the Epoch. It results in a very large number and there is a potential problem looming in 2038[3] when the number of seconds since the Epoch will be greater than 2,147,483,647, which is the maximum value that many computers can deal with as a signed 32-bit integer. Fortunately, this problem will not affect JavaScript dates because it uses floating-point numbers rather than integers, so it can handle bigger values.

Getter Methods

The properties of date objects are unable to be viewed or changed directly. Instead, they have a number of methods known as **getter methods** that return information about the date object, such as the month and year.

Once you have created a date object it will have access to all the getter methods. There are two versions of each method, one that returns the information in local time and the other that uses Coordinated Universal Time (UTC).

 Coordinated Universal Time

UTC is the primary time standard by which the world regulates clocks. It was formalized in 1960 and is much the same as Greenwich Mean Time (GMT). The main difference is that UTC is a standard that is defined by the scientific community, unlike GMT.

The getDay() and getUTCDay() methods are used to find the day of the week that the date object falls on. It returns a number, starting at 0 for Sunday, up to 6 for Saturday:

---

[3] http://en.wikipedia.org/wiki/Year_2038_problem

```
> diwali.getDay(); // it's on a Thursday
<< 4
```

The getDate() and getUTCDate()methods return the day of the month for the date object:

```
> diwali.getDate(); // it's on the 23rd
<< 23
```

The getMonth() and getUTCMonth() methods can be used to find the month of the date object. It returns an integer, but remember that JavaScript starts counting at 0, so January is 0, February is 1, and so on up to December being 11:

```
> diwali.getMonth(); // it's in October
<< 9
```

The getFullYear() and getUTCFullYear() methods return the year of the date object. There is also a getYear() method, but it isn't Y2K compliant, so shouldn't be used:

```
> diwali.getYear(); // broken for years after 2000
<< 114

> diwali.getFullYear(); // use this instead
<< 2014
```

There are also getHours(), getUTCHours(), getMinutes(), getUTCMinutes(), getSeconds(), getUTCSeconds, getMilliseconds(), and getUTCMilliseconds() methods that will return the hours, minutes, seconds and milliseconds since midnight.

The getTime() method returns a timestamp representing the number of milliseconds since the Epoch:

```
> diwali.getTime();
<< 1414018800000
```

This can be useful for incrementing dates by a set amount of time; for example, a day can be represented by 1000 * 60 * 60 * 24 milliseconds:

```
> christmasEve = new Date(christmas.getTime() - 1000 * 60 * 60 * 24)
<< [object Date]{

  }

> christmasEve.toString();
<< Fri Dec 26 2014 00:00:00 GMT+0000 (GMT)"
```

The getTimezoneOffset() method returns the difference, in minutes, between local time and UTC. For example, my timezone is currently British Summer Time:

```
> new Date().getTimezoneOffset()
<< -60
```

This shows that British Summer Time is one hour ahead of UTC.

Setter Methods

Most of the getter methods covered in the previous section have equivalent **setter methods**. These are methods that can be used to change the value of the date held in a Date object. Each of the methods takes an argument representing the value to which you update the date. The methods return the timestamp of the updated date object.

As an example, we can change the value of the date stored in the diwali variable so that it contains the date of Diwali in 2015, which is on Wednesday, November 11, 2015:

```
> diwali.setDate(11);
<< 1412982000000
```

```
> diwali.setMonth(10); // November is month 10
<< 1415664000000

> diwali.setFullYear(2015);
<< 1447200000000
```

Note that the values returned by these functions is the timestamp representing the number of milliseconds since the Epoch. To see the actual date, we need to use the toString() mehtod:

```
> diwali.toString();
<< "Wed Nov 11 2015 00:00:00 GMT+0000 (GMT)"
```

There are also setHours(), setUTCHours(), setMinutes(), setUTCMinutes(), setSeconds(), setUTCSeconds, setMilliseconds() and setUTCMilliseconds() methods that can be used to edit the time portion of a Date object.

Alternatively, if you know the date as a timestamp, you can use the setTime() method:

```
> diwali.setTime(1447200000000);
<< 1447200000000
```

The RegExp Object

A **regular expression** (or RegExp, for short) is a pattern that can be used to search or modify strings. A common use case is "find and replace" type operations. For example, say you were looking for any word ending in "ing," you could use the regular expression /\w+ing/.

If that example looks a bit confusing, don't worry, it will become clear as we move through this section. Regular expressions can look a little strange; in fact, they're something of a dark art that could easily fill a whole book! They are certainly useful when manipulating text strings, though, so we'll introduce some of the basics here and recommend that you carry out further reading once you've finished this book.

Here are a couple of resources for the curious:

▨ Mastering Regular Expressions by Jeffrey Fried[4]
▨ Regular Expressions Info[5]

Creating Regular Expressions

There are two ways to create a regular expression. The first, and preferred way, is to use the literal notation of writing the regular expression between forward slashes that we've already seen:

---

[4] http://www.amazon.com/Mastering-Regular-Expressions-Jeffrey-Friedl/dp/0596528124/
[5] http://www.regular-expressions.info/

```
var pattern = /\w+ing/;
```

Alternatively, you can create a new instance of the `RegExp` object using the `new` operator:

```
var pattern = new RegExp('\w+ing');
```

This permits you to create regular expressions using strings.

RegExp Methods

Once you have created a regular expression object, you can use the `test()` to see if a string (passed to the method as a parameter) matches the regular expression pattern. It returns `true` if the pattern is in the string, and `false` if it isn't:

```
var pattern = /.*ing/;
<< undefined

pattern.test("joke"); //testing if the string ends in 'ing'
<< false

pattern.test("joking");
<< true
```

The `exec()` method works the same as the `test()` method, but instead of returning `true` or `false`, it returns an array containing the first match found or `null` if there aren't any matches:

```
pattern.exec("joke"); //testing if the string ends in 'ing'
null

pattern.exec("joking");
["joking"]
```

Basic Regular Expressions

At the most basic level, a regular expression will just be a string of characters, so the following will match the string `'java'`:

```
/java/
```

Character Groups

Groups of characters can be placed together inside square brackets. This **character group** represents any *one* of the characters inside the brackets. For example, the following regular expression matches any vowel:

```
/[aeiou]/
```

A sequence of characters can also be represented by placing a dash [-] between the first and last characters; for example, all the uppercase letters can be represented as:

```
/[A-Z]/
```

The digits 0-9 can be represented as:

```
/[0-9]/
```

If a ^ character is placed at the start of the sequence of characters with the brackets, it negates the sequence, so the following regular expression represents any character that is *not* a capital letter:

```
/[^A-Z]/
```

These groups can be combined with letters to make a more complex pattern. For example, the following regular expression represents the letter J (lower case or capital) followed by a vowel, followed by a lowercase v, followed by a vowel:

```
var pattern = /[Jj][aeiou]v[aeiou]/;
<< undefined

pattern.test("JavaScript");
<< true

pattern.test("jive");
<< true
```

```
pattern.test("hello");
<< false
```

Regular Expression Properties

Regular expressions are objects and have the following properties:

- The `global` property makes the pattern return all matches. By default, the pattern only looks for the first occurrence of a match.

- The `ignoreCase` property makes the pattern case-insensitive. By default, they are case sensitive.

- The `multiline` property makes the pattern multiline. By default, a pattern will stop at the end of a line.

The following flags can be placed after a regular expression literal to change the default properties:

- g sets the `global` property to true

- i sets the `ignoreCase` property to true

- m sets the `multiline` property to true

For example, the following regular expression will match "`JavaScript`" or "`javascript`" because the `ignoreCase` property is set to `true`:

```
var pattern = /java/i
<< undefined

pattern.test("JavaScript");
<< true
```

These properties can be checked using the dot notation, but cannot be updated once the regular expression has been created, as can be seen in the following example:

```
var pattern = /java/i
<< undefined
```

```
pattern.ignoreCase // checking it is true
<< true

pattern.ignoreCase = false // this won't work
<< false

pattern.ignoreCase // has it changed?
<< true
```

The only way to change the ignoreCase property to false is to redefine the regular expression:

```
pattern = /java/
```

Special Characters

In a regular expression, there are a number of characters that have a special meaning, commonly known as **metacharacters**:

- ▒ . matches any character

- ▒ \w matches any word character, and is equivalent to [A-Za-z0-9_]

- ▒ \W matches any non-word character, and is equivalent to [^A-Za-z0-9_]

- ▒ \d matches any digit character, and is equivalent to [0-9]

- ▒ \D matches any non-digit character, and is equivalent to [^0-9]

- ▒ \s matches any whitespace character, and is equivalent to [\t\r\n\f]

- ▒ \S matches any non-whitespace character, and is equivalent to [^ \t\r\n\f]

Modifiers

Modifiers can be placed after a pattern to match multiple occurrences of that pattern:

- ▒ ? matches zero or one occurrence of the pattern

- ▒ * matches zero or more occurrences of the pattern

- ▒ + matches one or more occurrences of the pattern

- {n} matches *n* occurrences of the pattern

- {n,} matches at least *n* occurrences of the pattern

- {,m} matches at most *m* occurrences of the pattern

- {n,m} matches at least *n* and at most *m* occurrences of the pattern

- ^ specifies that the pattern must come at the beginning

- $ specifies that the pattern must come at the end

Any special characters or modifiers can be escaped using a backslash. So if you wanted to match a question mark, ?, you would need to use the regular expression /\?/.

For example, the following regular expression will match anything that starts with J followed by one or more vowels, then any letters or numbers ending in ing:

```
var pattern = /J[aeiou]+\w*ing/
```

As we can see, it matches the words "Joking" and "Jeering":

```
pattern.test("Joking");
<< true

pattern.test("Jeering");
<< true
```

A Practical Example

If we were looking for PDF files and had a list of filenames, this regular expression could be used to find them (assuming they have a **.pdf** extension, of course):

```
var pdf = /.*\.pdf$/;
```

This looks for zero or more occurrences of any character, followed by an escaped period, followed by the letters "pdf" that must come at the end of the string:

```
pdf.test("chapter1.pdf");
<< true

pdf.test("report.doc");
<< false
```

String Methods

There are a number of string methods that accept regular expressions as a parameter.

The `split()` method that we saw in Chapter 2 [14] can also accept a regular expression that's used to split a string into the separate elements of an array:

```
"Hello World   from JavaScript!".split(/\s+/) // splits the string
➥on one or more occurrences of a white space character
<< ["Hello", "World", "from", "JavaScript!"]
```

The `match()` method returns an array of all the matches:

```
"JavaScript".match(/[aeiou]/); // return the first vowel
<< ["a"]

"JavaScript".match(/[aeiou]/g); // return an array of all the vowels
➥- note the 'g' flag
<< ["a", "a", "i"]
```

The `search()` method returns the position of the first match:

```
"I'm learning JavaScript".search(/java/i);
<< 13
```

The `replace()` method replaces any matches with another string:

```
"JavaScript".replace(/[aeiou]/ig,"*"); // replace all vowels with *
<< "J*v*Scr*pt"
```

Roll the Dice!

We'll finish off by using what we have learned in the chapter to create a dice object.

The object will have a `roll()` method that returns a number between 1 and 6. Here's the code to create the dice object:

```
dice = {
    sides: 6,
    roll: function(){
        return Math.floor(6 * Math.random()) + 1;
    }
}
```

Let's take it for a spin:

```
dice.roll();
<< 5

dice.roll();
<< 3
```

This is an example of using JavaScript objects to model a real-world object. We'll develop this concept further in Chapter 13.

Quiz Ninja Project

Now it's time to take another look at our Quiz Ninja project. We're going to use an object to store the information about the quiz. Open up **scripts.js** in the **js** folder and enter the following at the top of the file:

```
                                                    scripts.js (excerpt)

quiz = {
"name":"Super Hero Name Quiz",
"description":"How many super heroes can you name?",
"question":"What is the real name of ",
"questions": [
    { "question": "Superman", "answer": "Clarke Kent" },
    { "question": "Batman", "answer": "Bruce Wayne" },
    { "question": "Wonder Woman", "answer": "Dianna Prince" }
]
}
```

This is an object that contains information about the quiz in its properties. For example there are `name` and `description` properties that contain string values about the quiz. There is also a `questions` property that contains an array of objects. These objects replace the nested arrays we used in the previous chapters and have properties of `question` and `answer`. This means that we can refer to a question as `quiz.questions[i].question` instead of `quiz[i][0]` and an answer as `quiz.questions[i].answer` instead of `quiz[i][1]`. So we also now need to make a change to the `for` loop in our code when we select the question:

scripts.js *(excerpt)*

```
for(var i=0, question, answer, max=quiz.questions.length; i<max;
➥i++) {
  question = quiz.questions[i].question;  // change is made here
  answer = ask(question);
  check(answer);
}
```

We also need to update the `ask()` function to use the question object notation instead of array notation:

scripts.js *(excerpt)*

```
function ask(question) {
  return prompt(quiz.question + question); // this line changes
}
```

The following line in the `check()` function also needs to be changed:

scripts.js *(excerpt)*

```
if(answer === quiz.questions[i].answer){
```

Save these changes then have a go at playing the game again. Once again, we haven't actually added any functionality, but we have started to make the program more modular by storing all the quiz information in a separate object. This will make it easier to expand on the functionality in later chapters

Summary

In this chapter we have learned the following:

■ Objects are a collection of key-value pairs placed inside curly braces `{}`.

- Objects have properties that can be any JavaScript value. If it is a function then it is known as a *method.*

- An object's properties and methods can be accessed using either dot notation or square bracket notation.

- Objects are mutable, which means that their properties and methods can be changed or removed.

- Objects can be used as parameters to functions, which allows arguments to be entered in any order, or omitted.

- Nested objects can be created by placing objects inside objects.

- JSON is a portable data format that uses JavaScript object literals to exchange information.

- The `Math` object gives access to a number of mathematical constants.

- The `Math` object can be used to perform mathematical calculations.

- The `Date` object can be used to create date objects.

- Once you've created a `Date` object, you can use the getter methods to access information about that date.

- Once you've created a `Date` object, setter methods can be used to change information about that date.

- The `Regex` object can be used to create regular expressions.

Now we've reached the end of the first part of the book, which means that you should have a good grasp of the JavaScript programming language basics. But JavaScript was originally designed to be used in the browser, so in the next chapter we'll look at how to use JavaScript to interact with web pages.

The Document Object Model

The Document Object Model (DOM) allows you to access elements of a web page and enable interaction with the page by adding and removing elements, changing the order of elements, changing the content of elements, changing element attributes, and even altering how elements are styled.

In this chapter, we'll be cover these topics:

- introduction to the DOM

- getting elements—`getElementById`, `getElementsByClassName`, `getElementsBy-TagName`, `querySelector`, and `querySelectorAll`

- navigating the DOM tree

- getting and setting an element's attributes

- updating the DOM by creating dynamic markup

- changing the CSS of an element

▓ our project—insert questions dynamically into the DOM to create a list of quiz questions

The Document Object Model

What is the Document Object Model?

The **Document Object Model**, or DOM for short, represents an HTML document as a network of connected nodes that form a tree-like structure[1].

Everything on a web page is represented by a **node**—HTML tags, the text inside these tags, even the attributes of a tag are all nodes. The HTML tag is the root node and every other part of the document is a child node of this.

Take the following piece of HTML as an example:

```
<p class="warning"> Something has gone <em>very</em> wrong! </p>
```

This can be represented as the tree diagram shown in Figure 6.1.

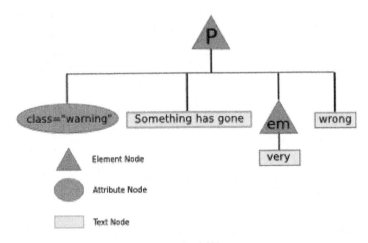

Figure 6.1. The DOM tree

The DOM is not actually part of JavaScript because it is *language agnostic*. This means that it can be used in any programming language, not just JavaScript. It is an

---

[1] The DOM can also be used to represent XML and XHTML documents.

Application Programming Interface (API) that lets us access and modify different parts of a web page using the built-in document object.

History of the DOM

In the early days of the Web, browser vendors such as Netscape and Microsoft developed their own distinct ways of accessing parts of a web page. In the beginning, they tended to focus on common page elements such as images, links, and forms. These methods became known as DOM level 0, or legacy DOM. Some of the more common methods can still be used in the current DOM API.

The World Wide Web Consortium (W3C) started to standardize the process and created the DOM API level 1 in 1998. This introduced a complete model for web pages that allowed every part of them to be navigated.

The DOM level 2 was published in 2000 and introduced the popular getElement-ById() method, which made it much easier to access specific elements on a web page.

The current standard is DOM level 3, although level 4 is in the process of being developed as a living standard, which means that it is being implemented in browsers before it is formalized and published.

Despite the standardization process, browsers have not always implemented the DOM consistently so it has been difficult to program for in the past. Fortunately, since Internet Explorer 8, DOM support has been much more consistent and most modern browsers implement the current DOM level 3 API reasonably well. They are also implementing more of the new DOM level 4 features with every update.

An Example Web Page

To illustrate the DOM concepts covered in this chapter, we'll use a basic web page that contains a heading and three paragraph elements. Save the following code in a file called **dom.htm**:

dom.htm

```
<!doctype html>
<html lang="en">
<head>
```

```
  <meta charset="utf-8">
  <title>Triathlon DOM</title>
</head>
<body>
  <header>
    <h1 id="title">Triathlon</h1>
  </header>
  <section id="sports">
    <p class="swim">Swim</p>
    <p id="bike">Bike</p>
    <p>Run</p>
  </section>
</body>
</html>
```

Figure 6.2 shows what this web page would look like as a node tree diagram.

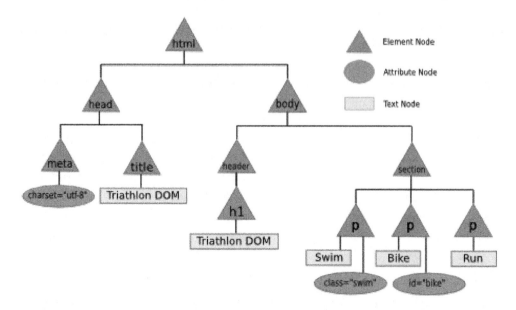

Figure 6.2. Our web page shown as a node tree

 This is a Simplified View

This is a slightly simplified diagram as the DOM also stores any whitespace that is in the HTML document as text nodes.

The best way to follow along with the examples in this chapter is to use the console built into the web browser (we discussed how to use this in Chapter 1). The screenshot in Figure 6.3 shows the page with the console open.

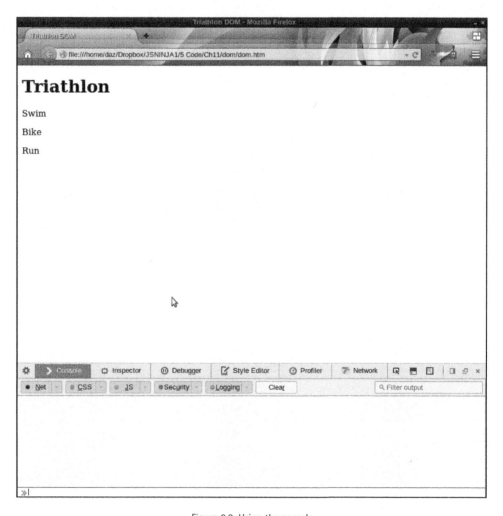

Figure 6.3. Using the console

Getting Elements

The DOM API provides several methods that allow us to access any element on a page. These methods will return a node object or a node list, which is an array-like object. These objects can then be assigned to a variable and be inspected or modified.

For example, we can access the body element of a web page and assign it to the variable body using the following code:

```
body = document.body;
<< <body>
```

Now that we have a reference to the body element, we can check its type:

```
typeof body;
<< "object";
```

This is a special Node object with a number of properties and methods that we can use to find information about, or modify, the body element.

For example, we can use the nodeType property to find out what type of node it is:

```
body.nodeType;
<< 1
```

All nodes have a numerical code to signify what type they are. These are summarised in the table below.

Code	Type
1	element
2	attribute
3	text
8	comment
9	document

There are other types not covered in the table, but these aren't used in HTML documents. As we can see from the table, a code of 1 confirms that body is an element node.

We can also use the nodeName property to find the name of the element:

```
body.nodeName;
<< "BODY"
```

Note that the element name is returned in upper-case letters.

Legacy DOM Shortcut Methods

There are some methods from DOM Level 0 that can still be employed to access commonly used elements:

■ `document.body` returns the body element of a web page, as we saw in the previous example.

■ `document.images` returns a node list of all the images contained in the document.

■ `document.links` returns a node list of all the `<a>` elements and `<area>` elements that have an `href` attribute.

■ `document.anchors` returns a node list of all the `<a>` elements that have a `name` attribute.

■ `document.forms` returns a node list of all the forms in the document. This will be used when we cover forms in Chapter 8.

 Array-*like*, but not an Array

Node lists are array-like objects, but they are not arrays. You can access each item using index notation. For example, `document.images[0]` will return the first image in the node list of all the images in the document.

They also have a `length` property, which can be used to iterate through every element using a `for` loop, like so:

```
for (var i=0 ; i < document.images.length ; i++) {

  // do something with each image using document.images[i]

}
```

Node lists don't have any other array methods such as `slice`, `splice`, and `join`.

Getting an Element by Its ID

The `getElementById()` method does exactly what it says on the tin. It returns a reference to the element with a unique `id` attribute that is given as an argument. For example, we can get a reference to the `h1` element with the `id` of `'title'` in the **dom.htm** page by writing this in the console:

```
title = document.getElementById('title');
<< <h1 id="title">
```

Every `id` attribute should be unique to just one element, so this method will return a reference to that element. For this reason, it's a very quick way of finding elements in a document. It is also supported in all the major browsers.

If no element exists with the given ID, `null` is returned.

Get Elements by Their Tag Name

`getElementsByTagName()` will return a live node list of all the elements with the tag name that is provided as an argument. For example, we can get all the paragraphs in the document using this code:

```
paragraphs = document.getElementsByTagName('p');
<< HTMLCollection [ <p.swim>, <p#bike>, <p> ]
```

As this is a node list, we can use the the index notation to find each individual paragraph in the list:

```
swim = paragraphs[0];
<< <p class="swim">

bike = paragraphs[1];
<< <p id="bike">

run = paragraphs[2];
<< <p>
```

If there are no elements in the document with the given tag name, an empty node list is returned.

document.getElementsByTagName() is supported by all major browsers and in Internet Explorer from version 6 onwards.

Get Elements by Their Class Name

getElementsByClassName() will return a live node list of all elements that have the class name that is supplied as an argument. For example, we can return a collection of all elements with the class of 'swim' using the following:

```
document.getElementsByClassName('swim');
<< HTMLCollection [   ]
```

There is only one element on the page that has the class name of swim, but a node list (with a length of 1) will still be returned:

```
document.getElementsByClassName('swim').length;
<< 1
```

Note that if there are no elements with the given class, an HTML collection is still returned, but it will have a length of 0:

```
document.getElementsByClassName('walk').length;
<< 0
```

To access the paragraph element node, we use the index notation to refer to the first element in the collection:

```
swim = document.getElementsByClassName('swim')[0];
<< <p class="swim">
```

This now refers to the actual paragraph element with a class of swim.

document.getElementsByClassName is supported in all the major modern browsers, but was only supported in Internet Explorer 9 and later.

Query Selectors

The document.querySelector() method allows you to use CSS notation to find the first element in the document that matches a CSS query selector criteria provided as an argument. If no elements match, it will return null.

The `document.querySelectorAll()` method also uses CSS notation but returns a node list of *all* the elements in the document that match the CSS query selector. If no elements match, it will return an empty node list.

These are both very powerful methods that can emulate all the methods discussed, as well as allowing more fine-grained control over which element nodes are returned.

Know Your Selectors

You do have to know about CSS query selectors to be able to use this method! If you don't know, or just need a reminder, you might want to check this page out at SitePoint.[2]

For example, the following could be used instead of `document.getElementById()`:

```
bike = document.querySelector('#bike');
<< <p id="bike">
```

And this could be used instead of `document.getElementsByClassName`:

```
swim = document.querySelectorAll('.swim');
<< NodeList [ <p.swim> ]
```

Note that this is not a *live* node list. See the section later in this chapter for more details about live node lists.

CSS query selectors are a powerful way of specifying very precise items on a page. For example, CSS pseudo-selectors can also be used to pinpoint a particular element. The following code, for example, will return only the last paragraph in the document:

```
run = document.querySelector('p:last-child');
```

All modern browsers support these methods and Internet Explorer supported it from version 8 onwards. Version 8 of Internet Explorer only understands CSS2.1 selectors (what it supports), so complex CSS3 notations such as `x ~ y:empty` will fail to work.

---

[2] http://www.sitepoint.com/web-foundations/css-selectors/

jQuery

jQuery is a popular JavaScript framework that makes it very easy to find elements on a page using a CSS-style syntax. It uses `document.querySelectorAll()` in the background whenever it can.

Navigating the DOM Tree

Node objects have a number of properties and methods for navigating around the document tree. Once you have a reference to an element, you can walk along the document tree to find other nodes. Let's focus on a particular part of the document tree in our example. The relationship each node has with the `bike` node is shown in Figure 6.4.

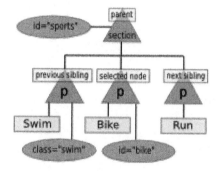

Figure 6.4. Navigating the DOM tree

The `childNodes` property is a list of all the nodes that are children of the node concerned. The following example will return all the child nodes of the element with an `id` of `sports`:

```
var sports = document.getElementById('sports');
<< undefined
sports.childNodes;
<< NodeList [ #text "
", <p.swim>, #text "
```

```
",  <p#bike>, #text "
",  <p>, #text "
"  ]
```

Note that the `childNodes` property returns *all* the nodes that are children of an element. This will include any text nodes and since whitespace is treated as a text node, there will often be empty text nodes in this collection.

The `children` property only returns any *element* nodes that are children of that node, so will ignore any text nodes. Note that this is only supported in Internet Explorer from version 9 onwards:

```
sports.children // this will only contain paragraph elements
<< HTMLCollection [ <p>, <p>, <p> ]

sports.children.length
<< 3
```

The `firstChild` property returns the first child of a node:

```
sports.firstChild
<< #text "
"
```

And the `lastChild` property returns the last child of a node:

```
sports.lastChild
<< #text "
"
```

Be careful when using these properties—the first or last child node can often be a text node, even if it's just an empty string generated by some whitespace.

For example, you might expect the first child node of the `sports` element to be the swim element and the last child to be the run element, but it is in fact a text node, generated by the whitespace characters in between the `<section>` and `<p>` tags:

The `parentNode` property returns the parent node of an element. The following code returns the `sports` node because it is the parent of the `bike` node:

```
bike.parentNode;
<< <section id="sports">
```

The `nextSibling` property returns the next adjacent node (that is, the same parent). It will return `null` if the node is the last child node of that parent:

```
bike.nextSibling;
<< #text "
   "
```

The `previousSibling` property returns the previous adjacent node. It will return `null` if the node is the first child of that parent:

```
bike.previousSibling
<< #text "
   "
```

Once again, these methods find the next and previous *node*, not element, so they will often return a blank text node as in the examples above.

Using these properties allows you to navigate around the whole of the document tree.

Finding the Value of a Node

Finding the text contained within an element is actually trickier than it sounds. For example, the variable `swim` has a DOM node that contains the following HTML:

```
<p class="swim">Swim</p>
```

It clearly contains the text "swim", but this is held in a text node, which is the first child of the `swim` node:

```
swimTextNode = swim.firstChild;
<< #text "Swim
```

Now that we have a reference to the text node, we can find the text contained inside it using the `nodeValue` method:

```
swimTextNode.nodeValue;
<< "Swim"
```

A quicker way of doing this is to use the `textContent` property. This will return the text content of an element as a string:

```
swim.textContent
<< "Swim"
```

Note that Internet Explorer version 8 does not support the `textContent` property, but has the `innerText` property, which works in a similar way.

Getting and Setting Attributes

All HTML elements have a large number of possible attributes such as `class`, `id`, `src`, and `href`. The DOM API contains getter and setter methods that can be used to view, add, remove, or modify the value of any of these attributes.

Getting an Element's Attributes

The `getAttribute()` method returns the value of the attribute provided as an argument:

```
swim.getAttribute("class");
<< "swim"

var meta = document.getElementsByTagName("meta")[0];
<< undefined

meta.getAttribute("charset");
<< "utf-8"
```

If an element does not have the given attribute, it returns `null`:

```
swim.getAttribute("stroke");
<< null
```

Setting an Element's Attributes

The `setAttribute` can change the value of an element's attributes. It takes two arguments: the attribute that you wish to change and the new value of that attribute.

For example, if we wanted to change the class of the `swim` element to `swimming`, we could do so using this code:

```
swim.setAttribute("class", "swimming");
<< undefined

swim.getAttribute("class");
<< "swimming"
```

If an element does not have an attribute, the `setAttribute` method can be used to add it to the element. For example, we can add an id of `"run"` to the `run` paragraph:

```
run.setAttribute("id","run");
<< undefined

run.getAttribute("id");
<< "run"
```

 Legacy DOM Attributes

The legacy DOM allows access to attributes using dot notation, like so:

```
bike.id;
<< "bike"
```

This notation is still supported, although some attribute names such as `class` and `for` are reserved keywords in JavaScript so we need to use `className` and `htmlFor` instead:

```
swim.className;
<< "swim"
```

Classes of an Element

The `className` Property

As we've seen, we can modify the class name of an element using the `setAttribute()` method. There is also a `className` property that allows the class of an element to be set directly. In addition, it can be used to find out the value of the class attribute:

```
swim.className;
<< "swimming"
```

We can change the class back to `swim` with the following code:

```
swim.className = "swim"
<< "swim"
```

The `classList` Property

The `classList` property is a list of all the classes an element has. It has a number of methods that make it easier to modify the class of an element. It's supported in all modern browsers and in Internet Explorer from version 10 onwards.

The `add` method works in a similar way to the `addClass` function we created above, and can be used to add a class to an element. For example, we could add a class of "sport" to the `run` element:

```
run.classList.add('run');
<< undefined
```

The `remove` method will remove a specific class from an element. For example, we could remove the class of "swim" from the `swim` element:

```
swim.classList.remove('swim');
<< undefined
```

The `toggle` method is a particularly useful method that will *add* a class if an element doesn't have it already and *remove* the class if it does have it. It returns `true` if the class was added and `false` if it was removed. For example:

```
swim.classList.toggle('sport'); // will remove the 'sport' class
<< false

swimm.classList.toggle('sport'); // will add the 'sport' class back
<< true
```

The `contains` method will check to see if an element has a particular class:

```
swim.classList.contains('sport');
<< true

swim.classList.toggle('sport');
<< false

swim.classList.contains('sport');
<< false
```

 Adding Classes in Old Versions of Internet Explorer

Unfortunately, the `classlist` property is only available in Internet Explorer version 10 and above, so if you want to support older versions of Internet Explorer, you could create a function that will add an extra class to an element, rather than just replace the current class. The `addClass` function takes the element and the new class name to be added as parameters. It uses a simple `if` block to check if the value of the `className` property is truthy. If it is, it will append the new class to the end of the current class; otherwise, it will simply set the new class as the element's class:

```
function addClass(element,newClass){
  if (element.className) {
    element.className = swim.className + " " + newClass;
  } else {
    element.className = newClass;
```

```
    }
    return element.getAttribute("class");
}
```

Let's test this out on the `swim` element, which already has a class of `'swim'`:

```
addClass(swim,"sport");
<< "swim sport"
```

Let's check that it works for the `run` element, which was without a `class` attribute:

```
addClass(run,"run");
<< "run"
```

Now the element has a class of `'run'`.

Updating the DOM by Creating Dynamic Markup

So far we've looked at how to gain access to different elements of a web page and find out information about them. We've also looked at how to change the attributes of elements. In this section, we're going to learn how to create new elements and add them to the page, as well as edit elements that already exist and remove any unwanted elements from the page.

Creating an Element

The document object has a `createElement()` method that takes a tag name as a parameter and returns that element. For example, we could create a new paragraph as a DOM fragment in memory by writing the following in the console:

```
var newPara = document.createElement('p');
```

At the moment, this paragraph element is empty. To add some content, we'll need to create a text node.

Creating a Text Node

A text node can be created using the `document.createTextNode()` method. It takes a parameter, which is a string containing the text that goes in the node. Let's create the text to go in our new paragraph:

```
var text = document.createTextNode('Transition 1');
```

Now we have an element node and a text node, but they are not linked together—we need to append the text node to the paragraph node.

Appending Nodes

Every node object has an `appendChild()` method that will add another node (given as an argument) as a child node. We want our newly created `text` node to be a child node of the `newPara` node. This means that it is `newPara` that calls the method with `text` as an argument:

```
newPara.appendChild(text);
```

Now we have a paragraph element that contains the text that we want. So the process to follow each time you want to create a new element with content is this:

1. create the element node
2. create the text node
3. append the text node to the element node

This can be made simpler by using the `textContent` property that every element object has. This will add a text node to an element without the need to append it:

```
var newPara = document.createElement('p');
newPara.textContent = 'Transition 1';
```

While this has cut the number of steps from three down to two, it can still become repetitive, so it's useful to write a function to make this easier. This is what we'll do next.

Putting It All Together in a Function

When we created our new paragraph element, all we specified were the type of tag we wanted to use and the text inside it. These will form the parameters of our function. The function will then perform the two steps we used to create the new element and then return that element:

```
function createElement (tag,text) {
  el = document.createElement(tag);
  el.textContent = text;
  return el
}
```

Let's try it out by creating another new paragraph element:

```
var anotherPara = createElement("p","Transition 2");
```

This means that we can now create new elements in a single line of code rather than three. It's time to add these new elements to our example page.

Adding Elements to the Page

We have already seen the appendChild() method. This can be called on a node to add a new child node. The new node will always be added at the end of the list of child nodes. The following example will add the newPara paragraph element we created above to the end of the sports section, as shown in Figure 6.5:

```
sports.appendChild(newPara);
<< <p>
```

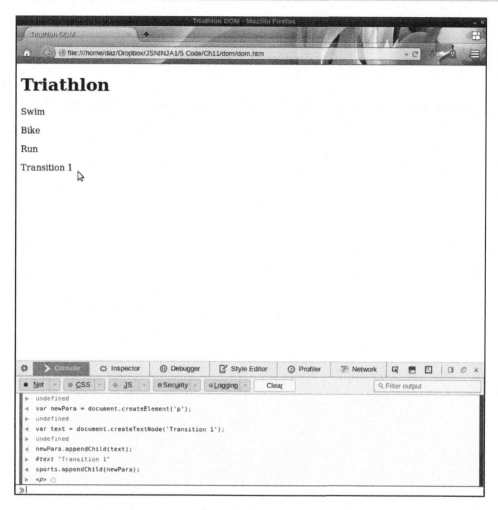

Figure 6.5. Append child

The appendChild method is useful as you'll often want to add a new element to the bottom of a list. But what if you want to place a new element in between two existing elements?

The insertBefore() will place a new element before another element in the markup. It's important to note that this method is called on the *parent node*. It takes two parameters: The first is the new node to be added and the second is the node that you want it to go before (it's helpful to think that the order of the parameters is the order they will appear in the markup). For example, we can place the `newPara` paragraph before the `bike` paragraph with the following line of code:

```
sports.insertBefore(newPara,bike);
<< <p>
```

This will produce the output shown in Figure 6.6.

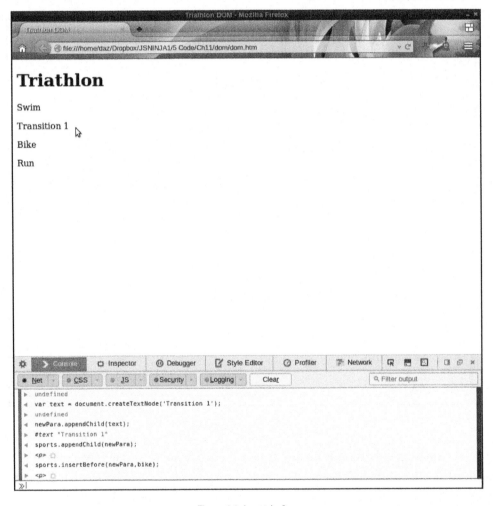

Figure 6.6. Insert before

Notice that even though the `newPara` paragraph had already been placed in the document, this method can still be used on it. This means that the `appendChild()` and `insertBefore()` methods can be used to move markup that already exists in the DOM. This is because a reference to a single DOM element can only exist once in the page, so if you use multiple inserts and appends, only the last one will have an effect. If an element is required to appear in several different places in the document, it would need to be cloned before each insertion.

This can be seen by using the `appendChild()` method on the `swim` paragraph. Since it already exists, it just moves its position to come after the `run` paragraph, as shown in Figure 6.7:

```
sports.appendChild(swim);
<< <p class="swim">
```

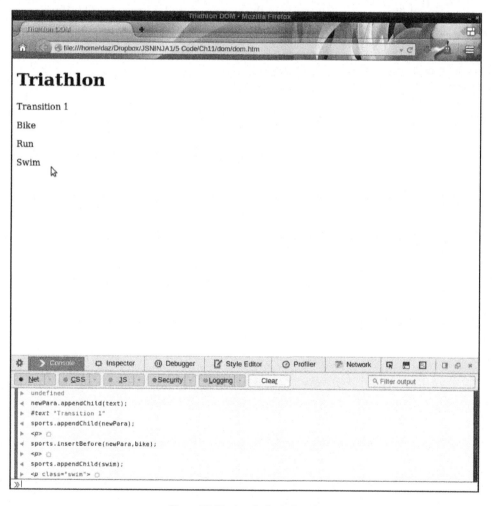

Figure 6.7. Moving the "swim" node

We can also use `insertBefore()` to move it back again:

```
sports.insertBefore(swim,newPara);
<< <p class="swim">
```

Interestingly, there is no `insertAfter` method, so you should ensure that you have access to the correct elements to place an element exactly where you want it.

Remove Elements from a Page

An element can be removed from a page using the `removeChild()` method. This method is called on the parent node and has a single parameter, which is the node to be removed. It returns a reference to the removed node. For example, if we wanted to remove the `swim` paragraph we would use the following code:

```
swim = sports.removeChild(swim);
<< <p class="swim">
```

As you can see in Figure 6.8, it's been removed.

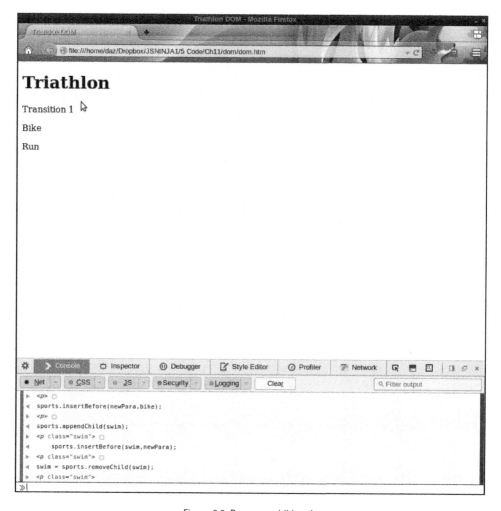

Figure 6.8. Remove a child node

Because we have a reference to the element, we can easily put it back into the document if we need to:

```
sports.insertBefore(swim,newPara);
<< <p class="swim">
```

Replacing Elements on a Page

The `replaceChild()` method can be used to replace one node with another. It is called on the parent node and has two parameters: the new node and the node that is to be replaced. For example, if we wanted to change the content of the `<h1>` tag that makes the title of the page, we could replace the text node with a new one, like so:

```
h1 = document.getElementById("title");
oldText = h1.firstChild;
newText = document.createTextNode("Iron Man Triathlon");
h1.replaceChild(newText,oldText)
```

Figure 6.9 shows that the text has now changed to "Iron Man Triathlon".

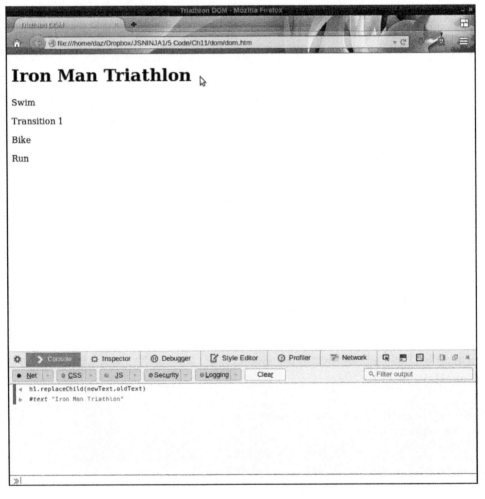

Figure 6.9. Replacing an element

innerHTML

The innerHTML node property is not part of the DOM standard, but it's supported by all the major browsers. It returns all the child elements of an element as a string of HTML. If an element contains lots of other elements, all of the raw HTML is returned. In the following example, we can see all the HTML that is contained inside the section element with a class of sports:

```
sports.innerHTML
<< "
    <p class="swim">Swim</p>
    <p id="bike">Bike</p>
    <p>Run</p>
    "
```

The innerHTML property is also writable and can be used to place a chunk of HTML inside an element. This will replace all of a node's children with the raw HTML contained in the string. This saves you having to create a new text node as it is done automatically and inserted into the DOM. It is also much quicker than using the standard DOM methods. For example, the heading text that we changed before could be changed in one line:

```
h1.innerHTML = "Biathlon";
```

This becomes an even more powerful method if you want to insert a large amount of HTML into the document. Instead of creating each element and text node individually, you can simply enter the raw HTML as a string. The relevant nodes will then be added to the DOM tree automatically. For example, we could change everything contained within the sports section:

```
sports.innerHTML = "<p>Skiing</p><p>Shooting</p>";
```

This will now remove all the paragraphs that were children of the sports section and replace them with two new child paragraph elements that contain a text node each, as shown in Figure 6.10.

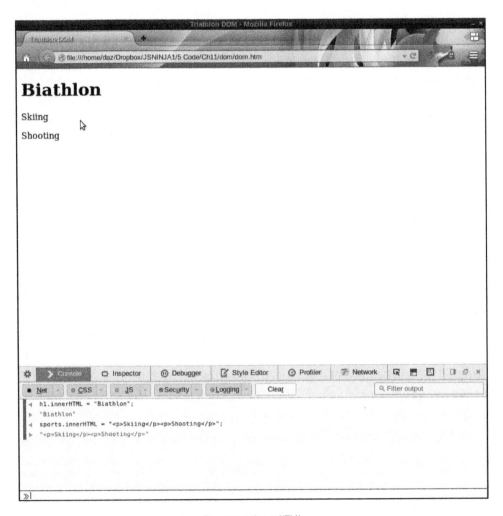

Figure 6.10. Inner HTML

innerHTML and User-generated Content

Be careful when using **innerHTML** to update a page with any user-generated content. A user is able to insert JavaScript as HTML, which can then be executed on your site ... possibly with disastrous consequences!

Live Collections

The node lists returned by the `document.getElementsByClassName()` and `document.getElementsByTagName()` methods are *live* collections that will update to reflect any changes on the page. For example, if a new element with the class swim

is added or an existing one is removed, the node list updates automatically. Therefore, its use is discouraged for performance reasons, but it can be useful.

To see an example of this, reload the page again to reset the DOM to its original
state. Let's take a look at how many elements are in the sports section:

```
var sports = document.getElementById("sports");
<< undefined

sports.children.length
<< 3
```

Now remove the swim paragraph:

```
var swim = document.getElementsByClassName('swim')[0];
<< undefined

sports.removeChild(swim);
<< <p class="swim">

sports.children.length
<< 2
```

You need to be careful when referring to elements by their index in a collection, as
this can change when markup is added or removed. For example, we saw earlier
that the run paragraph could be accessed using this line of code:

```
document.getElementsByTagName('p')[2];
<< undefined
```

Yet now it refers to undefined as nothing is at that index of 2 in the collection; this
is because the swim paragraph has been dynamically removed from the DOM. The
run paragraph isn't the third paragraph in the collection any more, it's the second.

Updating CSS

Every element node has a style property. These can be used to dynamically
modify the presentation of any element on a web page.

To see an example of this, reload the page again to reset the DOM. We can add a
border to the swim paragraph with the following code:

```
var swim = document.getElementsByClassName('swim')[0];
<< undefined

swim.style.border = "blue 2px solid";
<< "blue 2px solid"
```

Camel Case Properties

Any CSS property names that are separated by dashes must be written in camelCase notation, so the dash is removed and the next letter is capitalized because dashes are not legal characters in property names.

For example, `background-color` becomes `backgroundColor`. We can change the color of the `bike` background to green using this code:

```
var bike = document.getElementById("bike");
<< undefined

bike.style.backgroundColor = "green";
<< "green"
```

You can see this change in Figure 6.11.

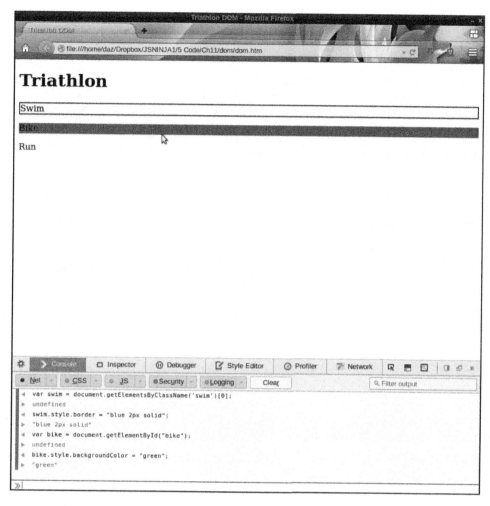

Figure 6.11. Green background

Disappearing Act

One particularly useful CSS property often employed is the `display` property. This can be used to make elements disappear and reappear on the page as needed:

```
var run = document.getElementsByTagName("p")[2];
<< undefined

run.style.display = "block";
<< "block"
```

You can hide the "run" paragraph with the following code:

```
run.style.display = "none";
<< "none"
```

You can see the effect in Figure 6.12.

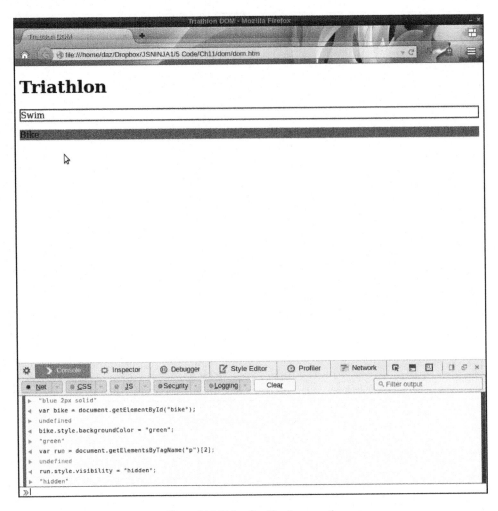

Figure 6.12. Hiding the "Run" paragraph

Checking Style Properties

The `style` property can also be used to see what CSS styles have been set on an element, but unfortunately it applies only to inline styles and styles set using JavaScript. This means that it excludes styles from external stylesheets, the most common way of setting styles.

There is a function called getComputedStyle() that will retrieve all the style information of an element that is given as a parameter. This is a read-only property, so is only used for finding out information about the style of an element.

For example, if you wanted all the styles applied to the bike paragraph, you could use the following:

```
bike = document.getElementById('bike');
<< <p id="bike">

styles = getComputedStyle(bike);
<< CSS2Properties { align-content: "stretch", align-items: "stretch"
➥, align-self: "stretch", animation-delay: "0s",
➥animation-direction: "normal", animation-duration: "0s",
➥animation-fill-mode: "none", animation-iteration-count: "1",
➥animation-name: "none", 203 more… }
```

As you can see, it returns an object (more specifically, it is a CSSStyleDeclaration object) that contains a list of property-value pairs of all the CSS styles that have been applied to the element given as an argument. In this example, there are over 200, although CSSStyleDeclaration objects have some built-in methods to help extract the information. For instance, if I wanted to find out about the element's color property I could use this code in the console:

```
styles.getPropertyCSSValue('color').cssText;
<< "rgb(0, 0, 0)"
```

This tells us that the color of the text is rgb(0, 0, 0), which is black.

You can read more on the Mozilla Developer Network about the getComputedStyle() function[3] and about CSSStyleDeclaration[4] objects.

Use with Caution

While it may seem useful to be able to edit the styles of elements on the fly like this, it is much better practice to dynamically change the class of an element and keep the relevant styles for each class in a separate stylesheet; however, there may be times when you have no access to a stylesheet or its classes.

---

[3] https://developer.mozilla.org/en/docs/Web/API/window.getComputedStyle
[4] https://developer.mozilla.org/en-US/docs/Web/API/CSSStyleDeclaration

For example, if you wanted to add a red border around one of the paragraphs (to highlight it for some reason), you could do it this way:

```
swim.style.border("red 2px solid");
```

But a better way would be to add a class of "highlighted":

```
swim.classList.add("highlighted");
```

And then add the following CSS in a separate stylesheet file:

```
.highlighted{
  border: red 2px solid;
}
```

This would give more flexibility if it was later decided to change the look of the highlighted elements. It could simply be changed at the CSS level, rather than having to dig around in the JavaScript code.

Quiz Ninja Project

Now that we've learned about the Document Object Model, we can start to add some dynamic markup to display the questions in our quiz. This will mean that there will be no need to rely on as many alert dialogs.

The first thing we need to do is add some empty section elements to the HTML in the **index.htm** file. Add the following after the closing </header> tag:

index.htm (excerpt)

```
<section id="question"></section>
<section id="feedback"></section>
```

These empty elements will be used to show the questions and provide feedback about whether the user has answered a question correctly or not. We'll also add a paragraph element inside the <header> tags that can be used to display the score as the game is being played:

---

index.htm *(excerpt)*

```
<p>Score: <strong id="score">0</strong></p>
```

The ID attributes of these elements will act as hooks that allow us to easily gain access to that element using the `document.getElementById()` method. Let's do that now by setting up some variables that we can use to access these elements near the start of the **scripts.js** file:

---

scripts.js *(excerpt)*

```
//// dom references ////
var $question = document.getElementById("question");
var $score = document.getElementById("score");
var $feedback = document.getElementById("feedback");
```

 Naming Conventions

You may have noticed that all of these variables have been prefixed with the $ symbol, which is a common convention used when naming variables that refer to DOM elements.

Our next job is to create a function called `update()` that can be used to update an element on the page. Add the following function to the top of the **scripts.js** file:

---

scripts.js *(excerpt)*

```
/// view functions ///

function update(element,content,klass) {
  var p = element.firstChild || document.createElement("p");
  p.textContent = content;
  element.appendChild(p);
  if(klass) {
    p.className = klass;
  }
}
```

This function has three parameters. The first parameterr is the element that is to be updated. The second parameter is for the content that it is to be updated with. A class can also be added to the content that is added using the third parameter, which is called `klass` because `class` is a reserved word in JavaScript.

The first line of the function checks to see if the element already has a first child and assigns it to the variable p. If it doesn't, then it creates a new paragraph element. The `textContent` property is then set to the content provided as an argument and it is added to the element using the `appendChild()` method.

Now we need to update some of our existingfunctions to use this new function to update the HTML instead of using dialogs. The first thing we need to do is udpate the score element with the score once the game starts. Add the following line of code to the start of the `play()` function, right after the `score` variable has been initialized:

scripts.js *(excerpt)*

```
update($score,score)
```

This will update the score element to display a score of 0 in the header.

The `ask()` function now needs an extra line so that the question is displayed in the HTML instead of the prompt dialog. Unfortunately we still need to use a prompt dialog to enter the answer (but don't worry, this will change in later chapters!):

scripts.js *(excerpt)*

```
function ask(question) {
    update($question,quiz.question + question);
    return prompt("Enter your answer:");
}
```

This will add a paragraph element to the question section that contains the question, with a prompt dialog asking for the answer.

Next we need to change the `check()` function so that it provides some feedback and updates the score element:

```
                                              scripts.js (excerpt)
function check(answer) {
if(answer === quiz.questions[i].answer){
  update($feedback,"Correct!","right");
  // increase score by 1
  score++;
  update($score,score)
} else {
    update($feedback,"Wrong!","wrong");
  }
}
```

Notice that the updates to the feedback element also contain a third argument of right or wrong that will be added as a class to the section. This means that we can style the feedback differently, depending on whether the player's answer is right or wrong.

Last of all we need to change the gameOver() function so it uses the update() function instead of an alert dialog. The game over message is placed inside the question element, so it replaces the last question asked:

```
                                              scripts.js (excerpt)
function gameOver(){
  // inform the player that the game has finished and tell them how
➥many points they have scored
  update($question,"Game Over, you scored " + score + " points");
}
```

Adding Some Style

Since we're now using a lot more HTML to display information, we need to add some extra styles to our CSS file. Open up the **styles.css** file and add the following:

```
                                              styles.css (excerpt)
section p {
  font: bold 24px/150% Arial, Helvetica, sans-serif;
  background: #ccc;
  border: #999 2px solid;
  color: #666;
  text-align: center;
```

```
    padding: 10px;
    margin: 10px;
    width: 300px;
}
```

This will style the paragraphs that are added to the question and feedback sections so that they appear in a gray box with a border, helping them to stand out and be easy to read.

The feedback paragraphs also have a class of `right` or `wrong` depending on whether the player answers the question correctly or not. We can use this to add some extra styles to give some visual feedback and color the boxes green for right answers and red for wrong answers by adding the following styles:

styles.css *(excerpt)*

```
.right {
    background: #0c0;
    border: #090 2px solid;
    color: #060;
}

.wrong {
    background: #c00;
    border: #900 2px solid;
    color: #600;
}
```

Now we've finished adding the styles, have a go at playing the quiz by opening **index.htm** in a browser. It should look similar to the screenshot shown in Figure 6.13.

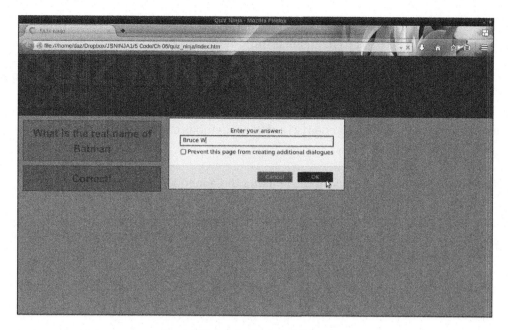

Figure 6.13. Quiz feedback via DOM updates

This looks much better than using the alert boxes, although, unfortuantely the messages can sometimes be slightly obscured because the prompt dialog darkens the screen slightly when it is open. Don't worry about this, because we'll not be using prompts for much longer.

Now we have successfully moved away from using alert dialogs to update the user and started to dynamically update the markup on the page instead. This task was made much easier by the fact that we already had functions for these jobs, meaning that all we had to do was update our functions to use the DOM instead of alerts.

Summary

In this chapter we have learned the following:

▨ The Document Object Model is a way of representing a page of HTML as a tree of nodes.

▨ The `document.getElementById`, `document.getElementsByClassName`, `document.getElementsByTagNames`, and `document.querySelector` can be used to access elements on a page.

- The `parentNode`, `previousSibling`, `nextSibling`, `childNodes`, and `children` methods can be used to navigate around the DOM tree.

- An element's attributes can be accessed using the `getAttribute()` method and updated using the `setAttribute()` method.

- The `createElement` and `createTextNode` methods can be used to create dynamic markup on the fly.

- Markup can be added to the page using the `appendChild` and `insertBefore` methods.

- Elements can be replaced using the `replaceChild` method and removed using the `removeChild` method.

- `innerHTML` can be used to insert a large chunk of raw HTML directly into the DOM.

- The CSS properties of an element can be changed by accessing the `style` property.

Now that we've learned how to find and change the markup of a web page, it's time to start interacting with it. In the next chapter we'll be covering a fundamental part of the JavaScript language: events.

Events

We saw in the last chapter how the DOM API links the JavaScript language to web pages. Events are another part of the DOM API and they are what provides the link between the web page and user interactions. Every time a user interacts with a web page, such as clicking on a link, pressing a key, or moving a mouse, an **event** occurs that our program can detect and then respond to.

In this chapter, we'll cover the following topics:

- introduction to events

- adding event listeners

- the event object

- mouse, keyboard and touch events

- removing event listeners

- stopping default behavior

- event propagation

Event Listeners

Imagine that you're waiting for a really important email message that you need to act upon as soon as it arrives, but you also have some JavaScript programming to do (you're working on the next big killer app). You could keep checking your email every couple of minutes to see if the important message has arrived, but this will cause lots of interruptions to your ninja training. Not to mention that you might be unable to check your email at the exact moment the message arrives, so it might be too late to act upon. The obvious answer to this dilemma is to set up a notification that will pop up as soon as the email arrives. You can happily program away, without being distracted by having to check your email.

Event listeners in JavaScript work in much the same way. They are like setting a notification to alert you when something happens. Instead of the program having to constantly check to see if an event has occurred, the event listener will let it know when the event happens and the program can then respond appropriately. The program can get on with the tasks while it waits for the event to happen.

For example, say in your program you want something to happen when a user clicks on the page. The code to check if a user has clicked might look like this example (JavaScript doesn't actually work like this, so this code would fail to work, although it is the way some applications work):

```
if (click) {

  doSomething();

} else {

  // carry on with rest of the program

}
```

The problem with this approach is that the program would have to keep returning to this if block to check if the click had happened. It's a bit like having to check your email every few minutes. This is known as a **blocking** approach to programming, as checking for the click is blocking the rest of the program from running.

Instead, we can use a **non-blocking** approach and set an **event listener** that will listen out for any clicks on the page. Every time this event occurs, a callback function will be called. So the program can continue processing the rest of the code while it is waiting for the click event to occur.

The following can be used to attach an event listener to the document that fires when the user clicks anywhere on the page:

```
document.body.addEventListener("click", doSomething);
```

Event listeners are added to elements on the page and are part of the DOM API that we met in the last chapter. In the example, the event listener has been added to the document's body element. It will call the function doSomething when any part of the page is clicked on. Until that happens, the program will continue to run the rest of the code.

Clickety Click

The click event occurs when a user clicks with the mouse, presses the **Enter** key, or taps the screen, making it a very useful all-round event covering many types of interaction.

Inline Event Handlers

The original way of dealing with events in the browser was to use **inline event attributes** that were added directly into the markup. Here's an example that adds an onclick event handler to a paragraph element:

```
<p onclick="console.log('You Clicked!')">Click Me</p>
```

The JavaScript code inside the quote marks will be run when a user clicks on the paragraph. This method will still work in modern browsers, but it isn't recommended for a number of reasons:

▨ The JavaScript code is mixed up with the HTML markup, breaking the concept of unobtrusive JavaScript, which says that any JavaScript code should be kept out of the HTML.

▨ Only one event handler can be attached to an element.

■ The code for the event handlers is hidden away in the markup, making it difficult to find where these events have been placed.

■ The JavaScript code has to be entered in a string, so you need to be careful when using apostrophes and quote marks.

I've included them here because you may see them in some code examples.

Older Event Handlers

Another method is to use the **event handler** properties that all node objects have. These can be assigned to a function that would be invoked when the event occurred. The following example would trigger an alert:

```
document.onclick = function (){ console.log("You clicked!"); }
```

This method is an improvement on the inline event handlers as it keeps the JavaScript out of the HTML markup. It is also well-supported and will work in all browsers, including older versions. Unfortunately, it still has the restriction that only one function can be used for each event.

Event Listeners

The recommended standard way of dealing with events is to use *event listeners*. These were outlined in DOM level 2 and allow multiple functions to be attached independently to different events. They are supported in all modern browsers, although only in Internet Explorer from version 9 onwards.

The addEventListener() method is called on a node object, the node to which the event listener is being applied. For example, this code will attach an event listener to the document's body:

```
document.body.addEventListener("click",doSomething);
```

The addEventListener() method can also be called without a node, in which case it is applied to the global object, usually the whole browser window.

Its first parameter is the type of event and the second is a callback function that is invoked when the event occurs. In this example, we are using the click event and an anonymous function that produces an alert dialog:

```
addEventListener("click", function(){
  alert("You Clicked!")
});
```

Alternatively, a named function could be used:

```
function doSomething() {
  alert("You Clicked!");
}

addEventListener("click",doSomething);
```

The parentheses are not placed after the function when it is used as the argument to an event listener; otherwise, the function will actually be called when the event listener is set, instead of when the event happens.

 Cross-browser Events

> All modern browsers now support the standard event listeners. Unfortunately, this has not always been the case, where older versions of Internet Explorer used a different syntax. If you need to support these browsers, JavaScript Rules has some suggestions for creating a cross-browser event listener function.[1]

Example Code

To test the examples in this chapter, create a file called **events.htm** that contains the following HTML. This includes some paragraph elements that we'll attach event listeners to throughout the chapter:

events.htm

```
<!doctype html>
<html lang="en">
<head>
  <meta charset="utf-8">
  <title>Events Examples</title>
  <link rel="stylesheet" href="css/styles.css">
</head>
<body>
```

---

[1] http://javascriptrules.com/2009/07/22/cross-browser-event-listener-with-design-patterns/

```
  <p id="click">Click On Me</p>
  <p id="dblclick">Double Click On Me</p>
  <p id="mouse">Hover On Me</p>
<script src="js/scripts.js"></script>
</body>
</html>
```

We'll also need a bit of styling, so create a **css** folder with a file inside called **styles.css** containing this code:

```
                                                                styles.css
p {
   width: 200px;
   height: 200px;
   margin: 10px;
   background-color: #ccc;
   float: left;
}

.highlight{
   background-color: red;
   }
```

Now create a **js** folder that contains a file called **scripts.js** for our JavaScript code. Place the following inside:

```
                                                                scripts.js
function doSomething(){
   console.log("Something Happened!");
}

addEventListener("click", doSomething);
```

Try opening **events.htm** in a browser with the console open and click anywhere on the page. You should see this message in the console:

```
"Something Happened!"
```

 Global Event Listeners

Event listeners are usually called as a method of a particular element on the page. If there's no element calling them, they are global and apply to the whole page.

The Event Object

Every time an event occurs, the callback function is called. This function is automatically passed an **event object** as a parameter that contains information about the event.

To see an example of this, change the doSomething() function in the **scripts.js** file to this:

```
function doSomething(event){
  console.log(event.type);
}
```

Now refresh the **events.htm** page in the browser and try clicking again. You should see the following appear in the console every time you click:

```
"click"
```

In the example, the event.type property is used to tell us that the type of event that was logged was a click event.

 What's in a Name?

The parameter does not have to be called **event**. It can be given any legal variable name, although calling it **event** can make it easier to read the code. Many developers often abbreviate it to just **e**.

Types of Event

The `event.type` property returns the type of event that occurred, such as `click` in the previous example. The different types of events will be discussed in the next section.

The Event Target

The `event.target` property returns a reference to the node that fired the event. If you change the `doSomething()` function to the following, it will show a message in the console telling us the node that was clicked on:

```
function doSomething(event){
    console.log(event.target);
}
```

For example, if you click on one of the paragraphs, you should see the following in the console:

```
<p id="click">
```

Coordinates of an Event

The `event.screenX` and `event.screenY` properties show the number of pixels from the left and top of the screen respectively where the event took place.

The `event.clientX` and `event.clientY` properties show the number of pixels from the left and top of the client that is being used (usually the browser window).

The `event.pageX` and `event.pageY` properties show the coordinates (in pixels) where the event took place from the left and top of the document respectively. This property takes account of whether the page has been scrolled.

All these event properties are similar, but subtly different. They are useful for finding out the place where a click happened or the position of the mouse cursor. To see the coordinates that are returned for these properties, change the `doSomething()` function to the following:

```
function doSomething(event){
    console.log("screen: (" + event.screenX + "," + event.screenY + ")
➥, page: (" + event.pageX + "," + event.pageY + "), client: (" +
➥event.screenX + "," + event.screenY + ")");
}
```

Which Mouse Button Was Pressed?

The event.which property returns which mouse button or key was pressed. Try pressing the different mouse buttons (including the middle button) to see what is returned when you change the doSomething() function to this:

```
function doSomething(event) {
    console.log(event.which);
};
```

You should see a "1" in the console if you press the left mouse button, "2" if you press the middle button, and "3" if you press the right button.

This is useful for finding out which mouse button was pressed, but there are more precise methods of doing so that are discussed in the next section.

Types of Events

There are several types of events, ranging from when a video has finished playing to when a resource has completed downloading. You can see a full list on the Events page of the Mozilla Developer Network.[2]

In this section we are going to focus on some of the more common events that occur using the mouse, the keyboard, and touch.

Mouse Events

We have already seen the click event that occurs when a mouse button is clicked. There is also the mousedown event, which occurs *before* the click and the mouseup event, occurring *after* the click.

This can be seen by adding this code to **events.js**:

---

[2] https://developer.mozilla.org/en-US/docs/Web/Events

```
var click = document.getElementById("click");

click.addEventListener("mousedown",function(){ console.log("down")
➥ });
click.addEventListener("click",function(){ console.log("click") });
click.addEventListener("mouseup",function(){ console.log("up") });
```

There is also the dblclick event, which occurs when the user double-clicks on the element to which the event listener is attached. To see an example of this, we'll attach an event listener to the second paragraph in our example (with an ID of 'dblclick'). Add the following code to scripts.js:

```
var dblclick = document.getElementById("dblclick");
dblclick.addEventListener("dblclick", highlight);

function highlight(event){
  event.target.classList.toggle("highlight");
  }
```

Now if you double click on the second paragraph, it should change color as the class of highlight is toggled on and off.

The mouseover event occurs when the mouse pointer is placed over the element to which the event listener is attached, while the mouseout event occurs when the mouse pointer moves away from an element. This example uses both the mouseover and mouseout events to change the color of the third paragraph (with an ID of "mouse") when the mouse pointer hovers over it, and back again when it moves away from the paragraph:

```
var mouse = document.getElementById("mouse");
mouse.addEventListener("mouseover", highlight);
mouse.addEventListener("mouseout", highlight);
```

The mousemove event occurs whenever the mouse moves. It will only occur while the cursor is over the element to which it is applied. The following line of code creates an alert dialog whenever the mouse moves over the third paragraph:

```
mouse.addEventListener("mousemove", function() { console.log(
➥"You Moved!"); } );
```

Keyboard Events

There are three events that occur when keys are pressed: keydown, keypress, and keyup. When a user presses a key, the events occur in that order. They are not tied to any particular key, although the information about which key was pressed is a property of the event object.

1. The keydown event occurs when a key is pressed and will *continue to occur* if the key is held down.

2. The keypress event occurs after a keydown event but before a keyup event. The keypress event only occurs for keys that produce character input. This means that it's the most reliable way to find out the character that was pressed on the keyboard.

3. The keyup event occurs when a key is released.

To understand the differences in these events, it is important to distinguish between a physical *key* on the keyboard and a *character* that appears on the screen. The keydown event is the action of pressing a key, whereas the keypress event is the action of a character being typed on the screen.

To see an example of this add the following to **scripts.js**:

```
addEventListener("keydown",highlight);
```

Pressing a key will result in the whole document changing color., because the event listener was applied to the whole document. If you hold a key down, the event will continue to fire, creating a psychedelic effect on the page.

To see the keyup event working, add the code that uses an anonymous function to show the exact time the key was released in the console:

```
addEventListener("keyup", function stop(event){
  var date = new Date;
  console.log("You stopped pressing the key on " + date);
});
```

The keydown and keyup event objects both have an event.keyCode property that returns a numerical code that represents the key that fired the event; for example, the J key has a key code of 74. You can find the code for each key on the JavaScript key code page.[3]

The keypress event object has an event.charCode property that returns a numerical Unicode character code representing the character that will be shown on the screen.

These two properties are similar, but not the same. For example, on a UK keyboard, pressing the **3** key results in a keyCode of 51 and a charCode of 51. But if the **Shift** key is held down while 3 is pressed the charCode will be 163, but the keyCode will still be 51.

The String.fromCharCode() method can then be used to convert the event.charCode property into a single-character string representation of the character that will appear on the screen.

This all means that if you want to know which *key* was pressed, you should use the keydown event and event.keyCode property. If you want to know which *character* will be displayed, you should use the keypress event and the event.keyChar property.

Add the code to see an alert dialog showing which character was pressed:

```
addEventListener("keypress", function (event){
  console.log("You pressed the " + String.fromCharCode
➥(event.charCode) + " character");
});
```

Now when you press a key, you should see a message similar to this in the console:

---

[3] http://www.javascriptkeycode.com

```
"You pressed the J character"
"You stopped pressing the key at Wed Aug 20 2014 15:46:42 GMT+0100
➥ (BST)"
```

Modifier Keys

Pressing the modifier keys such as **Shift**, **Ctrl**, **Alt**, and **meta** (**Cmd** on Mac) will fire the keydown and keyup events, but not the keypress event as they don't produce any characters on the screen.

The event object also contains information about whether a modifier key was held down when the key event occurred. The event.shiftKey, event.ctrlKey, event.altKey, and event.metaKey are all properties of the event object and return true if the relevant key is held down when the event occurred. For example, the following code will check to see if the user has pressed the **C** key (which has a keycode of 32) while holding down the **Ctrl** key:

```
addEventListener("keydown", function(event) {
  if (event.keyCode == 32 && event.ctrlKey)
    console.log("Action cancelled!");
});
```

The following code checks to see if the **Shift** key was held down when the mouse was clicked:

```
addEventListener("click", function(event) {
  if (event.shiftKey)
    console.log("A Shifty Click!");
});
```

 ### Take Care When Using Modifier Keys

Many of the modifier keys already have a purpose assigned in the browser or operating system. And although it's possible to prevent the default behavior in the browser (see later in this chapter), it's not considered best practice to do so.

Touch Events

Many modern devices now support **touch events**. These are used on smart phones and tablets, as well as touch-screen monitors, satellite navigators, and trackpads. Touch events are usually made with a finger, but can also be by stylus or another part of the body. There are a number of touch events that cover many types of touch interactions.

It's important to support mouse events as well as touch events, so that non-touch devices are also supported. With so many different devices available these days, you can't rely on users using just touch or just a mouse. In fact, some devices, such as touchscreen laptops, support both mouse and touch interactions.

The `touchstart` event occurs when a user initially touches the surface.

 Use touchstart with Caution

Be careful when using the `touchstart` event as it fires as soon as a user touches the screen. They may be touching the screen because they want to zoom in or swipe, and a `touchstart` event listener could prevent them from doing this.

The `click` event is often a much safer option as it still fires when the screen is touched, but there is a slight delay of 300 ms, allowing the user time to perform another action with the device. The `click` event can be though of as a "tap" in the context of a touch event.

The `touchend` event occurs when a user stops touching the surface:

```
addEventListener("touchend", function(){
    alert("Thank You");
  }
```

The `touchmove` event occurs after a user has touched the screen and then moves around without leaving. It will continue to occur as long as the user is still touching the screen, even if they leave the element to which the event listener is attached.

The `touchenter` event occurs when a user has already started touching the surface, but then passes over the element to which the event listener is attached.

The `touchleave` event occurs when the the user is still touching the surface, but leaves the element to which the event listener is attached.

The `touchcancel` event occurs when a touch event is interrupted, such as a user's finger moving outside the document window or too many fingers being used at once. A pop-up dialog will also cancel a touch event.

 Swiping

There are no "swipe" events. These need to be created by using a combination of `touchstart`, `touchmove`, and `touchleave` events that monitor the distance and direction moved from start to finish of a touch event.

There are proposals for `gesture` events[4] that may be supported in the future.

Touch Event Properties

Because it is possible to touch a surface many times at once, touch event objects have a property called `event.touches`. This is a list of touch objects that represents all the touches taking place on that device. It has a `length` property that tells you how many *touch points* (usually the user's fingers, but could be a stylus) are in contact with the surface. Each touch object in the list can be accessed using index notation. For example, if a user touches the screen with two fingers, `events.touches.length` would return 2. The first touch object can be accessed using `events.touches[0]` and the second using `events.touches[1]`.

Each touch object has a number of properties, many similar to the `event` object, such as `touch.screenX` and `touch.screenY` to find the coordinates where the finger is touching the screen. They have other properties such as `touch.radiusX` and `touch.radiusY`, which give an indication of the area covered by the touch, and `touch.force`, which returns the amount of pressure being applied by the touch as a value between 0 and 1.

Each touch object has a `touch.identifier` property, a unique ID that can be used to ensure you are dealing with the same touch.

---

[4] https://developer.mozilla.org/en-US/docs/Web/Guide/Events/Mouse_gesture_events

More information about touch events can be found on JavaScript Kit,[5] although, be warned, they are complex and difficult to implement. It can be handy to use a library such as Hammer JS that makes events such as swipe, pinch and rotate easy to implement.[6]

Removing Event Listeners

An event listener can be removed using the removeEventListener() method. To see an example, add this paragraph to **events.htm**:

```
<p id="once">A one time thing</p>
```

Now add the following code to **scripts.js**:

```
once = document.getElementById("once");
once.addEventListener("click", remove);

function remove(event) {
  console.log("Enjoy this while it lasts!");
  once.style.backgroundColor = "pink";
  once.removeEventListener("click",remove);
}
```

This adds a click event listener to a paragraph element, but then removes it in the callback function named remove. This means it will only be called once (try clicking on it again and nothing happens).

 Removal Reference

Note that you cannot use anonymous functions as an argument to addEventListener() if you want to remove it later. This is because there needs to be a reference to the same function name in the arguments of removeEventListener().

---

[5] http://www.javascriptkit.com/javatutors/touchevents.shtml
[6] http://hammerjs.github.io/

Stopping Default Behavior

Some elements have default behavior associated with certain events. For example, when a user clicks on a link, the browser redirects to the site in the `href` attribute, while a form is submitted when the user clicks on the submit button.

`preventDefault()` is a method of the `event` object that can be used inside the callback function to stop the default behavior occurring. To see an example, add the following line to the **events.htm** file:

```
<p>
  <a id="broken" href="http://sitepoint.com">Broken Link</a>
</p>
```

Then add the following event listener inside the `script.js` file:

```
var broken = document.getElementById("broken");

broken.addEventListener("click",function(event) {
    event.preventDefault();
    console.log("Broken Link!");
  });
```

This will stop the page from redirecting to the page specified in the `href` attribute and show the message in the console instead.

 Use `preventDefault()` with Caution

Make sure that you think carefully before using `preventDefault()` to change default behavior. Users will expect certain behaviors and preventing them may cause confusion.

Some events do not allow the default behavior to be prevented. This can vary from browser to browser, but each event object has a property called `cancellable` that returns `false` if it cannot be prevented.

You can also see if the default behavior has been prevented by checking the `defaultPrevented` property.

Event Propagation

When you click on an element, you are actually clicking on all the elements that it is nested in. Add the following piece of HTML to the **events.htm** file:

```
<ul id="list">
  <li>one</li>
  <li>two</li>
  <li>three</li>
</ul>
```

If you click on one of the list items, you are also clicking on the <ul> element and the <body> element. An event is said to *propagate* as it moves from one element to another.

Event propagation is the order that the events fire on each element. There are two forms of event propagation: bubbling and capturing.

Bubbling is when the event fires on the element clicked on first, then bubbles up the document tree, firing an event on each parent element until it reaches the root node.

Capturing starts by firing an event on the root element, then propagates downwards, firing an event on each child element until it reaches the target element that was clicked on.

Bubbling

The default behavior is bubbling, which we can see happen if we add the following code to **scripts.js**:

```
ul = document.getElementById("list");
li = document.querySelector("#list li");

ul.addEventListener("click", function(event){
  console.log("Clicked on ul");
});
```

```
li.addEventListener("click", function(event){
  console.log("Clicked on li");
});
```

Now try clicking on the first list item. There should be a message in the console saying "Clicked on li" because this was the target element. The event then bubbles up to the parent <ul> element and displays a message in the console saying "Clicked on ul". The event will continue to bubble all the way to the root HTML element, but nothing will happen because none of the other elements had event listeners attached to them.

Capturing

The addEventListener method has a third parameter, which is a Boolean value that specifies whether capturing should be used or not. It defaults to false, which is why bubbling happens by default. There may be instances when you would rather capture the events instead; for example, you might want events on outer elements to fire before any events fire on the element that was actually clicked on.

To implement capturing instead, change the code to the following:

```
ul.addEventListener("click", function(event){
  console.log("Clicked on ul");
},true);

li.addEventListener("click", function(event){
  console.log("Clicked on li");
},true);
```

Now if you click on the first list item, "Clicked on ul" will be logged to the console first. The events then propagate downwards to the child <li> element, so "Clicked on li" is logged to the console next.

If you want the event to both capture *and* bubble, you must set a separate event handler for both cases, like so:

```
// capturing

ul.addEventListener("click", function(event){
  console.log("Clicked on ul");
```

```
},true);

li.addEventListener("click", function(event){
  console.log("Clicked on li");
},true);

// bubbling

ul.addEventListener("click", function(event){
  console.log("Clicked on ul");
},false);

li.addEventListener("click", function(event){
  console.log("Clicked on li");
},false);
```

These event listeners will have to be removed separately by specifying the relevant third argument.

Stopping the Bubbling Phase

The bubble phase can be stopped from occurring by adding the `event.stopPropagation()` method into the callback function. In the following example, the event will fail to propagate as the third argument is `false`, which stops capturing, and the `event.stopPropagation()` method is called, which stops bubbling:

```
li.addEventListener("click", function(event){
  console.log("clicked on li");
  event.stopPropagation();
}, false);
```

Now clicking on the first list time will only produce one alert, since the click event will not propagate to the <ul> element.

 Keep Bubbling

Be very wary of using the `event.stopPropagation()` method to stop the bubble phase occurring. There may be other event listeners attached to elements further up the bubble chain that won't be fired as a result.

Event Delegation

Event delegation can be used to attach an event listener to a parent element in order to capture events that happen to its child elements.

Let's look at the list items in our example:

```
<ul id="list">
  <li>one</li>
  <li>two</li>
  <li>three</li>
</ul>
```

If we wanted to attach event listeners to all the `<li>` tags so that they were highlighted when they were clicked on, it would need more code to add a separate event listener to each element. In this case, it would only take a little more effort, but imagine if you had a 10 x 10 table with 100 elements!

A better way is to attach the event listener to the parent `<ul>` element and then use the `event.target` property to identify the element that was clicked on. Add the following to **scripts.js** to see this in action (remember that the `highlight` function used `event.target`):

```
ul.addEventListener("click",highlight);
```

Now clicking on any list item will highlight that list item as it was the target of the click event.

This is a useful method if you are adding extra list elements to the DOM dynamically. Any new list elements that are a child of the `<ul>` element will automatically inherit this event listener, saving you from having to add an event listener every time a new list item is added.

Quiz Ninja Project

Now that we've reached the end of the chapter, it's time to add some events to our Quiz Ninja Project. We're going to add a button that can be clicked on to start the game. This will replace the `confirm` dialog that we've been using so far.

To start, add this line of code to **index.htm**, just before the closing `<body>` tag:

```
<button id="button">Click To Play Quiz Ninja!</button>
```

This will add a button to the markup. Now we need a reference to it in **scripts.js**. Add the following line of code after the other DOM references:

```
var $start = document.getElementById("start");
```

Now we need to attach a `click` event listener to to the button that will start the game when the button is clicked. Add the following code after the view functions:

```
// Event listeners
$start.addEventListener('click', function() { play(quiz) } , false);
```

The only thing left to do is add some styles to the **styles.css** file to make the button stand out:

```
button {
    font: bold 24px/150% Arial, Helvetica, sans-serif;
    display: block;
    width: 300px;
    padding: 10px;
    margin: 10px auto;
}
```

And that's it — hopefully you can see that it wasn't too hard to implement a button to play the game, especially since all the functions we needed were already in place. Open **index.htm** and have a go at playing the game. It should look similar to Figure 7.1.

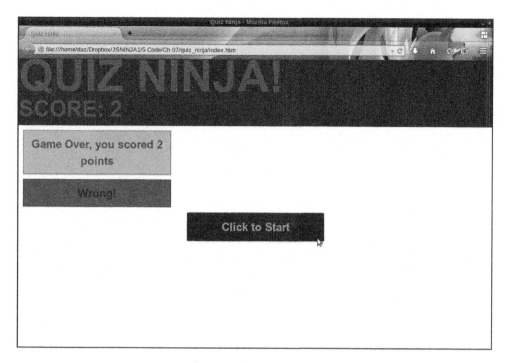

Figure 7.1. Playing Quiz Ninja

Summary

In this chapter, we have learned the following:

▨ Events occur when a user interacts with a web page.

▨ An event listener is attached to a node, watches for an event to happen and then invokes a callback function.

▨ The event object is passed to the callback function as an argument, and contains lots of properties and methods about the event.

▨ There are many types of event, including mouse events, keyboard events, and touch events.

▨ You can remove an event using the removeEventListener method.

▨ The default behavior of elements can be prevented using the preventDefault() function.

- Event propagation is the order that the events fire on each element.

- Event delegation is when an event listener is added to a parent element to capture events that happen to its children elements.

In the next chapter, we'll look at one of the biggest users of events: forms.

Forms

Forms are the most common method of interacting with a web page. A form is the main component of Google's home page, and most of us use forms every day to log into our favorite sites. In this chapter, we will look at how forms can be used to interact with a JavaScript program.

In this chapter, we'll cover these topics:

- form controls

- accessing form elements

- form properties and methods

- form events

- submitting a form

- retrieving and changing values from a form

- form validation

■ our project—add a form for answering questions and validation

Forms

Forms are made up of a `<form>` element that contains form controls such as input fields, select menus, and buttons. The form can be filled in by a user and is then submitted to a URL where it is processed on a server.

Each form control has an initial value that is specified in the HTML code and a current value. The current value can be changed by a user entering information or interacting with the form's interface (such as using a slider). Values in a form can also be changed dynamically using JavaScript.

When a form is submitted, it's sent to a server where the information is processed using a "back end" language such as PHP or Ruby. It's possible to process the information in a form on the "front end" *before* it is sent to the server using JavaScript, which is what we'll be focusing on in this chapter.

A Searching Example

We'll start off with a simple example of a form that contains one input field and a button to submit a search query, not unlike the one used by Google. This example doesn't use any styles; you just need to create a file called **index.htm** that contains the following code:

index.htm

```
<!doctype html>
<html lang="en">
<head>
  <meta charset="utf-8">
  <title>Search</title>
</head>
<body>
  <form name="search" action="search">
    <input type="text" name="searchBox">
    <button type="submit">Search</button>
  </form>
```

```
<script src="scripts.js"></script>
</body>
</html>
```

This form has a `name` attribute of "`search`" and contains two controls: an input field where a user can enter a search phrase and a button to submit the form. The form can also be submitted by pressing **Enter**.

The "`action`" attribute is the URL that the form will be submitted to so that it can be processed on the server side. The input field also has a "`name`" attribute of "`searchBox`" that is used to access the information inside it.

You should also create a file called **scripts.js** to put the JavaScript in. This can be saved in the same directory as **index.htm**.

Accessing Form Elements

The legacy DOM had a useful method called `document.forms` that returns an HTML collection of all the forms in the document in the order that they appear in the markup. Even though there is only one form in our example, a collection will still be returned, so we have to use index notation to return the first (and only) form object, like so:

```
var form = document.forms[0];
```

This is the equivalent of using the following method that we learned in chapter 6:

```
form = document.getElementsByTagname('form')[0]
```

Instead of using a numerical index, we can use the `name` attribute to identify a form:

```
var form = document.forms.search;
```

Be careful referencing elements in this way, however. If the form had the same name as any properties or methods of the `document.forms` object, such as "`submit`" for example, that property or method would be referenced instead of the `form` element. To avoid this, the square bracket notation can be used (this is also useful if the form's name attribute contains any invalid characters, such as spaces or dashes):

```
var form = document.forms['search'];
```

A form object also has a method called `elements` that returns an HTML collection of all the elements contained in the form. In this case the form contains two controls: an input element and a button element:

```
var input = form.elements[0];
var button = form.elements[1];
```

We can also access the form controls using their `name` attributes as if it was a property of the form object. So for example, the input field has a name attribute of `searchBox` and can be accessed using this code:

```
var input = form.searchBox
```

The square bracket notation can be used instead (again, this is useful if there are any naming clashes with existing property and method names, or if the name is an invalid variable name):

```
var input = form['searchBox']
```

Form Properties and Methods

Form objects have a number of useful properties and methods that can interact with the form.

The `form.submit()` method will submit the form automatically. Note that submitting a form using this method won't trigger a form "submit" event; that is covered in the next section.

A form can be submitted manually by the user employing a button or input element with a type attribute of `submit`, or even an input element with a `type` attribute of `image`:

```
<button type="submit">Submit</button>
<input type="submit" value="Submit">
<input type="image" src="button.png">
```

The form.reset() method will reset all the form controls back to their initial values specified in the HTML.

A button with the type attribute of reset can also be used to do this without the need for additional scripting:

```
<button type="reset">Reset</button>
```

 Avoid Reset Buttons

Reset buttons are generally considered poor for usability, as they are too easy to click and then wipe out all the data that's been entered. So think very carefully before using one in a form.

The form.action property can be used to set the action attribute of a form, so that it is sent to a different URL to be processed on the server:

```
form.action = "/alt/search"
```

Form Events

There are some events that are exclusive to forms.

The focus event occurs when the cursor is focused on that element. In the case of an input element, this is when the cursor is placed inside the element (either by clicking on it or navigating to it using the keyboard). To see an example, add the following code to **scripts.js**:

```
var input = form.elements.searchBox;

input.addEventListener('focus', function(){ alert("focused")},
➥false);
```

Open **search.htm** in your browser and place the cursor inside the input field. You should see an alert dialog similar to the one in the screenshot in Figure 8.1.

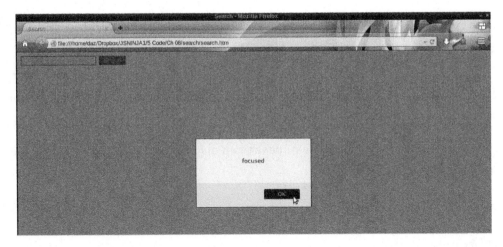

Figure 8.1. Focused!

The `blur` event occurs when the user moves the focus away from the form element. Add the following to **scripts.js**, reload the page, and then move the cursor away from the search box:

```
input.addEventListener('blur', function(){ alert("blurred")},
➥false);
```

The `change` event occurs when the user moves the focus away from the form element *after changing it*. So if a user clicks in an input field and makes no changes, and then clicks elsewhere, the `change` event won't fire but the `blur` event will.

Add the following code to **scripts.js** and reload the page. You'll notice that the alert message `"changed"` only appears if you actually change the value inside the search box, then move the cursor away from it:

```
input.addEventListener('change', function(){ alert("changed")},
➥false);
```

Note that the `blur` event will also fire, but after the `change` event.

Submitting a Form

Possibly the most important form event is the `submit` event, occurring when the form is submitted. Usually this will send the content of the form to the server to be processed, but we can use JavaScript to intercept the form before it's sent by adding a `submit` event listener. Add the following code to the **scripts.js** file:

```
var form = document.forms.search;
form.addEventListener ("submit", search, false);

function search() {
  alert("Submitted");
}
```

Now reload the page and click on the **Submit** button. You should see an alert dialog saying "Submitted." After you click **OK**, the browser tries to load a nonexistent page (the URL should end in something similar to ".../search?searchBox=hello"). This is because when the event fired, our `search()` function was invoked displaying the alert dialog; then the form was submitted to the page in its `action` attribute for processing, but unfortunately this page doesn't exist. We won't create that page either, since back-end processing won't be covered in this book. What we'll do instead is stop the form from being submitted to that URL altogether. This is done by using the `preventDefault()` method that we saw in the last chapter. Add the following line to the search function:

```
function search() {
  alert("Form Submitted");
  return false;
}
```

Now reload **search.htm** and try submitting the form. You'll see that the alert dialog still appears, but after you click **OK**, nothing else happens.

Retrieving and Changing Values from a Form

Text input element objects have a `value` property that can be used to find the text inside the field.

We can use this to report back what the user has searched for. Edit the `search()` function to the following:

```
function search(event) {
  alert("You Searched for: " + input.value);
  event.preventDefault();
}
```

Note that in this example, `input` is the global variable defined at the start of the **scripts.js** file. It points to the input element in our form, but it could have been called anything.

Now refresh the page, enter some text in the search box, and you should see a similar sight to the screenshot shown in Figure 8.2:

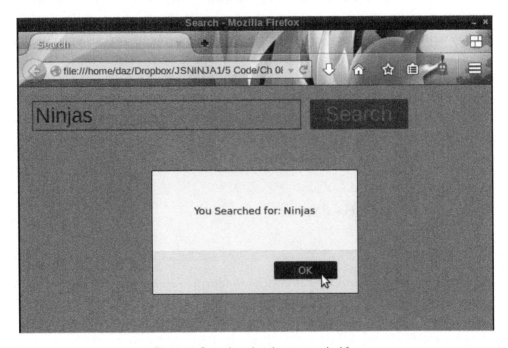

Figure 8.2. Reporting what the user searched for

It's also possible to set the value using JavaScript. Add the following line of code to the **scripts.js** file:

```
input.value = "Search Here";
```

Now refresh the page and you should see that the string "Search Here" is displayed in the input field, as in the screenshot shown in Figure 8.3.

Figure 8.3. Search Here

The problem with this is that the text remains in the field when the the user clicks inside it, so it has to be deleted before the user can enter their own text. This is easily remedied by adding these event handlers:

```
input.addEventListener('focus', function(){
  if (input.value==="Search Here") {
    input.value = ""
    }
  }, false);

input.addEventListener('blur', function(){
  if(input.value == "") {
    input.value = "Search Here";
    } }, false);
```

Now the default text will disappear when the user clicks inside the input field (the focus event) and reappear if the users leaves the field blank and clicks away from it (the blur event).

 Placeholder Text

Similar functionality can be produced in modern browsers using the `placeholder` attribute in the HTML markup. Simply change the input field to the following in **index.htm**:

```
<input type="text" name="search-box"
➥placeholder="Search Here">
```

This has slightly different behavior in that the placeholder text is not actually a value of the input field, so it won't be submitted as the field's value if the user fails to fill it in.

Form Controls

In our previous search example we only used the input and button form controls, but there are others that can help to make our web pages more interactive.

The different types of form controls are:

- input fields, including text, passwords, check boxes, radio buttons, and file uploads

- select menus for drop-down lists of options

- textarea for longer text entry

- button for submitting and resetting forms

To demonstrate all of these HTML form controls, we'll create another form that contains all these elements. Back in Chapter 5, we created a superman object that had lots of properties associated with the Man of Steel. We're going to create a form that allows a user to enter all these details into a browser, so we'll create a similar hero object that describes a superhero (or villain).

Create a new project folder that contains the following code in a file called **hero.htm**:

hero.htm

```
<!doctype html>
<html lang="en">
<head>
  <meta charset="utf-8">
  <title>Hero Form</title>
  <link rel="stylesheet" href="css/styles.css">
</head>
<body>
```

```
<form id="hero">
  <label for="name" class="break">Name:</label>
  <input type="text" name="name" autofocus placeholder=
➥"Your Super Hero Name" maxlength=5>
  <button type="submit">Submit</button>
</form>
<script src="js/scripts.js"></script>
</body>
</html>
```

We'll start with a basic form that's fairly similar to our previous search example, containing a text input field and button to submit the form.

 HTML5 Attributes

The `input` element includes some of the new attributes introduced in HTML5.

The `autofocus` attribute give focus to this element when a page loads. It is the equivalent to putting the following line of JavaScript in **scripts.js**:

```
forms.hero.name.focus();
```

The `placeholder` attribute will insert the value provided in the input field until the user enters some text. This can be useful to place hints about how to fill in the form.

The `maxlength` attribute will limit the number of characters that can be entered in the field to the value given (in this case 32).

There are many new attributes that can be employed to make forms more user-friendly. A good roundup of all the new form elements can be in this article on the SitePoint website.[1]

We'll also need a **css** folder containing a file called **styles.css** that contains the following code (it makes the form look a bit neater by displaying some of the controls as block elements):

[1] http://www.sitepoint.com/html5-forms-markup

```
                                                          styles.css
label.break, button{
    display: block;
}
```

And last of all we'll need a **js** folder that contains a file called **scripts.js**. In this file, let's start off by assigning the form to a variable and then adding an event listener for when the form is submitted:

```
var form = document.forms.hero;
form.addEventListener("submit", makeHero, false);
```

The event listener will call the makeHero() function when the form is submitted. In this function, we want to create an object from the information provided in the form. Let's implement that function by adding this code to **scripts.js**:

```
function makeHero(event) {

    event.preventDefault(); // prevent the form from being submitted

    var hero = {}; // create an empty object

    hero.name = form.name.value; // create a name property based on
➥the input field's value

    alert(JSON.stringify(hero)); // convert object to JSON string and
➥display in alert dialog
}
```

This function uses the event.preventDefault() method to stop the form from being submitted. We then create a local variable called hero and assign it to an empty object literal. We'll then augment this object with properties from the form, although we only have the name property at the moment. Once the hero object is created, it could be returned by the function and then used in the rest of the program. Since this is just for demonstration purposes, we simple use the JSON.stringify() method to convert the hero object into a JSON string and then display it in an alert dialog.

Open up **hero.htm** in a browser and enter the name of a superhero and you should see a screenshot similar to Figure 8.4.

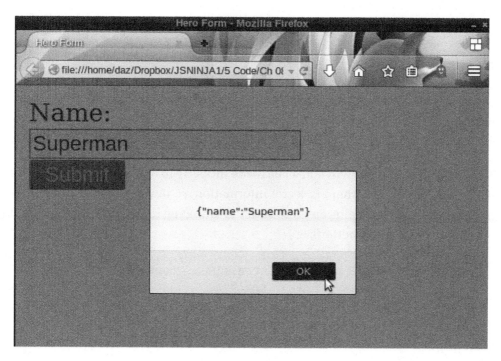

Figure 8.4. Hero's name

Now that we know our code is working, let's look at some of the other types of form controls.

Input Fields

Input fields are the most common types of form control, but there are several categories of input field as you'll soon see:

Text Input Fields

The default type of input field is `"text"` which is used for entering a short piece of text, such as a username or phone number. In our example, we use a text input field to enter the name of the superhero. The `type="text"` attribute isn't imperative (we didn't use it in the search example as `"text"` is the default), but it is advisable to use it as it makes the intended purpose of the field explicit, helping with maintenance, readability, and future-proofing.

The initial value of this field can be set in the HTML using the `"value"` attribute:

```
<input type="text" name="name" value="Enter your name">
```

Password Input Fields

input type="password" is used to enter passwords or secret information. This works in the same way as an input field with type="text", except that the characters are concealed as they are entered so they're unable to be read on the screen.

To see this in action, we will add a realName property to our hero object. Obviously the real name of a superhero is secret information, so it needs to be hidden from prying eyes when it is being entered. Add the following line to the form in **hero.htm** (just before the submit button):

```
<label for="realName" class="break">Real Name:</label>
<input type="password" name="realName">
```

To process this information, we add the following line to the makeHero() function in **scripts.js**:

```
hero.realName = form.realName.value;
```

As you can see, values from a password input field are accessed in exactly the same way as text input fields using the value property.

Checkbox Input Fields

Check boxes are created using input fields with type="checkbox". They are used to select different options that can be checked (true) or left unchecked (false). The user can select *more than one checkbox* from a list.

We'll use checkboxes to add a list of powers that the superhero can have. Add the following lines of code to the form in **hero.htm**:

```
<p>Super Powers:</p>
<label for="flight">Flight:</label>
<input type="checkbox" value="Flight" name="powers">
<label for="strength">Super Strength:</label>
<input type="checkbox" value="Strength" name="powers">
<label for="speed">Super Speed:</label>
<input type="checkbox" value="Super Speed" name="powers">
```

```
<label for="energy">Energy Blasts:</label>
<input type="checkbox" value="Energy Blasts" name="powers">
<label for="telekinesis">Telekinesis:</label>
<input type="checkbox" value="Telekinesis" name="powers">
```

Notice that all the checkbox elements have the same name property of "powers".
This means that they can be accessed as an HTML collection like so:

```
form.powers;
```

We can then iterate over this collection using a for loop to see if each checkbox
was checked. Checkbox objects have a checked property that tells us if it has been
checked or not. It is a Boolean property, so can only have the values true or false.
The value property is used to set the name of the power that can be used if the
checkbox has been checked. Add the following code to the makeHero() function in
scripts.js:

```
hero.powers = [];
for (i=0; i < form.powers.length; i++) {
  if (form.powers[i].checked) {
    hero.powers.push(form.powers[i].value);
  }
}
```

This creates a powers property for our hero object that starts as an empty array. We
then iterate over each checkbox to see if it was checked in the form. If it was, we
add the value property of the checkbox to the powers array using the push method.

Note that a checkbox can be set to true using JavaScript by setting its checked
property to true. For example, we could make the first checkbox in the list of powers
appear checked with this line of code:

```
document.forms.hero.powers[0].checked = true
```

Checkboxes can also be checked initially using the "checked" attribute in the HTML:

```
<input type="checkbox" value="Flight" name="powers" checked>
```

Radio Button Input Fields

Radio buttons are created using input fields with `type="radio"`. Like checkboxes they allow users to check an option as `true`, but they only give an exclusive choice of options, so *only one option* can be selected.

This type of mutually exclusive option could be whether a superhero is a hero or a villain ... or even an antihero (you know, those ones that are unable to decide whether to be good or bad). Add this line of code to the form in **hero.htm**:

```
<p>What type of hero are you?</p>
<label>Hero:</label>
<input type="radio" name="type" value="Hero">
<label>Villain:</label>
<input type="radio" name="type" value="Villain">
<label>Anti-Hero:</label>
<input type="radio" name="type" value="Antihero">
```

All these radio buttons have the same `name` attribute of `"type"`. This is used to group them together—only one radio button can be checked in a group that have the same name. It also means we can access an HTML collection of all the radio buttons in that group using this line of code:

```
form.type;
```

Because this is an array-like object, we can use index notation to access each radio button in the group. For example, the first radio button is:

```
form.type[0];
```

Each radio button has a `value` property that is equal its `value` attribute. We can use this to set a `type` property in our `hero` object to the value of the radio button that is selected. Add the following code to the `makeHero()` function in **scripts.js**:

```
for (i=0 ; i < form.type.length ; i++) {
  if (form.type[i].checked) {
    hero.type = form.type[i].value;
```

```
    break;
    }
}
```

This uses a `for` loop to iterate over the collection of radio buttons to see which one has been checked. If it is checked, the `hero.type` property is set to the radio button's `value` property. Note the use of the `break` statement. This is because there is no point continuing the search for a checked radio button once one has been found since only one of them can be checked.

Radio buttons also have a `checked` property that returns the Boolean values `true` and `false`, depending on if it has been selected or not. It's possible to change the `checked` property to `true`, but because only one radio button can be checked at once, all the others with the same `name` property will change to `false`. So the following line of code would check the `"antihero"` radio button, but the `"hero"` and `"villain"` radio buttons would then be unchecked:

```
form.type[2].checked = true;
```

Radio buttons can also be checked initially using the "checked" attribute in the HTML:

```
<input type="radio" name="type" value="Villain" checked>
```

Hidden Input Fields

Hidden fields can be created using input fields with `type="hidden"`. These are not displayed by the browser but have a "value" attribute that can contain information that is submitted with the form. They are often used to send information such as settings or information that the user has already provided. Note that the information in these fields is in no way secret as it is visible in the HTML, so they shouldn't be used for sensitive data. The value of a hidden input field can be changed using JavaScript.

File Input Fields

A file input field can be created using input fields with `type="file"`. They are used to upload files and most browsers will provide a **Browse** button or similar that lets users select a file from their file system.

HTML5 Input Types

There are lots of new input types included in HTML5 such as `number`, `tel`, and `color`. As browsers start to support these, they will implement different user interface elements depending on the input type. So a number field might use a slider, whereas a date field will show a calendar. They will also validate automatically, so an email input field will show an error message if it there is no valid email address.

Let's add an input type of "`number`" to our form. Add the following to **hero.htm**:

```
<label for="age" class="break">Age:</label>
<input type="number" name="age" min=0 step=1>
```

Number input fields also have optional `min` and `max` attributes that can be used to limit the input given. The `step` attribute is used to specify how much the value changes by on each click. Most modern browsers will add controls at the side of the input field so that the value can be increased or decreased, as shown in Figure 8.5.

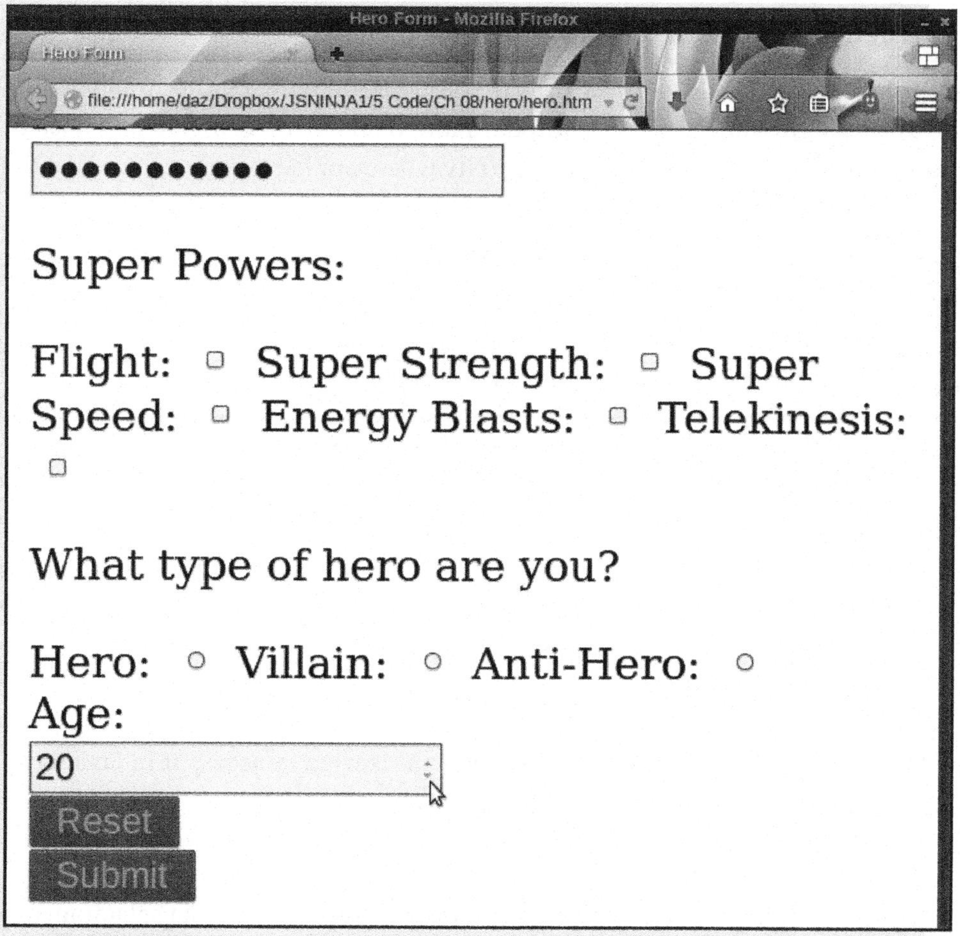

Figure 8.5. Using the number input field to specify our hero's age

We'll also need some JavaScript to process the age information. Add the following line to the makeHero() function in **scripts.js**:

```
hero.age = form.age.value;
```

These new input types are yet to be all supported, but the good news is that you can start using them now because they will still work; the browser will just display a normal text input field if it doesn't support a particular type. A good roundup of all the new form elements can be found in this article on SitePoint.[2]

---

[2] http://www.sitepoint.com/html5-forms-markup

Select Drop-down List

Select drop-down lists can be used to select one or more options from a list of values. The `multiple` attribute is required if more than one option is to be selected. We'll use one in our example to choose the city where our hero operates. Add the following line of code to the form in **hero.htm**:

```
<label for="City" class="break">Base of Operations:</label>
<select name="city">
  <option value="" selected>Choose a City</option>
  <option value="Metropolis">Metropolis</option>
  <option value="Gotham City">Gotham City</option>
  <option value="Keystone City">Keystone City</option>
  <option value="Coast City">Coast City</option>
  <option value="Star City">Star City</option>
</select>
```

Note that the `selected` attribute can be used to set the initial value in the HTML. In this example, the blank option that provides the instructional message "Choose a City" has this attribute, so it is shown when the page loads.

The `name` attribute of the `<select>` element is used to access it in JavaScript:

```
form.city;
```

If only one item was selected, this will return a reference to that selection; otherwise a collection will be returned containing each selection.

Each selection object has a `value` property that returns the `value` attribute of the `<option>` tag that was selected. Add the following code to the `makeHero()` function to set the `city` property:

```
hero.city = form.city.value;
```

It is also possible to find out the index of the option that has been selected using the `selectedIndex` property. For example, if a user selected "Gotham City" from the menu, `form.city.selectedIndex` would return `two` because it is the third option in the list.

Text Areas

A `<textarea>` element is used to enter long pieces of text over multiple lines such as a comment or blog post. They work in much the same way as input fields. We access them using the `name` attribute, and use the `value` property to see what text was entered in the form.

For example, we can add a text area to our form for the origin story of our superhero. Add the following lines of code to the form in **hero.htm**:

```
<label for="origin" class="break">Origin Story:</label>
<textarea name="origin" rows="20" cols="60"></textarea>
```

This can easily be added to the `hero` object by placing the following line of code to the `makeHero()` function:

```
hero.origin = form.origin.value;
```

It is also possible to change the value in the form directly:

```
form.origin.value = "Born as Kal-El on the planet Krypton..."
```

The initial value of a text area can be set in the HTML by placing the text between the opening and closing tags:

```
<textarea name="origin" rows="20" cols="60">Born as Kal-El on the
➥planet Krypton...</textarea>
```

Buttons

We've already used a button to submit a form, but there are different types of button. The default type is `submit`, which is why we didn't have to specify the type in our search example earlier. Another type is `reset`, which will reset all the form fields to their initial settings. Let's add a reset button to our example by adding the following line to **hero.htm**, just before the submit button:

```
<button type="reset">Reset</button>
```

Now have a go at filling in part of the form and pressing the reset button; all the form fields should clear. Remember: this is *not* recommended good practice for usability reasons!

The other type is simply `button`. This doesn't need to be inside a form element and has no default behavior. It simply creates a clickable button that can have an event listener attached to it:

```
<button type="button">Click Me</button>
```

I Need a Hero!

Now that our example form is complete, have a go at filling it in and pressing the **Submit** button. You should see something similar to the screenshot in Figure 8.6.

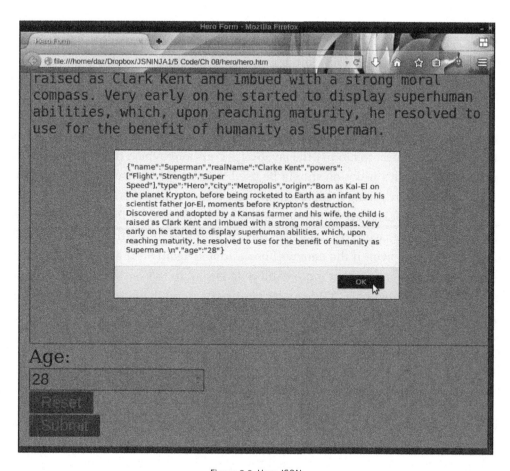

Figure 8.6. Hero JSON

We've successfully created a JavaScript object from form inputs that could then be used in the rest of our program. In this example we've used the JSON.stringify() method to convert the object into a JSON string, which could then be stored in a database or exported to an external web service.

Form Validation

Form validation is the process of checking whether a user has entered the information into a form correctly. Examples of the types of validation that occur include ensuring that:

- a required field is completed

- an email address is valid

- a number is entered when numerical data is required

- a password is at least a minimum number of characters

Validation can occur on the client side using JavaScript and on the server side. It is advisable to use both client-side and server-side validation; JavaScript should not be relied upon to validate any data before it is saved to a database. This is because it's possible for a user to modify the JavaScript code and bypass the validation rules. Instead, JavaScript validation should be used to enhance the user experience when filling in a form by giving feedback about any errors before it is submitted. This should then be backed up with more validation performed on the server before the data is eventually saved to a database. Having said that, it is still useful to validate on the client side even if the data will be validated again on the server side. This is because it will ensure that more valid data is sent to the server, which helps to cut down the number of HTTP requests required to send the form back and forward from the server to be corrected.

HTML5 has its own validation API that can be used, although it lacks the full support from all browsers at the moment. The error messages that it produces can look inconsistent across browsers and are difficult to style.

The API works by simply adding relevant attributes to the form fields. For example, if a field is a required field that must be filled in, all you need to do is add a "required" attribute to that field and the browser will take care of the rest.

To see an example of this in action, add a `required` attribute to the `name` field in our hero form:

```
<input type="text" name="name" required>
```

Now refresh the page and leave the name field blank. As you click in another field, you'll notice that the blank name field is highlighted because it is a required field, similar to the screenshot in Figure 8.7.

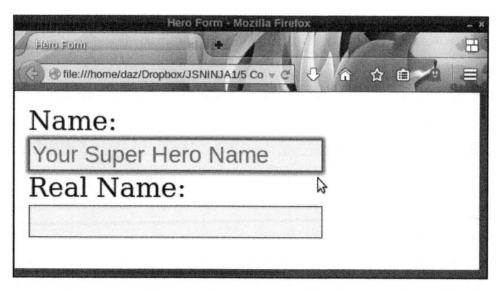

Figure 8.7. This is a required field

You can find more information about the HTML5 validation API in this article by Craig Buckler on SitePoint.[3]

It is also possible to implement custom form validation using JavaScript. For example, say we wanted to exclude any superhero names that begin with an "X." This is not a standard form of validation, so we'd have to write our own. Add this code to **scripts.js** to see an example of custom validation:

```
form.addEventListener("submit",validate,false);

function validate(event) {
  var firstLetter = form.name.value[0];
  if (firstLetter.toUpperCase() === "X") {
      event.preventDefault();
      alert("Your name is not allowed to start with X!");

  }
}
```

This starts by finding the first letter of the value entered in the name field using the index notation (an index of 0 represents the first letter in a string). It then checks to see if the first letter is an "X" and alerts the user to the mistake. It also uses the

---

[3] http://www.sitepoint.com/html5-forms-javascript-constraint-validation-api

preventDefault() method to stop the form from being submitted. Otherwise it returns true, which means the form is submitted as normal.

If you refresh the page and enter a name beginning with "X" in the name field and then try submitting the form, you should receive an error alert dialog as in the screenshot shown in Figure 8.8.

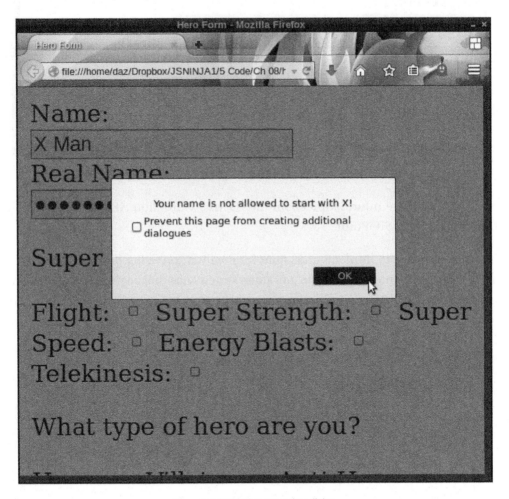

Figure 8.8. Validation error alert dialog

We can improve the usability of the form further by giving instant feedback instead of waiting for the form to be submitted. This can be achieved by adding the event listener directly to the input field that will fire when the user leaves the field (using the blur event). The feedback can then be inserted into the label for the input field (along with a class of error for styling purposes) for more direct feedback. Add the following code to **scripts.js**:

```
form.name.addEventListener("blur",validateInline,false);

function validateInline(event) {
  // get the fist letter of the name input field
  var firstLetter = form.name.value[0];
  // get a reference to the label for the name input field
  var label = document.querySelector("label[for='name']");
  if (firstLetter.toUpperCase() === "X") {
    label.classList.add("error");
    label.textContent = "Your name is not allowed to start with X!";
  } else { // the error hasn't happened or has been fixed
    label.classList.remove("error");
    label.textContent = "Name:";
  }
}
```

The else block ensures that if the error has been fixed, the error class is removed and the label text is returned to normal.

We also should add some styling to the error message so that it stands out. Add the following to **styles.css**:

```
.error{
  background: #f99;
  border: #900 1px solid;
}
```

Now if you refresh the page and try to enter a name beginning with "X," you should see an error message above the input field as soon as you try to move to another field. This can be seen in the screenshot in Figure 8.9.

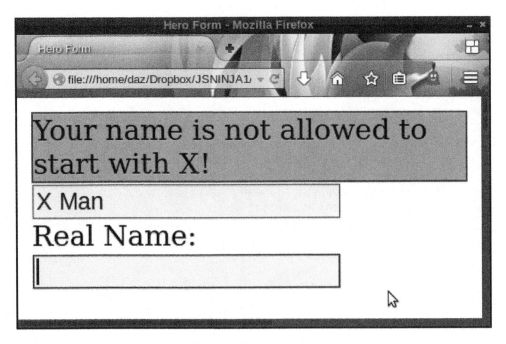

Figure 8.9. Inline error message

Quiz Ninja Project

Now we can use forms in our Quiz Ninja game so that players can enter their answers without using prompt dialogs. Our first task is to add a form element with an ID of answer in the HTML. This goes in between the question and feedback sections in the **index.htm** file:

```
<form id="answer">
  <input type="text">
  <button>Submit Answer</button>
</form>
```

Now we add a reference to the form in our JavaScript. Add this line to the end of the DOM references in **scripts.js**:

```
var $form = document.getElementById("answer");
```

The next task to do is remove the for loop that we've been using to loop through each question. This is because the prompt dialogs that we've been using pause the execution of the program and wait until the player has entered the answer. This won't happen if we use a form, so the program would just loop through each question without giving the player a chance to answer!

Instead, we're going to use a counter to keep track of which question the player is up to. Remove the following main game loop code from the **scripts.js** file:

```
// main game loop
for(var i=0, question, answer, max=quiz.questions.length; i<max;
➥i++) {
  question = quiz.questions[i].question;
  answer = ask(question);
  check(answer);
}
// end of main game loop
```

And replace it with this:

```
var i = 0;
chooseQuestion();
```

This sets a variable i to 0, which will keep track of how many questions have been asked. We then invoke the `chooseQuestion()` function. This is a new function that's used to select the next question; we then ask it by invoking the `ask()` function. The code for this function goes with the other nested functions inside the `play()` function:

```
function chooseQuestion() {
  var question = quiz.questions[i].question;
  ask(question);
}
```

Next, we remove the following from the `ask()` function, because it uses a prompt dialog to ask for an answer:

```
return prompt("Enter your answer:");
```

We'll replace it with a couple of lines that give focus to the form's input field and also remove any previous answer. The input field is the first element in the form, so has an index of 0:

```
$form[0].value = "";
$form[0].focus();
```

We need to wait for the player to enter an answer and submit the form before we check the answer. We can use an event listener to check when the form has been submitted and then invoke the check() function. Add the following code to the beginning of the play() function—it has to go inside the play() function so that it can invoke the nested check() function:

```
$form.addEventListener('submit', function(event) {
   event.preventDefault();
   check($form[0].value);
   }, false);
```

This uses the preventDefault() method to stop the default form behavior; then it invokes the check() function, passing $form[0].value as an argument. This is the value that is entered in the input field by the player and it will be passed to the the check() function to see if it's correct.

Next, we add this code to the end of the check() function to increase the value of i, and then choose the next question:

```
i++;
if(i === quiz.questions.length) {
   gameOver();
} else {
   chooseQuestion();
}
```

Players can now use the form instead of prompt dialogs to enter their answers, but a lot of the elements are displayed when they are unnecessary. For example, when the page loads the form is displayed, event though there is no question to answer, and the start button remains on the page, even after the game has started. To remedy this, we can create a couple of helper functions to hide and show elements as we need them. Add the following to **scripts.js**, before the play() function:

```
function hide(element) {
   element.style.display = "none";
}
```

```
function show(element) {
  element.style.display = "block";
}
```

These functions change the `display` CSS property of the element to `"none"`, which effectively hides the element, although it is still contained in the markup. Now we can use these functions to hide certain elements at the relevant times. To hide the form when the page loads, add the following code just before the `play()` function:

```
// hide the form at the start of the game
hide($form);
```

This should mean that only the start button is shown prior to the game commencing. When the player clicks on the button, the `play()` function is called and the game starts. At this point, we want the start button to be hidden and the form to be shown, so add this at the beginning of the `play()` function:

```
// hide button and show form
hide($start);
show($form);
```

At the end of the game, we want to hide the form and show the start button so that the player can choose to play again. Add the following to the end of the `gameOver()` function:

```
hide($form);
show($start);
```

Finally, we'll add some CSS to style the form in **styles.css**. The input field is actually styled the same way as the button, so we can simply add the input selector to the beginning of the declaration:

```
input, button {
  .... styles remain the same
```

The following styles will center the quiz playing area:

```
body{
    width: 400px;
    margin: 0 auto;
    background: #fff;
    height:100vh;
}

html{
    background: #444;
}
```

Let's have a go at playing it. Open up **index.htm** and it should look similar to the screenshot shown in Figure 8.10.

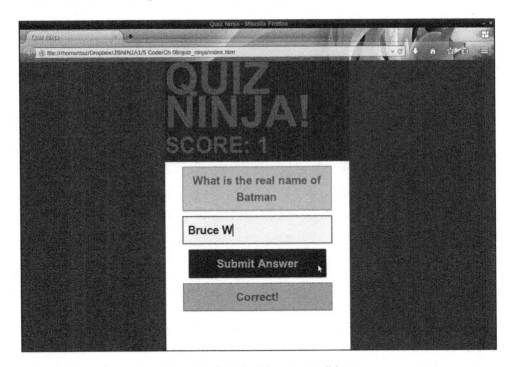

Figure 8.10. Our quiz with no prompt dialogs

Our quiz is now shaping up nicely and looking much more professional without all the alert and prompt dialogs.

Summary

In this chapter, we have learned the following:

- Forms are the primary method used for entering data into a browser.

- Forms have a variety of controls that are used for entering different types of information.

- HTML5 has a large number of new input types that are beginning to be implemented in modern browsers.

- `document.forms` will return an HTML collection of all the forms on a page.

- `form.elements` will return an HTML collection of all the elements contained within a form.

- Forms have `focus`, `blur`, and `change` events that fire as a user interacts with the form.

- Forms also have a `submit` event that can be used to intercept a form before it has been submitted.

- The information entered into a form can be read or updated using the `value` property of the form controls.

- The HTML5 form validation API can be used to automatically validate a form, but only at a basic level, so a custom validation script may be required.

In the next chapter, we'll look at the `window` object.

The Window Object

The window object represents the browser window that contains a web page. It is also used to represent the global object in a browser environment.

In this chapter, we'll cover these topics:

- the Browser Object Model

- finding out browser information

- browser history

- controlling windows

- cookies

- timing functions

- Our project — using cookies to welcome back the user

The Browser Object Model

The Browser Object Model (or BOM for short) is a collection of properties and methods that contain information about the browser and computer screen. For example, we can find out which browser the users are utilising (though, this method is unreliable), the dimensions of their screens, and which pages they have visited before the current page. It can also be used for the rather dubious practice of creating pop-up windows, if you're into annoying your users.

There is no official standard for the BOM, although there are a number of properties and methods that are supported by all the major browsers, making a sort of de facto standard. These properties and methods are made available through the `window` object. Every browser window, tab, popup, frame, and iframe has a `window` object.

There Isn't Always a BOM

Remember that JavaScript can be run in different environments. The BOM only makes sense in a browser environment. This means that other environments (such as Node.js) may not have a `window` object, although they will still have a global object; for example, Node.js has an object called `global`.

Going Global

All the way back in Chapter 2, we introduced the concept of global variables. These are variables that are created without using the `var` keyword. Global variables can be accessed in all parts of the program.

Global variables are actual properties of a global object. In a browser environment, the global object is the `window` object. This means that any global variable created is actually a property of the `window` object:

```
x = 6;
<< 6

window.x;
<< 6
```

In general, you should refer to global variables without using the `window` object (it's less typing and your code is more portable between environments). An exception is if you need to check whether a global variable has been defined. For example, the following code will throw an exception if x has not been defined:

```
if (x) {
  // do something
  }
```

However, if the variable is accessed as a property of the window object, an exception will not occur (although the block of code will still not be evaluated without x being defined):

```
if (window.x) {
  // do something
}
```

Some functions that we've already met such as parseInt() and isNaN() are global functions, which in a browser environment makes them methods of the window object:

```
window.parseInt(4.2);
<< 4

window.isNaN(4.2);
<< false
```

Like variables, it is customary to omit accessing them through the window object.

Dialogs

In Chapter 1, we introduced three functions that produced dialogs in the browsers: alert(), confirm(), and prompt(). These are not part of the ECMAScript standard, although all major browsers support them as methods of the window object.

The window.alert() method will stop the execution of the program and display a message in a dialog box. The message is provided as an argument to the method and undefined is always returned:

```
window.alert("Hello")
```

The `window.confirm()` method will stop the execution of the program and display a confirmation dialog that shows the message provided as an argument and giving the options of **OK** or **Cancel**. It returns the Boolean values of `true` if the user clicks **OK** and `false` if the user clicks **Cancel**:

```
window.confirm("Do you wish to continue?")
```

The `window.prompt()` method will stop the execution of the program. It displays a dialog that shows a message provided as an argument as well as an input field that allows the user to enter text. This text is then returned as a string when the user clicks **OK**. If the user clicks **Cancel**, `null` is returned:

```
window.prompt("Please enter your name?")
```

 Dialogs Stop Processing

It is worth reiterating again that these methods will stop the execution of a program in its tracks. This means that everything will stop processing at the point the method is called, until the user clicks **OK** or **Cancel**. This can cause problems if the program needs to process something else at the same time or the program is waiting for a callback to be called.

Browser Information

The `window` object has a number of properties and methods that provide information about the user's browser.

Which Browser?

The `window` object has a `navigator` object that contains information about the browser being used. Its `userAgent` property will return information about the browser and operating system being used. For example, if I run the following line of code, it shows that I am using Firefox version 31.0 on Linux:

```
window.navigator.userAgent
<< "Mozilla/5.0 (X11; Linux i686; rv:31.0) Gecko/20100101
➥Firefox/31.0"
```

Don't rely on this information though, as it can be modified by a user to masquerade as a different browser. It's also difficult to make any sense of the string returned, because all browsers pretend to be others to some degree. For example, every browser will include the string "Mozilla" in its userAgent property for reasons of legacy Netscape compatibility.

Location, Location, Location

The window.location property is an object that contains information about the URL of the current page. It contains a number of properties that provide information about different fragments of the URL.

The href property returns the full URL as a string:

```
window.location.href
<< "https://learnable.com/topics/all/book?utm_source=sitepoint&
➥utm_medium=link&utm_content=top-nav"
```

This property (as well as most of the others in this section) is a read/write property, which means that it can also be changed by assignment. If this is done, the page will be reloaded using the new property. For example, the following line will redirect the page to the SitePoint home page:

```
window.location.href = "http://www.sitepoint.com/"
<< "http://www.sitepoint.com/"
```

The protocol property returns a string describing the protocol used (such as http, https, pop2, ftp etc.). Note that there is a colon (:) at the end:

```
window.location.protocol
<< "https:"
```

The host property returns a string describing the domain of the current URL *and* the port number (this is often omitted if the default port 80 is used):

```
window.location.host
<< "learnable.com"
```

The `hostname` property returns a string describing the domain of the current URL:

```
window.location.host
<< "learnable.com"
```

The `port` property returns a string describing the port number. It will return an empty string if the port is not explicitly stated in the URL:

```
window.location.port
<< ""
```

The `pathname` property returns a string of the path that follows the domain:

```
window.location.pathname:
<< "/topics/all/book"
```

The `search` property returns a string that starts with a `"?"` followed by the query string parameters. It returns an empty string if there are no query string parameters:

```
window.location.search
<< "?utm_source=sitepoint&utm_medium=link&utm_content=top-nav"
```

The `hash` property returns a string that starts with a `"#"` followed by the fragment identifiers. It returns an empty string if there are no fragment identifiers:

```
window.location.hash
<< ""
```

The `origin` property returns a string that shows the protocol and domain where the current page originated from. This property is read-only, so cannot be changed:

```
window.location.origin
<< "https://learnable.com"
```

The `window.location` object also has these methods:

- The `window.location.reload()` method can be used to force a reload of the current page. If it's given a parameter of `true`, it will force the browser to reload the page from the server, instead of using a cached page.

- The `window.location.assign()` method can be used to load another resource from a URL provided as a parameter, for example:

```
window.location.assign("http://www.sitepoint.com/")
```

- The `window.location.replace()` method is almost the same as the `window.location.assign()` method, except that the current page will not be stored in the session history, so the user will be unable to navigate back to it using the back button.

The Browser History

The `window.history` property can be used to access information about any previously visited pages in the current browser session. Avoid confusing this with the new HTML5 History API.[1]

The `window.history.length` property shows how many pages have been visited before arriving at the current page.

The `window.history.go()` method can be used to go to a specific page, where 0 is the current page:

```
window.history.go(1); // goes forward 1 page
window.history.go(0); // reloads the current page
window.history.go(-1); // goes back 3 pages
```

There are also the `window.history.forward()` and `window.history.back()` methods that can be used to navigate forwards and backwards by one page respectively, just like using the browser's forward and back buttons.

---

[1] See this SitePoint post for details. [http://www.sitepoint.com/javascript-history-pushstate/]

Controlling Windows

A new window can be opened using the `window.open()` method. This takes the URL of the page to be opened as its first parameter, and a list of attributes as the second parameter. This can also be assigned to a variable, so the window can then be referenced later in the code:

```
popup = window.open('https://sitepoint.com','SitePoint','width=400,
➥height=400,resizable=yes');
```

The `window.close()` method can be used to close a window:

```
popup.close();
```

It is also possible to move a window using the `window.move()` method. This takes two parameters that are the X and Y coordinates of the screen that the window is to be moved to:

```
window.moveTo(0,0); // will move the window to the top-left corner
➥of the screen
```

You can resize a window using the `window.resizeTo()` method. This takes two parameters that specify the width and height of the resized window's dimensions:

```
window.resizeTo(600,400);
```

 Avoid Popups!

These methods were largely responsible for giving JavaScript a bad name as they were used for creating annoying pop-up windows. It's also a bad idea from a usability standpoint to resize or move a user's window.

Many browsers block pop-up windows and disallow some of these methods to be called in certain cases. For example, you can't resize a window if more than one tab is open.

It's rare that it would be sensible to use any of these methods, so think very carefully before using them. There will almost always be a better alternative, and a ninja will find it.

Screen Information

The `window.screen` object contains information about the screen that the browser is displayed on. You can find out the height and width of the screen in pixels using the `height` and `width` properties respectively:

```
window.screen.height;
<< 1024

window.screen.width;
<< 1280
```

The `availHeight` and `availWidth` can be used to find the height and width of the screen, excluding any operating system menus:

```
window.screen.availWidth;
<< 1280

window.screen.availHeight;
<< 995
```

The `colorDepth` property can be used to find the color bit depth of the user's monitor, although there are few use cases for doing this other than collecting user statistics:

```
window.screen.colorDepth;
<< 24
```

The Document Object

Each `window` object contains a `document` object. This object has properties and methods that deal with the page that has been loaded into the window. In Chapter 6, we covered the Document Object Model and the properties and methods used to manipulate items on the page. The `document` object contains other methods that are worth looking at.

document.write()

The `write()` method simply writes a string of text to the page. If a page has already loaded, it will completely replace the current document:

```
document.write("Hello, world!");
```

This would replace the whole document with the string "Hello, world!". It is possible to include HTML in the string and this will become part of the DOM tree. For example, the following piece of code will create an <h1> tag node and a child text node:

```
document.write("<h1>Hello, world!</h1>");
```

The document.write() method can also be used within a document inside <script> tags to inject a string into the markup. This will not overwrite the rest of the HTML on the page. The following example will place the text "Hello, world!" inside the <h1> tags and the rest of the page will display as normal:

```
<h1>
<script>document.write("Hello, world!")</script>
</h1>
```

The use of document.write() is heavily frowned upon as it can only be realistically used by mixing JavaScript within an HTML document. For this reason, there should be no reason for a ninja to use it, although you might come across it in some old (I hope) tutorials on the Web.

Cookies

Cookies are small files that are saved locally on a user's computer. They were invented by Netscape as a way of getting round HTTP being a **stateless** protocol. This means that a browser does not remember anything from one request to another. So every time a user visits a page, nothing about any previous visits is remembered. Cookies can be used to sidestep this problem by storing information that can then be retrieved between requests.

A restriction of cookies is that they can only be read by a web page from the same domain that set them. This is to stop sites being able to access information about users, such as other sites they have visited. Cookies are also limited to storing up to 4KB of data, although 20 cookies are allowed per domain, which can add up to quite a lot of data.

Cookies can be used for personalising a user's browsing experience, storing user preferences, keeping track of user choices (such as a shopping cart), authentication and tracking users. The use of cookies for tracking purposes has been much maligned in recent years.

Their use for data storage is starting to be replaced in many cases by the new HTML5 localStorage API as it allows more data to be stored; this is covered in Chapter 14. Cookies are still useful for retaining state information (such as if a user is logged in) because they're passed between the client and server on every HTTP request.

Cookies take the form of a text file that contain a list of name/value pairs separated by semicolons. For example, a cookie file might contain the following information:

```
"name=Superman; hero=true; city=Metropolis"
```

Creating Cookies

To create a cookie, you assign it to JavaScript's "cookie jar," the document.cookie property, like so:

```
document.cookie = "name=Superman"
<< "name=Superman"
```

The document.cookie property acts like a special type of string. Assigning another cookie to it won't overwrite the entire property, it will just append it to the end of the string. So we can add more cookies by assigning them to document.cookie:

```
document.cookie = "hero=true"
<< "hero=true"

document.cookie = "city=Metropolis"
<< "city=Metropolis"
```

Changing Cookie Values

A cookie's value can be changed by reassigning it to document.cookie using the same name but a different value. The following code will update the value of both the cookies that we set in the previous section:

```
document.cookie = "name=Batman"
<< "name=Batman"
document.cookie = "city=Gotham"
<< "city=Gotham"
```

Reading Cookies

To see the current contents of the cookie jar, simply enter `document.cookie`:

```
document.cookie:
<< "name=Batman; hero=true; city=Gotham"
```

We can use the `split` method to break the string into an array containing each name/value pair, and then use a `for` loop to iterate through the array:

```
var cookies = document.cookie.split("; ");
for (var i=0, max=cookies.length; i < max; i++){
  var crumbs = cookies[i].split("=");
  console.log("The value of " + crumbs[0] + " is " + crumbs[1]);
}
```

To see an example of cookies used in the wild, you can visit nearly any website, open the console, and type `document.cookie`.

Cookie Expiry Dates

Cookies are **session cookies** by default. This means that they are deleted once a browser session is finished (when the user closes the browser tab or window). Cookies can be made **persistent**—that is, lasting beyond the browser session—by adding "`; expires=date`" to the end of the cookie when it is set, where `date` is a date value in the UTC String format `Day`, `DD-Mon-YYYY HH:MM:SS GMT`. The following example sets a cookie to expire in one day's time:

```
var expiryDate = new Date();
var tomorrow = expiryDate.getTime() + 1000 * 60 * 60 * 24;
expiryDate.setTime(tomorrow);
```

```
document.cookie = "name=Batman; expires=" + expiryDate.
➡toUTCString();
```

An alternative is to set the max-age value. This takes a value in seconds, but is not supported in Internet Explorer version 9 or earlier:

```
document.cookie = "name=Batman; max-age=86400" // 86400 secs = 1 day
```

The Path and Domain of Cookies

By default, cookies can only be read by pages inside the same directory and domain as the file was set. This is for security reasons so that access to the cookie is limited.

The path can be changed so that any page in the root directory can read the cookie. It's done by adding "; path=/" to the end of the cookie when it is set:

```
document.cookie = "name=Batman; path=/"
```

It's also possible to set the domain by adding "; domain=domainName" to the end of the cookie:

```
document.cookie = "name=Batman; domain=sitepoint.com";
```

A cookie can only be read by the domain that created it anyway, but doing this will allow all **subdomains** of sitepoint.com (such as javascript.sitepoint.com and books.sitepoint.com) to read it.

Secure Cookies

Adding "; secure" to the end of the cookie will ensure that it's only transmitted over a secure HTTPS network:

```
document.cookie = "name=Batman; secure"
```

Deleting Cookies

To remove a cookie, simply set it to expire at a time in the past:

```
document.cookie = "name=Batman; expires=Thu, 01 Jan 1970
➥00:00:01 GMT"
```

If a cookie is a session cookie, it will expire when the tab or window is closed.

 A Cookie Library

JavaScript's cookie handling is quite basic and can also be quite cumbersome. Many developers use a library such as Cookies.js[2] or jsCookie.[3] You could even develop your own set of functions to make dealing with cookies easier.

Timing Functions

The `window` object provides some useful methods for scheduling the execution of a function and for repeatedly executing functions at regular intervals.

The `window.setTimeout()` method accepts a callback to a function as its first parameter and a number of milliseconds as its second parameter. Try entering the following example into a console. It should show an alert dialog after three seconds (that's 3000 milliseconds):

```
window.setTimeout(function(){ alert("Time's Up!") }, 3000);
<< 4
```

Notice that the method returns an integer. This is an ID used to reference that particular timeout. It can also cancel the timeout using the `window.clearTimeout()` method. Try calling the code again:

```
window.setTimeout(function(){ alert("Time's Up!") }, 3000);
<< 5
```

Now quickly enter the following code before the alert pops up:

---

[2] https://github.com/ScottHamper/Cookies

[3] http://codecanyon.net/item/jscookie-easy-to-use-javascript-cookie-library/308627

```
window.clearTimeout(5); // make sure you use the correct ID
<< undefined
```

If you were quick enough, and used the correct ID, the alert was prevented from happening.

The `window.setInterval()` method works in a similar way to `window.setTimeout()`, except that it will continue to invoke the callback function after every given number of milliseconds.

The previous example used an anonymous function, but it is also possible to use a named function like so:

```
function hello(){ console.log("Hello"); };
```

Now we can set up the interval and assign it to a variable:

```
repeat = window.setInterval(hello,1000)
<< 6
```

This should show the message "Hello" in the console every second (1,000 milliseconds).

To stop this, we can use the `window.clearInterval()` method and the variable `repeat` as an argument (this is because the `window.setInterval()` method returns its ID, so this will be assigned to the variable `repeat`):

```
window.clearInterval(repeat);
```

Animation

The `setTimeOut()` and `setInterval()` methods can be used to animate elements on a web page. As an example, let's create a web page that shows a colored square, and make it rotate. Create a folder called **animation** that contains **index.htm**, a **css** folder containing **styles.css**, and a **js** folder containing **scripts.js**. Place this code inside **index.htm**:

```
                                                                    index.htm
<!doctype html>
<html lang="en">
<head>
  <meta charset="utf-8">
  <title>Animation Example</title>
  <link rel="stylesheet" href="css/styles.css">
</head>
<body>
  <div id="square"></div>
  <script src="js/scripts.js"></script>
</body>
</html>
```

This places a div on the page with an ID of square. Add the following **styles.css**:

```
                                                                    styles.css
#square {
  margin: 100px;
  width: 100px;
  height: 100px;
  background: #d16;
}
```

This will set the position, dimensions, and color of the div. Now for the animation—add the following code to **scripts.js**:

```
                                                            scripts.js (excerpt)
var square = document.getElementById("square");
var angle = 0;

setInterval(function() {
  angle = (angle + 5)%360
  square.style.transform = "rotate(" + angle + "deg)"
}, 1000/6)
```

This code receives a reference to our square div and then sets a variable called angle to 0. We then use the setInterval() method to increase the value of angle by 5 (we also use the % operator so that it resets to 0 at 360), then set the transform CSS3 property to rotate that number of degrees. The second argument is 1000/60, which equates to a frame speed of 60 frames per second.

Open **animation.htm** in your browser and you should see a rotating square, although it will probably be quite slow and not very smooth. This was the only way to achieve animation using JavaScript until the `window.requestAnimationFrame()` method was developed.

requestAnimationFrame

This method of the `window` object works in much the same way as the `window.setInterval()` method, although it has a number of improvements to optimize its performance. These include making the most of the browser's built-in graphics-handling capabilities and not running the animation when the tab is inactive, resulting in a much smoother performance. It is supported in all major browsers, including Internet Explorer from version 10 onwards. Change the code in **scripts.js** to the following:

```
var square = document.getElementById("square");
var angle = 0;

function rotate() {
  angle = (angle + 5)%360
  square.style.transform = "rotate(" + angle + "deg)"
  window.requestAnimationFrame(rotate);
}

id = window.requestAnimationFrame(rotate);
```

This is similar to the earlier code, but this time we place the rotation code inside a function called `rotate`. The last line of this function uses the `window.requestAnimationFrame()` method and takes the `rotate()` function as an argument. This will then call the `rotate()` function recursively. The frame rate cannot be set using `requestAnimationFrame()`; it's usually 60 frames per second, although it's optimized for the device being used.

To start the animation, we need to call the `window.requestAnimationFrame()` method, giving the `rotate()` function as an argument. This will return a unique ID that can be employed to stop the animation using the `window.cancelAnimationFrame()` method:

```
window.cancelAnimationFrame(id);
```

Refresh the **animation.htm** page and you should notice that the animation is much faster and smoother, as shown in Figure 9.1.

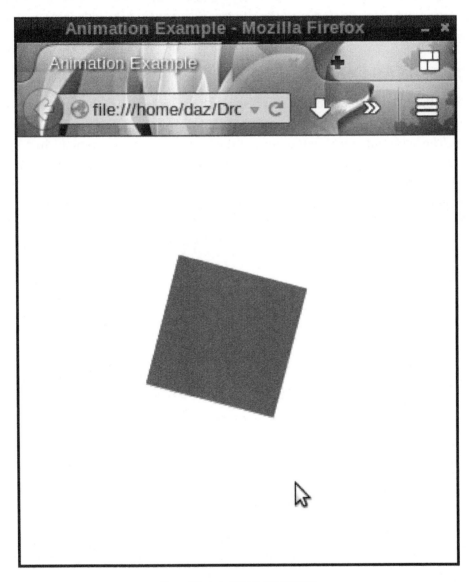

Figure 9.1. Animation in the browser

CSS Animation

The rotation animation example demonstrates how JavaScript can be used to perform animations in the browser. It could also be achieved using pure CSS animation with the following style rules in **styles.css**:

```css
#square {
    margin: 100px;
    width: 100px;
    height: 100px;
    background: #cc0;
    animation: spin 4s linear infinite;
}

@keyframes spin { from { transform:rotate(360deg); } to
↳{ transform:rotate(0deg); } }
```

In general, it is typically better to use CSS for any animation effects, although there are times when JavaScript will be the better solution.

Quiz Ninja Project

We're now going add a timer to our quiz game with a "beat the clock" element to it. We'll do this using the `window` object's `setInterval()` method to add a time limit to the game. First of all, we'll add an element to the HTML for the timer. Add the following line to the end of the `<header>` element inside the **index.htm** file:

```html
<p id="timer"></p>
```

We also need to add this code inside the **styles.css** file to make the timer display in the center of the header:

```css
#timer{
    text-align: center;
}
```

Using its ID, add a reference to this element to the other DOM references in the **scripts.js** file:

```javascript
var $timer = document.getElementById("timer");
```

We'll also add the following code to the start of the `play()` function:

```
// initialize timer and set up an interval that counts down
var time = 20;
update($timer,time);
var interval = window.setInterval( countDown , 1000 );
```

This sets a variable called `time` to 20. It is used to measure, in seconds, how the game will last. The next line updates the timer element with the initial time allowed for the game. The last line sets up an interval that calls a function called `countdown()` every second (1,000 milliseconds). Let's write that function now. It can be placed anywhere inside the `play()` function, but it is probably best placed near the end with all the other functions:

```
// this is called every second and decreases the time
function countDown() {
  // decrease time by 1
  time--;
  // update the time displayed
  update($timer,time);
  // the game is over if the timer has reached 0
  if(time <= 0) {
    gameOver();
  }
}
```

This function decreases the `time` variable that we initialized earlier by 1, and then calls the `update()` so that the time the player has left is updated and shown in the header. Last of all, we check to see if the time has reached zero and, if it has, we call the `gameOver()` function.

Finally, we have to add a line to the `gameOver()` function that will remove the interval when the game has finished, otherwise it will continue to keep counting down past zero! To stop this from happening, we place the following line of code anywhere inside the `gameOver()` function:

```
// stop the countdown interval
window.clearInterval(interval);
```

Try playing the game now by opening **index.htm** in a browser and see how you go with the added pressure of beating the clock. It should look similar to Figure 9.2.

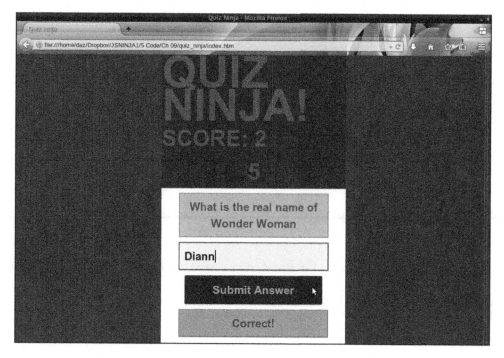

Figure 9.2. A countdown timer

Summary

In this chapter we have learned the following:

- The window object is the global object in a browser.

- Global variables are actually properties of the window object.

- alert, confirm(), and prompt() are all methods of the window object, and open dialogs that halt the execution of the program.

- The navigator object gives information about the user's browser and operating system, although it can be unreliable.

- The location object provides information about the URL of the current page.

- The history object keeps information about the pages that have been visited in the session.

- You can open, close, resize, and move windows (although, this doesn't mean that you should!).

- The `screen` object provides information about the user's screen.

- The `document.write()` is an archaic method of writing text to the document and should be avoided.

- Cookies can be used to store small pieces of information between requests using the `document.cookie` property.

- The `window.setTimeout()` method can be used to invoke a function after a set amount of time.

- The `window.setInterval()` method can be used to repeatedly invoke a function.

In the next chapter, we'll be looking at how to handle errors and write tests in JavaScript.

Testing and Debugging

Errors and bugs are a fact of life in programming—they will always be there. A ninja programmer will try to do everything to minimize errors occurring, and find ways to identify and deal with them quickly when they do occur.

In this chapter, we'll cover these topics:

- errors, exceptions, and warnings

- the importance of testing and debugging

- strict mode

- debugging in the browser

- error objects

- throwing exceptions

- exception handling

- testing frameworks

■ our project—add exception handling and write tests for the Quiz Ninja application

Errors, Exceptions, and Warnings

Errors are caused when something goes wrong in a program. They are usually caused by one of the following:

■ system error—there is problem with the system or external devices with which the program is interacting

■ programmer error—the program contains incorrect syntax or faulty logic.; it could even be as simple as a typo

■ user error—the user has entered data incorrectly that the program is unable to handle

As programmers, we often have little influence over how external systems work, so it can be difficult to fix the root cause of system errors. Despite this, we should still try to catch them and attempt to reduce their impact by working around the problems they cause. Programmer errors are our responsibility, so we must ensure they are minimized as much as possible and fixed promptly. We also should try to limit user errors by predicting any possible interactions that may throw an error, and ensure they are dealt with in a way that doesn't negatively affect the user experience.

When an error occurs in JavaScript, an **exception** is thrown that will cause the program to terminate. For example, trying to call a method that is nonexistent will result in an exception:

```
document.unicorn();
<< TypeError: document.unicorn is not a function
```

An exception will also produce a **stack trace**. It is often not just a single function or method call that causes an error, but a sequence of function and method calls. A stack trace will work backwards from the point at which the error occurred to identify the original function or method that started the sequence.

JavaScript will also show a **warning** if there is an error in the code that fails to stop the program from running. This means that the program will continue to run after a warning; this can be problematic, though, since the issue that produced the warning may cause the program to run incorrectly.

An example of a mistake that causes a warning is assigning a value to a variable that's undeclared:

```
pi = 3.142;
<< JavaScript Warning: assignment to undeclared variable
```

Warnings and exceptions are presented differently in various browser environments. Some of them will show a small icon in the corner of the browser window to indicate that an exception or warning has occurred, whereas others require the console to be open to see any warnings or exceptions.

When an exception occurs, the HTML will still appear but the JavaScript code will stop working, which isn't always obvious. If a warning occurs, the JavaScript will continue to run (although possibly incorrectly).

The Importance of Testing and Debugging

JavaScript is a fairly forgiving language when it comes to errors; it didn't implement exceptions at all until ECMAScript version 3. Instead of alerting a user to an error in a program it just failed silently in the background, and this is sometimes still the case. It might seem like a good idea at first, but the error might give unexpected or incorrect results that nobody spots, or lurk in the background for a long time before causing the program to crash spectacularly. Failing silently makes errors difficult to spot and longer to track down.

For this reason, ninjas should ensure that the code they write fails loudly in development so that any errors can be identified and fixed quickly. In production, a ninja should try to make the code fail gracefully (although not completely silently—we still need to know there's been an error) so that the user experience is not affected, if possible. This is achieved by making sure exceptions are caught and dealt with and code is tested rigorously.

Strict Mode

ECMAScript 5 includes a **strict mode** that produces more exceptions than warnings and prohibits the use of some deprecated features. For example, trying to assign a value to a variable that is undeclared will result in an exception:

```
e = 2.718;
<< ReferenceError: e is not defined
```

Increasing the chance of errors might seem like a bad idea at first, but it's much better to spot errors earlier on, rather than have them cause problems later. Writing code in strict mode can also help to improve its clarity and speed, since it follows conventions and will throw exceptions if any sloppy code practices are used.

Not using strict mode is often referred to as "sloppy mode" as it is forgiving of sloppy programming practices. Strict mode encourages a better quality of JavaScript to be written that befits a ninja programmer, so its use is recommended.

Strict mode simply requires the following string to be added to the first line of a JavaScript file:

```
"use strict";
```

This will be picked up by any JavaScript engine that uses strict mode. If the engine does not support strict mode, this string will simply be ignored.

You can even use strict mode on a per-function basis by adding the line inside a function. Strict mode will then only be applied to anything inside that function:

```
function strictly(){
    "use strict";
}
```

In fact, the recommended way to invoke strict mode is to place all of your code into a self-invoking function (covered in more detail in Chapter 12), like so:

```
(function() {
    "use strict";
```

```
// All your code would go inside this function

}());
```

Placing `"use strict"` at the beginning of a file will enforce strict mode on all the JavaScript in the file, and if you are using anybody else's code, there's no guarantee that they've coded in strict mode. This technique will ensure that only your code is forced to use strict mode.

Linting Tools

Linting tools such as JS Lint,[1] JS Hint,[2] and ES Lint[3] can be used to test the quality of JavaScript code, beyond simply using strict mode. They are designed to highlight any sloppy programming practices or syntax errors, and will complain if certain style conventions are not followed, such as how code is indented. They can be very unforgiving and use some opinionated coding conventions, such as not using the ++ and -- increment operators (in the case of JS Lint).

Passing a lint test is no guarantee that your code is correct, but it will mean it will be more consistent and less likely to have problems. Some of the errors and warnings that these tools produce can be difficult to understand, but the brilliant JS Lint Error Explanations[4] site is a helpful resource when trying to interpret them.

Feature Detection

Programming in JavaScript can be something of a moving target as the APIs it uses are in a constant state of flux. And there are new APIs being developed as part of the HTML5 specification all the time (more on these in chapter 14). Browser vendors are constantly adding support for these new features, but they don't always keep up. What's more, some browsers will support certain features and others won't. You can't always rely on users having the most up-to-date browser, either.

One way of circumventing this problem is through **browser sniffing**. This involves using the string returned by `window.navigator.userAgent` property that we met

---

[1] http://jslint.com/
[2] http://jshint.com/
[3] http://eslint.org/
[4] http://jslinterrors.com/

in the last chapter to identify the user's browser. The relevant methods can then be used for that browser. This approach is problematic, however, and not recommended because the user agent string cannot be relied upon. Additionally, the pace of browser development makes it difficult to keep up with what features are supported across browser versions.

A better way to determine browser support for a feature is to use **feature detection**. This is done using an `if` statement to check whether an object or method exists before trying to actually call the method. For example, say we want to use the shiny new `unicorn` API, we would wrap any method calls inside the following `if` block:

```
if (window.unicorn) {
    unicorn();
}
```

This ensures that no error occurs if the browser doesn't support the method, because referencing a nonexistent method such as `window.unicorn` (without the parentheses) will return `undefined`. As it's a falsy value, the `if` block won't run, but calling the method `unicorn()` (with parentheses) will cause an exception to be thrown. This guarantees that the method is only called if it actually exists and avoids any exceptions being thrown.

Debugging in the Browser

Debugging is the process of finding out where bugs occur in the code and then dealing with them. In many cases, the point at which an error occurs is not always where it originated, so you'll need to run through the program to see what's happening at different stages of its execution. When doing this, it can be useful to create what are known as **breakpoints**, which halt the progress of the code and allow us to view the value of different variables at that point in the program. There are a number of options for debugging JavaScript code in the browser.

The Trusty Alert

The most basic form of debugging is to use the `alert()` method to show a dialog at certain points in the code. Because `alert()` stops a program from running until **OK** is clicked, it allows us to effectively put breakpoints in the code that let us check the value of variables at that point to see if they're what we expect them to be. Take the following example that checks to see if a person's age is appropriate:

```
function amIOldEnough(age){
  alert(age);
  if (age < 12) {
    return "No, sorry.";
  } else if (age < 18) {
    return "Only if you are accompanied by an adult.";
  }
  else {
    return "Yep, come on in!";
  }
}
```

The `alert` method at the start of the function will allow us to see the value of the age variable at that point; once we click on **OK** we can check that the correct string is returned. Using alerts for debugging was the only option in the past, but JavaScript development has progressed since then and their use is discouraged for debugging purposes today.

Using the Console

Most modern browsers have a `console` object that provides a number of methods for logging information and debugging. It is not part of the official ECMAScript specification, but is well supported in all the major browsers.

- The `console.log()` method can be used to log the value of variables at different stages of the program, although it will not actually stop executing the program.

- The `console.trace()` method will log an interactive stack trace in the console. This will show the functions that were called in the lead up to an exception occurring while the code is running.

This SitePoint post[5] also lists a few other useful but little-known methods of the `console` object.

Debugging Tools

Most modern browsers also have a debugging tool that allows you to set breakpoints in your code that will pause it at certain points. You can then see the values of all the variables at those points and modify them. This can be very useful when trying

---

[5] http://www.sitepoint.com/three-little-known-development-console-api-methods/

to track down bugs. Here are the links to the debugger documentation for each of the major browsers:

- Firefox[6]
- Internet Explorer[7]
- Chrome[8]
- Safari[9]

Error Objects

An `error` object can be created by the host environment when an exception occurs, or it can be created in the code using a constructor function, like so:

```
var error = new Error();
```

This constructor function takes a parameter that's used as the error message:

```
error = new Error("Oops, something went wrong");
```

There are six more error objects used for specific errors:

- `EvalError` is not used in the current ECMAScript specification and only retained for backwards compatibility. It was used to identify errors when using the global `eval()` function.

- `RangeError` is thrown when a number is outside an allowable range of values.

- `ReferenceError` is thrown when a reference is made to an item that doesn't exist. For example, try calling the function `unicorn()` in the console (assuming you haven't defined a function called `unicorn()`).

- `SyntaxError` is thrown when there's an error in the code's syntax.

---

[6] https://developer.mozilla.org/en-US/docs/Tools/Debugger
[7] http://msdn.microsoft.com/en-us/library/z959x58c.aspx
[8] https://developer.chrome.com/devtools/docs/javascript-debugging
[9] https://developer.apple.com/library/mac/documentation/AppleApplications/Conceptual/Safari_Developer_Guide/Debugger/Debugger.html

- TypeError is thrown when there's an error in the type of value used; for example, a string is used when a number is expected.

- URIError is thrown when there's a problem encoding or decoding the URI.

These error functions can also be used as constructors to create custom error objects:

```
error = new TypeError("You need to use numbers in this function")
```

All error objects have a number of properties, but they are often used inconsistently across browsers. The only properties that are generally safe to use are:

- The name property returns the name of the error constructor function used as a string, such as "Error" or "ReferenceError".

- The message property returns a description of the error and should be provided as an argument to the Error constructor function.

- The stack property will return a stack trace for that error.

Throwing Exceptions

So far we have seen errors that are thrown automatically by the JavaScript engine when an error occurs. It's also possible to throw your own exceptions using the throw statement. This will allow for any problems in your code to be highlighted and dealt with, rather than lurk quietly in the background.

The throw statement can be applied to any JavaScript value and the execution of the program will still stop:

```
throw 5;
throw "JavaScript"
throw { name: "Ninja" }
```

It is best practice, however, to throw an error object. This can then be caught in a catch block, which is covered later in the chapter:

```
throw new Error("Something has gone badly wrong!"
```

As an example, let's write a function called `squareRoot()` to find the square root of a number. This can be done using the `Math.sqrt()` method, but it returns NaN for negative arguments. This is not strictly correct (the answer should be an imaginary number, but these are unsupported in JavaScript). Our function will throw an error if the user tries to use a negative argument:

```
function squareRoot(number) {
  "use strict";
  if (number < 0) {
    throw new Error("You can't square root negative numbers")
    }
  return Math.sqrt(number);
};
```

Let's test it out:

```
squareRoot(121);
<< 11

squareRoot(-1);
<< "You can't square root negative numbers"
```

Exception Handling

When an exception occurs, the program terminates with an error message. This is ideal in development as it allows us to identify and fix errors. In production, however, it will appear as if the program has crashed, which does not reflect well on a ninja programmer.

It is possible to handle exceptions gracefully by **catching** the error. Any errors can be hidden from users, but still identified. We can then deal with the error appropriately—perhaps even ignore it—and keep the program running.

try, catch, and finally

If we suspect a piece of code will result in an exception, we can wrap it in a `try` block. This will run the code inside the block as normal, but if an exception occurs it will pass the error object that is thrown on to a `catch` block. Here is a simple example using our `squareRoot()` function from earlier:

```
function imaginarySquareRoot(number) {
  "use strict";
  try {
    return String(squareRoot(number));
  } catch(error) {
    return squareRoot(-number)+"i";
  }
}
```

The code inside the `catch` block will only run if an exception is thrown inside the `try` block. The error object is automatically passed as a parameter to the `catch` block. This allows us to query the error name, message, and stack properties and deal with it appropriately. In this case, we actually return a string representation of an imaginary number:

```
imaginarySquareRoot(-49) // no error message shown
<< "7i"
```

A `finally` block can be added after a `catch` block. This will always be executed after the `try` or `catch` block, regardless of whether an exception occurred or not. It is useful if you want some code to run in both cases. We can use this to modify the `imaginarySquareRoot()` function so that it adds "+ or -" to the answer before returning it:

```
function imaginarySquareRoot(number) {
  "use strict";
  try {
    var answer = String(squareRoot(number));
  } catch(error) {
    answer = squareRoot(-number)+"i";
  } finally {
```

```
        return "+ or -" + answer;
    }
}
```

Tests

Testing is an important part of programming that can often be overlooked. Writing good tests means that your code will be less brittle as it develops, and any errors will be identified early on.

A test can simply be a function that tests that a piece of code runs as it should. For example, we could test that the squareRoot() returns the correct answer with the following function:

```
function itSquareRoots4() {
    return squareRoot(4) === 2;
}
```

Here we're comparing the result of squareRoot(4) with the number 2. This will return true if our function works as expected, which it does:

```
itSquareRoots4();
<< true
```

Clearly this is in no way a thorough test of the function, but I hope it illustrates how it works.

Test-driven Development

Test-driven development (TDD) is the process of writing tests before any code. Obviously these tests will initially fail, because there is no code. The next step is to write some code so that the tests pass. After this the code is refactored to make it more readable, faster, and remove repetition. This process should be followed in small piecemeal chunks every time a new feature is implemented. It gives the following workflow:

1. write tests (that initially fail)
2. write code to pass the tests
3. refactor the code

4. write more tests for new features

This is often referred to as the "red-green-refactor" cycle of TDD, as failing tests usually show up as red and tests that pass show as green.

Testing Frameworks

It is possible to write your own tests, as we've seen, but this can be a laborious process. Testing frameworks provide a structure to write meaningful tests and then run them. There are a large number of frameworks available for JavaScript that can be seen on Ahref magazine.[10] We'll be focusing on the Jasmine framework by Pivotal Labs, which was originally known as JsUnit.

Jasmine

Jasmine[11] is one of the most popular JavaScript TDD frameworks. It uses the concept of **specs**, which are short descriptions of what the code should do. A typical spec looks like this:

```
describe("The squareRoot function", function() {
  var number;

  it("square roots 4", function() {
    answer = squareRoot(4);

    expect(answer).toBe(2);
  });
});
```

This spec is made up of a `describe` function and a function called `it`, which contains the actual spec. There's another function called `expect` that's used for the actual tests. There are also some thoughtfully named functions called **matchers.** One example is `toBe()`, seen in the previous code sample. These are placed one after the other so that they read like an English sentence, making them easier to understand (even for non-programmers) and the feedback they provide more meaningful. It's important to recognise that they are just functions at the end of the day, so they

---

[10] http://www.ahrefmagazine.com/web-development/javascript-testing-frameworks
[11] http://jasmine.github.io/

behave in exactly the same way as any other function in JavaScript. This means that any valid JavaScript code can be run inside the spec.

Crunching Some Numbers

To demonstrate the TDD process, we'll have a go at creating a small library called "Number Cruncher" that will contain some functions that operate on numbers. The first function we'll try to implement will be called `factorsOf()`. This will take a number as a parameter and return all the factors of that number as an array.[12]

To start, download the Jasmine library from GitHub.[13] This is a zip file that needs to be extracted. Then open the directory called **dist**. This contains more zip files of all the recent versions of Jasmine. Choose the latest version and extract it . These files should then be copied into our project folder, called **numberTest**. The file structure should look similar to the one in the screenshot in Figure 10.1.

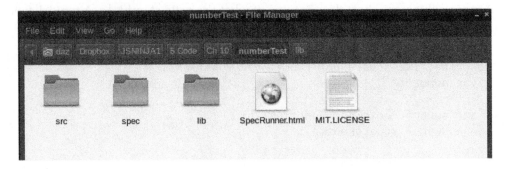

Figure 10.1. File structure

Delete all the files inside the **spec** and **src** folders as these are just useful examples that are provided by Jasmine, and we're going to create our own. Inside the **src** folder, create a blank file called **numberCruncher.js**; this is where our functions will go. Inside the **spec** folder, create a blank file called **numberSpec.js**, which is where the tests will go.

The **SpecRunner.html** file is the file that runs the tests. The script tags will need changing so that they refer to the correct files:

---

[12] The factors, or divisors, of a number are any integers that divide exactly into the number without leaving a remainder, for example, the factors of 6 are 1, 2, 3, and 6

[13] https://github.com/pivotal/jasmine/archive/master.zip

```
                                              specRunner.html (excerpt)

<!-- include source files here... -->
<script type="text/javascript" src="src/numberCruncher.js"></script>

<!-- include spec files here... -->
<script type="text/javascript" src="spec/numberSpec.js"></script>
```

Now, since we're doing TDD, we need to start writing the tests. Open up
numberSpec.js and add the following code:

```
                                          spec/numberSpec.js (incomplete)

describe("The factorsOf() function", function() {

    it("should find the factors of 12", function() {
        expect(factorsOf(12)).toEqual([1,2,3,4,6,12]);
    });

});
```

This is one description and one spec that says our `factorsOf()` function should
return an array containing the factors of 12 when 12 is provided as an argument.
Let's run the test now by opening **SpecRunner.html** in a browser. It should look
similar to the screenshot in Figure 10.2.

Figure 10.2. Our first test fails

This shows that our test has failed. Well, what did you expect? We've yet to write any code! Let's have a go at writing the `factorsOf()` function in the **numberCruncher.js** file:

src/numberCruncher.js *(incomplete)*

```
"use strict";

function factorsOf(n) {
  var factors = [];
  for (var i=1; i < n ; i++) {
    if (n/i === Math.floor(n/i)){
      factors.push(i);
    }
```

```
    }
    return factors;
}
```

This function creates a local variable called `factors` and initializes it to an empty array. It then loops through every integer value from 1 up to n (the number that was given as an argument) and adds it to the array of factors using the `push()` method if it's a factor. We test if it's a factor by seeing if the answer leaves a whole number with no remainder when n is divided by the integer i (the definition of a factor).

Try running the test again by refreshing the **SpecRunner.html** page. It should look similar to the screenshot in Figure 10.3.

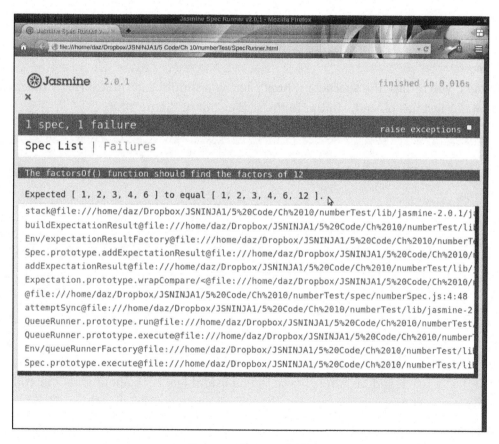

Figure 10.3. Our test still fails

Oh dear, it still failed. This time, the failure message is a bit more specific. It says that it was expecting the array [1,2,3,4,6,12] but received the array [1,2,3,4,6]—the last number 12 is missing. Looking at our code, this is because the loop only continues while i < n. We need i to go all the way up to and including n, requiring just a small tweak to our code:

src/numberCruncher.js *(incomplete)*

```javascript
function factorsOf(n) {
  var factors = [];
  for (var i=1; i <= n ; i++) { // change on this line
    if (n/i === Math.floor(n/i)){
      factors.push(i);
    }
  }
  return factors;
}
```

Now if you refresh the **SpecRunner.html** page, you should get a nice page confirming that our test has passed, similar to the screenshot in Figure 10.4.

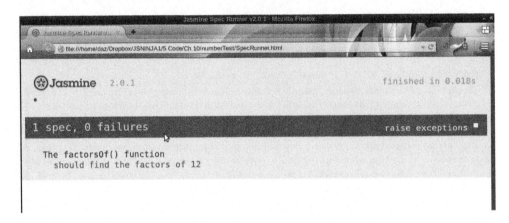

Figure 10.4. Success at last!

Our test passed, and Jasmine gives us some useful feedback about what our code does. But just because our test passed, doesn't mean we can stop there. There is still one more step of the TDD cycle: refactoring.

There are a few places where we can tidy the code up. First of all we should only really be testing for factors up to the square root because if n/i is a whole number, not only is i a factor, but n/i will be too. This will cut down the number of steps in the `for` loop dramatically. Secondly, the test to see if `i` is a factor of `n` can be written more succinctly using the `%` operator. If `i` is a factor of `n`, then `n%i` will equal 0 because there's no remainder.

```
                                              src/numberCruncher.js (incomplete)
function factorsOf(n) {
  var factors = [];
  for (var i=1 , max = Math.sqrt(n); i <= max ; i++) {
    if (n%i === 0){
      factors.push(i,n/i);
    }
  }
  return factors.sort(function(a,b){ return a > b; });
}
```

We'll also sort the array at the end using the `sort()` method with a callback we saw in Chapter 4.

Refresh **SpecRunner.html** to confirm that the tests still pass.

Now that our tests are passing and our code has been refactored, it's time to add some more functionality. Let's write another function called `isPrime()` that will return `true` if a number is prime and `false` if it isn't. Let's start by writing the test by adding the following code to the **numberSpec.js** file:

```
                                              spec/numberSpec.js (incomplete)
describe("The isPrime() function", function() {

  it("should say 2 is prime", function() {
    expect(isPrime(2)).toBe(true);
  });

  it("should say 10 is not prime", function() {
    expect(isPrime(10)).not.toBe(true);
  });


});
```

We're using a new `describe` block because we are testing a different function. This block has two specs—one to check whether `true` is returned when a prime number

(2) is provided as an argument and another to check that `true` is not returned if a non-prime number (10) is given as an argument. These specs use the `toBe()` matcher, which allows you to check if something is `true` or `false`. Note the nice use of negation using the `not` matcher (although we should probably be checking if it is `false` because this test will pass if anything but `true` is returned).

If you refresh the page, you'll see that our new tests are failing, as shown in Figure 10.5. This is to be expected, since we're yet to write any code for them.

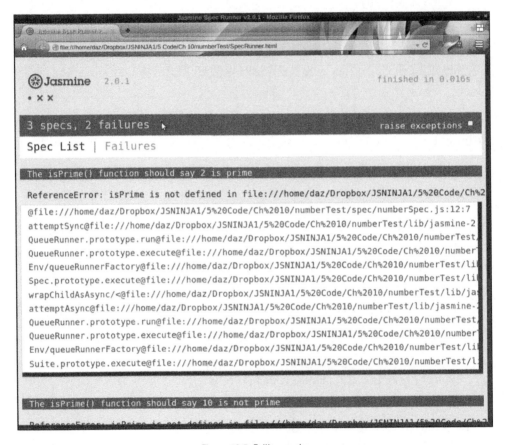

Figure 10.5. Failing again

We'd better write the `isPrime()` function. This will use the `factorsOf()` function and check to see if the number of factors in the array returned by the `factorsOf()` function is 2. This is because all prime numbers have precisely two factors. Add the following code to the bottom of the **numberCruncher.js** file:

```
                                    src/numberCruncher.js (incomplete, excerpt)
function isPrime(n) {
  return factorsOf(n).length === 2
};
```

Now if we refresh the **SpecRunner.html** page, we should receive a message telling us that all three of our specs have passed, similar to the screenshot in Figure 10.6.

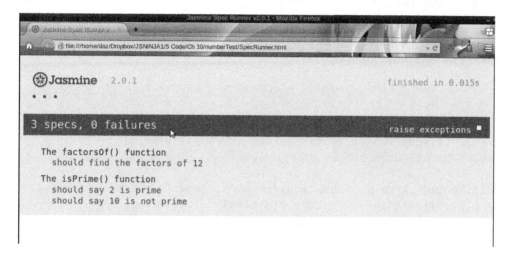

Figure 10.6. Back to the winners' list

Great, our library of functions is growing! The next step is to once again refactor our code. It's a bit brittle at the moment, because both functions accept negative and non-integer values, which have no factors and aren't prime. It turns out that the factorsOf() function fails silently and returns an empty array if either of these are passed. It would be better to throw an exception to indicate that an incorrect argument has been used. Let's create some specs to check that this happens. Open up **numberSpec.js** and add the following function at the top of the file:

```
                                              spec/numberSpec.js (excerpt)
var int, negative, decimal;

beforeEach(function() {
  int = Math.floor(100*Math.random());
```

```
    negative = int*-1;
    decimal = Math.floor + 0.5;
});
```

This is a setup function and it contains any code that will be run before every spec. In this case we're using it to create three random numbers that are assigned to variables with global scope. The first, `int`, is an integer between 1 and 100. The second, `negative`, is the negative of that number, and the last, `decimal`, is the same number, plus `0.5`. These numbers can now be used in the specs and will use a different number in each test. Now add the following specs inside the "The `factorsOf()` function" describe function:

spec/numberSpec.js (excerpt)

```
it("should throw an exception for negative numbers", function() {
    expect(function(){ factorsOf(negative) }).toThrow();
});

it("should throw an exception for non-integer numbers", function() {
    expect(function(){ factorsOf(decimal) }).toThrow();
});
```

These specs use the `toThrow()` method to check that an exception has been thrown. One point to note here is that the `factorsOf()` function being tested needs to be wrapped in an anonymous function for it to work.

While we're at it, we can add some extra specs in the "The `isPrime()` function" describe function that deal with these numbers. No exceptions are necessary in these cases; negative numbers and non-integers are simply not prime, so the function should return `false`:

spec/numberSpec.js (excerpt)

```
it("should say a negative number is not prime", function() {
    expect(isPrime(negative)).toBe(false);
});
```

```
it("should say a non-integer is not prime", function() {
  expect(isPrime(decimal)).toBe(false);
});
```

If you reload the **SpecRunner.html** file, you'll see that the tests for the `factorsOf()` function fail as expected, but the tests for the `isPrime()` function pass. This is by a happy accident because the `factorsOf()` function is returning an empty array that is not of length 2, so `false` is returned as expected.

Let's try and make all the tests pass by throwing some exceptions in the `factorsOf()` function. Change the `factorsOf()` function to the following in **numberCruncher.js**:

src/numberCruncher.js *(incomplete, excerpt)*

```
function factorsOf(n) {

  if (n < 0) {
    throw new RangeError("Argument Error: Number must be positive");
  }

  if (Math.floor(n) !== n) {
    throw new RangeError("Argument Error: Number must be an
➥integer");
  }

  var factors = [];
  for (var i=1 , max = Math.sqrt(n); i <= max ; i++) {
    if (n%i === 0){
      factors.push(i,n/i);
    }
  }
  return factors.sort(function(a,b) { return a > b; });
}
```

Now the function checks to see if a negative number or non-integer has been provided as an argument and throws an exception in both cases. Let's run our tests again by refreshing the **SpecRunner.html** page in the browser. If you then click on the "**Spec List**" tab you can see the feedback about each spec. It should look similar to the screenshot in Figure 10.7.

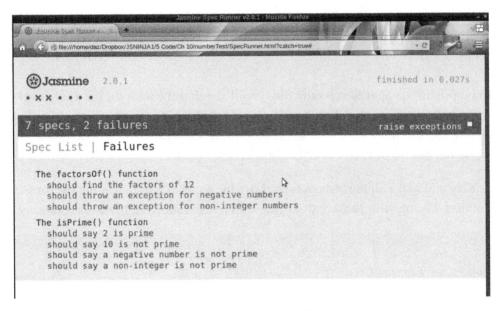

Figure 10.7. An unexpected fail

Oh, no! Our tests for the `factorsOf()` function all pass ... but the exceptions have caused the `isPrime()` function to choke and fail the tests. We need to add code that handles any exceptions that might be thrown when the `factorsOf()` function is called from within the `isPrime()` function. This sounds like a job for a `try...catch...finally` block. Change the `isPrime()` function in the **numberCruncher.js** file to the following:

```
                                                    src/numberCruncher.js (excerpt)

function isPrime(n){
    var result;
    try{
      result = factorsOf(n).length === 2;
    } catch(e){
      result = false;
    } finally{
      return result;
    }
}
```

Now we've placed the original code inside a `try` block, so that if `factorsOf()` throws an exception, we can pass it on to the `catch` block and handle the error. We know that if there is an error, all we need to do is return false, so we set the variable `result` to be false. Then in the `finally` block, we simply return `result`, which should be true or false.

Now we'll test our code again by refreshing the **SpecRunner.html** page. I trust your results are similar to the screenshot in Figure 10.8.

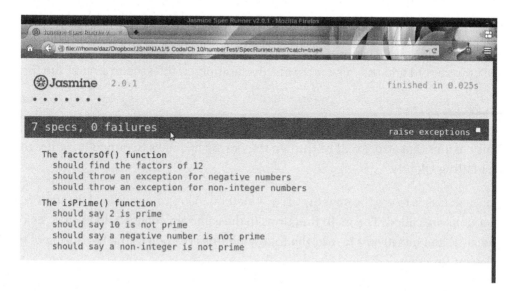

Figure 10.8. Passing with flying colors

Hooray! All our tests are now passing. We'll stop there, but I hope that this demonstrates how TDD can be used to keep adding functionality in small increments using the fail, pass, refactor cycle.

Quiz Ninja Project

We're now going to use some of the techniques we've learned in this chapter to improve the quality of our code in the Quiz Ninja project, making it easier to debug. First of all, we'll ensure that we use strict mode by wrapping all the code inside an immediately invoked function expression that's anonymous. To do this, place this line of code on the very first line of the **scripts.js** file:

```
(function () {
```

Then place the following line on the very last line of the file:

```
}())
```

This function call is invoked as soon as the file loads, running the code exactly the same way as usual; however, now all the variables are wrapped up within the scope of this anonymous function. So if this file is used in conjunction with another JavaScript file, there will be no problems if any variables in either file share the same name.

We now should add the `"use strict"` declaration on the second line of the file:

```
"use strict";
```

This ensures that errors will be thrown if there are mistakes in our code, rather than just failing silently.

The next task is to use the `console.log()` method to log when some of the important functions are called. The main functions in the game are `chooseQuestion()`, `ask()`, `check()`, and `gameOver()`. Add the following lines of code to the beginning of the relevant functions:

```
console.log("chooseQuestion() invoked");

console.log("ask() invoked");

console.log("check() invoked");

console.log("gameOver() invoked");
```

These log messages the console to say that a particular function has been invoked, so we can see where the program is at in its runtime. There will be no impact on the player, though, as we're just using the console.

Try playing the game with the console open in the browser. You should see the messages logged in the console as the program runs, as in the screenshot shown in Figure 10.9.

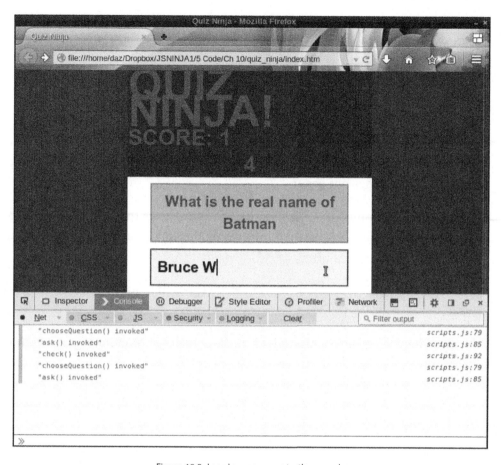

Figure 10.9. Logging messages to the console

Summary

In this chapter, we've learned the following:

■ Bugs are unavoidable in code and it's best to find them early rather than later.

■ JavaScript can be put into strict mode using the string `"use strict"`. This can be used in a whole file or just a single function.

■ Linting tools can be used to ensure that your code follows good practice and conventions.

■ Feature detection can check whether a method is supported before calling it, helping to avoid an exception being thrown.

- The console and browser's built-in debugging tool can be used to interactively find and fix bugs in code.

- Exceptions can be thrown using the `throw` statement.

- An error object is created when an exception occurs.

- Any code placed inside a `try` block will pass any error objects to a `catch` block when an exception occurs. Any code inside a `finally` block will run if an exception does or does not occur.

- Test-driven development is the practice of writing tests that fail, then writing the code that passes the test, then refactoring the code every time a new feature is implemented.

- The Jasmine framework can be used to write specs that test code in a structured way.

In the next chapter, we'll be taking a look at the concept of functional programming in JavaScript.

Chapter **11**

Functional JavaScript

Functional programming uses functions as the building blocks of a program and avoids changing the state of data. This means that a program becomes a sequence of expressions based on the return values of functions. The return value of a function should only depend on the values provided as arguments.

Functional programming has gained momentum in recent years with a dedicated following. The popularity of purely functional languages such as Clojure, Scala, and Erlang sparked an interest in functional programming techniques that continues to grow. JavaScript has always supported functional-style programming due to functions being first-class objects. This facilitates some of JavaScript's most interesting techniques—such as callbacks and closures—that can be used to create cleaner code that is flexible and powerful.

In this chapter, we'll cover the following topics:

- introduction to functional programming

- function properties and methods

- functions that return functions

- callbacks

- closures

- immediately Invoked function expressions

- self-defining functions

- recursive functions

- currying

- our project—improve some of the functions using techniques from this chapter

What is Functional Programming?

In JavaScript, functions are first-class objects, which means that they behave the same way as every other value. So they can have their own properties and methods, as well as accepting other functions as parameters and being returned by other functions. This makes them a very flexible tool to work with in JavaScript, and there are a variety of techniques and patterns that can be used to make code cleaner.

Functional programming involves using functions to perform a series of operations. Each function forms an abstraction that should perform a single task, while encapsulating the details of its implementation inside the body of the function.

Here's an example of a `random()` function that will return a random integer between two arguments, a and b; if only one argument is supplied, it will return a random number between 1 and that argument's value:

```
function random(a,b) {
  if (b === undefined) b = a, a = 1; // if only one argument is
➥supplied, assume the lower limit is 1
  return Math.floor((b-a+1) * Math.random()) + a;
}

random(6);
<< 4
```

```
random(10,20);
<< 13
```

This is an example of an **abstraction**, as it wraps all the logic cleanly away inside the function.

Functions should not alter the underlying data they deal with—they should simply return a different value, rather than change the value itself. This is known as **non-destructive data transformation**. For example, the following function will return a string written backwards:

```
function reverse(string) {
  var array = string.split("");
  array.reverse();
  return array.join("");
}
```

The function does not change the actual value of the string that's provided as an argument, however:

```
var message = "Hello";
reverse(message);
<< "olleH"

message; // hasn't changed
<< "Hello"
```

Functions should, as much as possible, only perform a single operation. They can then be used as building blocks to create other functions that represent more complex abstractions and extend the functionality further. By only performing a single task the function becomes more flexible, as it can be used as a building block in many situations rather than be tightly coupled with one particular operation. It also makes the code more modular as each function can be improved or replaced as required, without having to interfere with any of the other functions. This makes it easy to replace one function with another that either improves the behavior, modifies it slightly, or even changes it completely.

As an example, we can use the square() function that we created in Chapter 4:

```
function square(x){
  return x*x;
}
```

This function can then be used to create a `hypotenuse()` function that returns the length of the hypotenuse of a right-angled triangle,[1] given the lengths of the other two sides as parameters:

```
function hypotenuse(a,b) {
  total = square(a) + square(b);
  return Math.sqrt(total);
  }

hypotenuse(3,4);
<< 5
```

The `hypotenuse()` function uses the `square()` function to square the numbers, rather than hard coding `a*a` and `b*b` into the function. This means that if we find a more optimal way to square a number, we only have to improve the implementation of the `square()` function. Or if we find an alternative way of calculating the hypotenuse (however unlikely that is!), we could just swap the `square()` function for another.

To illustrate the point further, we can create another function called `sum()` that takes an array as an argument as well as a callback. The callback is used to transform the value of each item in the array using the `map()` method, and then the `reduce()` method is used to find the sum of all items in the array:

```
function sum(array, callback) {
  if(typeof callback === "function") {
    array = array.map(callback);
```

---

[1] The hypotenuse is the longest side of a right-angled triangle. Its length can be found using the formula $a^2 + b^2 = c^2$, which is commonly known as Pythagoras' Theorem.

```
  }
    return array.reduce( function(a,b) { return a + b });
}
```

The callback makes the function more flexible as it allows a transformation to be performed on all the numbers in the array before finding the sum. This means it can be used to find the sum of a set of numbers:

```
sum([1,2,3]); // returns 1 + 2 + 3
<< 6
```

Or the sum of a set of numbers after they've been squared (here we're using the square function as the callback):

```
sum([1,2,3], square); // returns 1^2 + 2^2 + 3^2
<< 14
```

This function can then be used to create a mean() function that calculates the mean of an array of numbers:

```
function mean(array) {
  return sum(array)/array.length;
}
```

And last of all, we can reuse the sum(), square(), and mean() functions together to make a standardDeviation() function that calculates the standard deviation of an array of numbers:

```
function standardDeviation(array) {
  return sum(array,square)/array.length - square(mean(array))
}
```

By separating each piece of functionality into individual functions, we're able to put together a more complex function. These functions can also be used to create other functions that require the mean, sum, or square values.

Functions that Return Functions

As functions are first-class objects is that they can accept a function as an argument as well as return another function.

This is the essence of functional programming: it allows generic higher-order functions to be used to return more specific functions based on particular parameters. For example, we can create a power() function that returns a function that calculates values to the power of a given parameter:

```
function power(x) {
  return function(power) {
    return Math.pow(x,power);
  }
}
```

Now we can create some more specific functions that use this generic function to build them. For example, we could implement a twoExp() function that returns powers of 2, like so:

```
twoExp = power(2);
<< function (power) {
    return Math.pow(x,power);
  }

twoExp(5);
<< 32
```

We can create another function called tenExp() that returns powers of 10:

```
tenExp = power(10);
<< function (power) {
    return Math.pow(x,power);
  }

tenExp(6);
<< 1000000
```

If a function returns another function, instead of assigning the returned function to a variable then calling it, the returned function can be invoked immediately using double parentheses:

```
power(3)(5);
<< 243
```

Function Properties and Methods

The fact that functions are first-class objects means that they can have properties and methods themselves. For example, all functions have a `length` property that returns the number of parameters the function has. In the following code, the `square` function takes one parameter:

```
square.length
<< 1
```

Call and Apply Methods

The `call()` method allows a function to be called by an object that is provided as the first argument. Inside the body of the function, the keyword `this` is used to refer to the object the function is called on.

In this example, the `sayHi()` function refers to an unspecific object called `this` that has a property called `name`:

```
function sayHi(){
    return "Hi " + this.name;
}
```

We can create some objects that have a `name` property and then use the `call()` method to invoke the `sayHi()` function, providing an object as an argument. This object will then take the value of `this` in the function:

```
alfie = { name: "Alfie" };
betty = { name: "Betty" };

sayHi.call(alfie);
<< "Hi Alfie"
```

```
sayHi.call(betty);
<< "Hi Betty"
```

If the function has arguments, these are given in the same order *after* the first argument:

```
function greet(greeting){
    return greeting + " " + this.name;
}

greet.call(alfie, "Hello");
<< "Hello Alfie"

greet.call(betty, "Yo");
<< "Yo Betty"
```

If a function does not refer to an object as this in its body, null can be provided as the first argument:

```
square.call(null, 4)
<< 16
```

The apply method works in the same way, except the arguments of the function are provided as an array, even if there is only one argument:

```
square.apply(null, [4])
<< 16
```

This can be useful if the data you're using as an argument is already in the form of an array.

These two methods allow generalized functions to be written that are not tied to specific objects by being methods of that object, giving more flexibility over the usage of the function.

Custom Properties

There is nothing to stop from you adding your own properties to functions. For example, you could add a `description` property to a function that describes what it does:

```
square.description = "Squares a number that is provided as an
➥argument"
<< "Squares a number that is provided as an argument"
```

A useful feature of this is that it provides result caching, or **memoization**.

If a function takes some time to compute a return value, we can save the result in a `cache` property. Then if the same argument is used again later, we can return the value from the cache, rather than having to compute the result again. For example, say that squaring a number was an expensive computational operation that took a long time. We could rewrite the `square()` function so that it saved each result in a `cache` object that is a property of the function:

```
function square(x){

    square.cache = square.cache || {}; // initialize the cache as an
➥empty object if it doesn't already exist
    if (!square.cache[x]) { // check to see if this value has already
➥been saved in the cache
        square.cache[x] = x*x; // if not then calculate the value and
➥save it in the cache
    }
    return square.cache[x]
}
```

If we try calling the function a few times, we can see that the `cache` object stores the results:

```
square(3);
<< 9

square(-11);
<< 121
```

```
square.cache;
<< {"3": 9, "-11": 121}
```

 Customize with Care

Adding your own custom properties to built-in objects can be risky. A ninja developer should be careful not to override default properties or methods.

Callbacks

We covered callbacks way back in Chapter 4. You'll recall that they're functions that are passed to other functions as arguments.

Event-driven Asynchronous Programming

Callbacks facilitate event-driven asynchronous programming. JavaScript is a **single-threaded environment**, which means that only one piece of code will ever be processed at a time. This may seem like a limitation, but non-blocking techniques can be used to ensure that the program continues to run. Instead of waiting for a event to occur, a callback can be created that's invoked when the event happens. This means that the code is able to run out of order, or *asynchronously*. Events can be DOM events, such as the `click` and `keyPress` that we looked at in Chapter 7, but they can also be events such as waiting for a file to load, waiting for data from a database or other website, or waiting for the program to complete a complex operation. By using callbacks, we ensure that these events don't hold up the execution of other parts of the program. Once the event occurs, the callback will be invoked before returning to the rest of the program.

Here's an example of a function called `wait()` that accepts a callback. To simulate an operation that takes some time to happen, we can use the `setTimeout()` function to call the callback after a given number of seconds:

```
function wait(message, callback, seconds){
  setTimeout(callback,seconds * 1000);
  console.log(message);
}
```

Now let's create a callback function to use:

```
function selfDestruct(){
  console.log("BOOOOM!");
}
```

If we invoke the `wait()` function and then log a message to the console, we can see how JavaScript works asynchronously:

```
wait("This tape will self-destruct in five seconds ... ",
➥selfDestruct, 5);
console.log("Hmmm, should I accept this mission or not ... ?");

<< "This tape will self-destruct in five seconds ... "
<< "Hmmm, should I accept this mission or not ... ? "
<< "BOOOOM!"
```

When the `wait()` function is invoked, any code inside it is run, so the message `"This tape will self destruct in five seconds ... "` is displayed. But when the `setTimeout()` function is invoked with a callback, control is handed back to the program and the next line in the program is run, which displays the message `"Hmmm, should I accept this mission or not ... ?"`. After five seconds, the callback is then called. This demonstrates that the `setTimeout()` function did not block the rest of the program from running.

Remember, though, that JavaScript is still single-threaded, so only one task can happen at once. If an event takes little time to happen, it may still have to wait until other parts of the program have executed before the callback occurs. For example, let's see what happens if we set the waiting time to be zero seconds:

```
wait("This tape will self-destruct immediately ... ", selfDestruct,
➥0);
console.log("Hmmm, should I accept this mission or not ... ?");

<< "This tape will self-destruct immediately ... "
<< "Hmmm, should I accept this mission or not ... ?"
<< "BOOOOM!"
```

Notice the callback in the `wait()` function is still invoked last, despite the wait time being set to zero seconds. We would have expected the callback to have been invoked immediately, but a callback always has to wait for the current execution stack to complete before it's invoked. In this case, the current execution stack is the rest of the function and and code already entered in the console. Once these have executed, the callback is invoked before handing control back to the main program.

Generalized Functions

Callbacks can be used to build more generalized functions. Instead of having lots of specific functions, one function can be written that accepts a callback. For example, we could add a callback parameter to the `random()` function, so that a calculation is performed on the random number that's returned:

```
function random(a,b,callback) {
  if (b === undefined) b = a, a = 1; // if only one argument is
➥supplied, assume the lower limit is 1
  result = Math.floor((b-a+1) * Math.random()) + a
  if(typeof callback === "function") {
    result = callback(result);
  }
  return result;
}
```

Now we have a function where more flexibility can be added using a callback. For example, we can have a random square number from one to 100:

```
random(1,10,square);
<< 49
```

Or a random even number from two to ten:

```
random(1,5, function(n) { return 2 * n });
<< 8
```

Closures

A **closure** is a reference to a free variable that was created inside the scope of another function, but is then kept alive and used in another part of the program. They're one of JavaScript's most powerful features, but they can be difficult to get your head round initially.

Function Scope

Back in Chapter 4, we saw that the value of a variable was only available inside the body of a function if the var keyword was used. In the following example, there are two variables: global, which is available everywhere, and local, which is only available inside the function:

```
var outside = "I'm a global variable";
function fun() {
  var inside = "I'm a global variable";
}

outside;
<< "I'm a global variable"

inside;
<< Error: "local is not defined"
```

It appears that we're unable to access the variable local outside of the function. It turns out, however, that we can gain access to it outside of its function using a closure.

The Ninja Training Temple

Imagine a temple where people go to train to be a ninja. When they enter the temple, new ninjas learn how to use weapons. Once they have mastered these skills, they move into the inner sanctum to learn about the skills of stealth. A person who has never entered the temple has neither the weapons nor stealth skills. A ninja who is inside the temple but not the inner sanctum only knows about the weapon skills. Once ninjas enters the inner sanctum they learn the stealth skills *and* still have the weapons skills. This can be represented by the following function:

```
function temple(){
  var weapons = "Katana, Bo, Shuriken, Yuri";

  function innerSanctum(){
    var stealth = "Cho Ho, Shinobi-Iri, Henso-Jutsu";
```

```
    }

}
```

Outside the `temple` function, the `weapons` and `stealth` variables are unable to be accessed. Inside the `temple()` function, the `weapons` variable can be accessed, and inside the `innerSanctum()` function, both the `weapons` and the `stealth` variable can be accessed.

A ninja who leaves the temple will still have all the skills that were learned there and be able to use them outside the temple. This is the concept of a closure: if a value or function is returned from a function, it maintains the references to the scope in which it was created. In the example, we can return the `innerSanctum()` function that has access to the `weapons` and `stealth` variables:

```
function temple(){
    var weapons = "Katana, Bo, Shuriken, Yuri";

    function innerSanctum(){
        var stealth = "Cho Ho, Shinobi-Iri, Henso-Jutsu";
        return "Ninja Skills " + weapons + " " + stealth;
    }

    return innerSanctum();

}
```

When the `temple()` function is called, it can be assigned to a `ninja` variable that will have access to the information contained in the `weapons` and `stealth` variables outside the `temple()` function:

```
ninja = temple();
<< "Ninja Skills Katana, Bo, Shuriken, Yuri Cho Ho, Shinobi-Iri,
➥Henso-Jutsu"
```

The `ninja` variable represents a closure, as it has access to the variables that were created inside the `temple()` function.

A Basic Closure Example

A simple closure involves returning the value of a variable that was created inside the function's scope to make it available outside the function:

```
function closure(){
  var inside = "I was created inside the function";
  return inside;
}
```

The value of the `inside` variable is unavailable outside the `closure()` function:

```
inside;
<< Error: "inside is not defined"
```

But we can create a closure by invoking the `closure()` function, which will return the value of `inside` and make it available outside the function:

```
outside = closure();
<< "I was created inside the function"
```

Returning a Function

A function can form a closure that maintains access to *all* the variables created in the original function's scope by returning a function instead of a single value:

```
function closure() {
  var a = 1.8;
  var b = 32;
  return function(c){
    return c * a + b;
  }
}
```

Now a new function can be created by invoking this function and assigning the return value to a variable:

```
toFahrenheit = closure();
```

This new function can then be invoked with its own argument, but the values of a and b from the original function are still remembered:

```
toFahrenheit(30);
<< 86
```

A Counter Example

Closures not only maintain the value of a variable from another function; this value can also be subsequently changed. It can be used to create a counter() function that starts a count using the variable i. It then returns a function that uses a closure to trap the value of i, which can then be incremented every time the new function is invoked. The reference to the variable i that is defined in the original function is maintained in the new function via a closure:

```
function counter(start){
  i = start;
  return function() {
    return i++;
  }
}

var count = counter(1); // start a counter at 1
count();
<< 1
count();
<< 2
```

A Functional Example

It's also possible to create a closure around the arguments provided to a function. This allows us to create a generic function that can be used to then return more specific functions based on its arguments. For example, consider this generic multiplier() function:

```
function multiplier(x){
  return function(y){
    return x*y;
  }
}
```

This function returns another function that traps the argument x in a closure, which is then used in the returned function. It can be used to create another function:

```
doubler = multiplier(2);
```

This creates a new function called doubler() that takes a parameter that's multiplied by the argument provided to the multiplier() function—which was 2 in this case—making a function that multiplies its argument by two:

```
doubler(10);
<< 20
```

This makes the multiplier() function a generic abstraction that can be used to build more specific abstractions, such as a tripler() function:

```
tripler = multiplier(3);

tripler(10);
<< 30
```

 arguments Object Cannot Be Trapped in a Closure

The arguments object cannot be trapped in a closure and returned in a function as it is not available inside nested functions. Hence, the following would fail:

```
function multiplier(){
  return function(x){
    return x * arguments[0]; // arguments is not available
➥in this nested function
  }
}
```

This can be fixed by using another closure:

```
function multiplier(){
  var args = arguments; // the variable args will be
➥available in the return function
  return function(x){
    return x * args[0];
  }
}
```

Check out this useful video about closures on Learnable.[2]

Immediately Invoked Function Expressions

An **Immediately Invoked Function Expression** (or IIFE, pronounced "iffy") is a function that, as the name suggests, is invoked as soon as it's defined. This is easily achieved by placing parentheses at the end of the function definition (remember that we use parentheses to invoke a function). The function also has to be made into an expression, which is done by placing the whole declaration inside parentheses, as can be seen in this example:

```
(function(){
  var temp = "world";
  console.log("Hello " + temp);

}());
<< "Hello world"
```

IIFEs are a useful way of performing a task while keeping any variables wrapped up within the scope of the function. This means that the global namespace is not polluted with lots of variable names.

Temporary Variables

There is no way to remove a variable from a scope once it's been declared. If a variable is only required temporarily, it may cause confusion if it's still available later in the code. Even worse, the name of the variable may clash with another piece of code (an external JavaScript library, for example) resulting in errors. Placing any code that uses the temporary variable inside an IIFE will ensure that it's only

---

[2] https://learnable.com/hub/play/63

available while the IIFE is invoked, and then it will disappear. The example that follows uses an IIFE to swap the value of two global variables, a and b. This process requires the use of a temporary variable, called temp, which only exists while the IIFE is invoked:

```
a = 1;
b = 2;
(function(){
  var temp = a;
  a = b;
  b = temp;
}());

console.log(a);
<< 2

console.log(b);
<< 1

console.log(temp);
<< Error: "temp is not defined"
```

Mimicking Block Scope

In most other languages, a variable has scope inside a code block—that's what's known as **block scope**. But this does not happen in JavaScript; variables only have a limited scope inside functions. This means that when a temporary variable is created inside an if block or a for loop, the variable will still be available outside of that block:

```
var list = [1,2,3];
for (var i = 0, max = list.length ; i < max ; i++ ){
  console.log(list[i]);
}
console.log(i); // i is still available outside the for block
<< 1
<< 2
<< 3
<< 3
```

The solution to this is to place the for block inside an IIFE to mimic block scope:

```
var list = [1,2,3];
(function(){for (var i = 0, max = list.length ; i < max ; i++ ){
  console.log(list[i]);
}}());
console.log(i); // i is not available outside the for block
<< 1
<< 2
<< 3
<< Error: "i is not defined"
```

 Using `let` for Block Scoping

The next version of ECMAScript supports block scoping if the `let` keyword is used instead of `var`. This has already been implemented in many modern browsers. Try the following example to see if it works in your browser:

```
var list = [1,2,3];
for (let i = 0, max = list.length ; i < max ; i++ ){
  console.log(list[i]);
}
console.log(i); // i is not available outside the for block
```

Initialization Code

An IIFE can be used to set up any initialization code that there'll be no need for again. Because the code is only run once, there's no need to create any reusable, named functions, and all the variables will also be temporary. An IIFE will be invoked once and can set up any variables, objects, and event handlers when the page loads. The following example logs a welcome message to the console and then eliminates all the temporary variables that are used in putting the message together:

```
(function() {
  var name = "Bart"; // This might be obtained from a cookie in
➥reality
  var days = ["Sunday","Monday","Tuesday","Wednesday","Thursday",
➥"Friday","Saturday"];
  date = new Date();
  today = days[date.getDay()];
  console.log("Welcome back " + name + ". Today is " + today);
```

```
})();
<< "Welcome back Bart. Today is Sunday"
```

Safe Use of Strict Mode

In the last chapter we discussed using strict mode to avoid any sloppy coding practices. One of the problems with simply placing `"use strict"` at the beginning of a file is that it will enforce strict mode on all the JavaScript in the file, and if you're using other people's code, there's no guarantee that they've coded in strict mode.

To avoid this, the recommended way to use strict mode is to place all your code inside an IIFE, like so:

```
(function() {
  "use strict";

  // All your code would go inside this function

  }());
```

This ensures that only your code inside the IIFE is forced to use strict mode.

Creating Self-contained Modules

An IIFE can be used to enclose a block of code inside its own private scope. This effectively creates a self-contained module that will not interfere with any other part of the program. Using IIFEs in this way means that code can be added or removed in a modular fashion. The example shows two modules, A and B, that are able to run code independently of each other:

```
(function() {
// Module A
  var name = "Module A";
  console.log("Hello from " + name);
}());

(function() {
// Module B
  var name = "Module B";
```

```
    console.log("Hello from " + name);
}());

<<  "Hello from Module A"
    "Hello from Module B"
```

Notice that both modules include a variable called name, but the modules don't interfere with each other. This is a useful approach for separating parts of a program into discrete modules, especially for testing purposes.

Functions that Define and Rewrite Themselves

The dynamic nature of JavaScript means that a function is able to not only call itself, but define itself, and even redefine itself. This is done by assigning a variable to an anonymous function that has the same name as the function.

Consider the following function:

```
function party(){
  console.log("Wow this is amazing!");
  party = function(){
    console.log("Been there, got the T-Shirt");
  }
}
```

This logs a message in the console, then redefines itself to log a different message in the console. When the function has been called once, it will be as if it was defined like this:

```
function party() {
  console.log("Been there, got the T-Shirt");
}
```

Every time the function is called after the first time, it will log the message "Been there, got the T-Shirt":

```
party();
<< "Wow this is amazing!"

party();
<< "Been there, got the T-Shirt"

party();
<< "Been there, got the T-Shirt"
```

If the function is also assigned to another variable, then this variable will maintain the original function definition and not be rewritten. This is because the rewriting depends on the name of the function. You can see an example of this if we create variable called `beachParty` that is assigned to the `party()` function *before* it is called for the first time and redefined:

```
function party(){
  console.log("Wow this is amazing!");
  party = function(){
    console.log("Been there, got the T-Shirt");
  }
}

var beachParty = party; // note that the party function is not
➥ invoked

beachParty(); // the party() function has now been redefined, even
➥though it hasn't been called explicitly
<< "Wow this is amazing!"

party();
<< "Been there, got the T-Shirt"

beachParty(); // but this function hasn't been redefined
<< "Wow this is amazing!"
```

```
beachParty(); // no matter how many times this is called it will
➥remain the same
<< "Wow this is amazing!"
```

 Properties Will Be Lost

If any properties have previously been set on the function, these will be lost when the function redefines itself. In the previous example, we can set a `test` property and see that it no longer exists after the function has been invoked and redefined:

```
function party() {
  console.log("Wow this is amazing!");
  party = function(){
    console.log("Been there, got the T-Shirt");
  }
}

party.music = "Classical Jazz"; // set a property of the
➥function

party();
<< "Wow this is amazing!"

party.music; // function has now been redefined, so the
➥property doesn't exist
<< undefined
```

Init-Time Branching

This technique can be used with the feature detection that we discussed in the last chapter to create functions that rewrite themselves, known as **init-time branching**. This enables the functions to work more effectively in the browser, and avoid checking for features every time they're invoked.

Let's take the example of our fictional `unicorn` method that's yet to have full support in all browsers. In the last chapter, we looked at how we can use feature detection to check if this object is supported. Now we can go one step further: instead of just running the relevant code, we can rewrite the function so that it only runs the relevant code without the need to check for support every time it's called:

```
function ride(){

    if (window.unicorn) {
      ridePony = function(){
        return "Riding on a unicorn is great fun!";
      }
    } else {
        ridePony = function(){
        return "Riding on a standard pony is only okay";
      }
    }
    return ride();
}
```

After we've checked whether the `window.unicorn` object exists (by checking to see if it's truthy), we've rewritten the `ride()` function according to the outcome. Right at the end of the function, we call it again so that the rewritten function is now invoked and the relevant value returned. The downside is that the function is invoked twice the first time it's used, although it becomes more efficient each subsequent time it's invoked. Let's take a look at how it works:

```
ride(); // the function rewrites itself, then calls itself
<< "Riding on a bog standard horse is only okay"
```

Once the function has been invoked once, it's rewritten based on the browser's capabilities. We can check this by inspecting the function without invoking it:

```
ride;
<< function (){
    return "Riding on a bog standard horse is only okay"
  }
```

This is a very useful pattern to initialize functions the first time they're called, optimizing them for the browser in use.

Recursive Functions

A **recursive function** is one that invokes itself until a certain condition is met. It is a useful tool to use when iterative processes are involved. A common example is a function that calculates the factorial[3] of a number:

[3] http://en.wikipedia.org/wiki/Factorial

```
function factorial(n) {
  if (n === 0) {
    return 1
  } else {
    return n * factorial(n - 1);
  }
}
```

This function will return 1 if 0 is provided as an argument (0 factorial is 1), otherwise it will multiply the argument by the result of invoking itself with an argument of one less. The function will continue to invoke itself until finally the argument is 0 and 1 is returned. This will result in a multiplication of 1, 2, 3 and all the numbers up to the original argument.

Another example from the world of mathematics is the Collatz conjecture.[4] This is a problem that is simple to state, but, so far, has not been solved. It involves taking any positive integer and following these rules:

▪ if the number is even, divide it by two
▪ if the number is odd, multiply it by three and add one

For example, if we start with the number 18, we would have the following sequence:

18, 9, 28, 14, 7, 22, 11, 34, 17, 52, 26, 13, 40, 20, 10, 5, 16, 8, 4, 2, 1, 4, 2, 1, ...

As you can see, the sequence becomes stuck in a loop at the end, cycling through "4,2,1". The Collatz conjecture states that every positive integer will create a sequence that finishes in this loop. This has been verified for all numbers up to 5×2^{60}, but there is no proof that it will continue to be true for all the integers higher than this. To test the conjecture, we can write a function that uses recursion to keep invoking the function until it reaches a value of 1 (because we want our function to avoid being stuck in a recursive loop at the end!):

```
function collatz(n,sequence) {
  var sequence = sequence || [n]; // the sequence should be an array
➥or start with first value
  if (n%2 === 0) {// n is even
    m = n/2;
```

---

[4] http://en.wikipedia.org/wiki/Collatz_conjecture

```
  } else { // n is odd
    m = 3*n + 1;
  }
  sequence.push(m); // add the current value to the sequence
  if (m === 1) { // sequence has reached the end
    return "Sequence took " + sequence.length + " steps";
    } else { // carry on by invoking the sequence again
      return collatz(m,sequence);
    }
}

collatz(18);
<< "Sequence took 21 steps. It was 18,9,28,14,7,22,11,34,17,52,26,13
➥,40,20,10,5,16,8,4,2,1"
```

Have a go at using the function and see if you can find a value above 5×2^{60} that doesn't end in the loop—you'll be famous if you do!

Currying

Currying is a process that involves the partial application of functions. It's amed after the logician Haskell Curry[5]—not the spicy food—just like the programming language Haskell is. His work on a paper by Moses Schönfinkel lead to the development of this programming technique.

A function is said to be curried when not all arguments have been supplied to the function, so it returns another function that retains the arguments given and expects the remaining arguments. Here is a `multiplier` function that expects two arguments and multiplies those numbers together. If only one argument is provided, it returns a function that expects only one argument and will multiply it by the argument supplied to the first function:

```
function multiplier(x,y) {
  if (y === undefined) {
    return function(z) {
      return x * z;
    }
  } else {
```

---

[5] http://en.wikipedia.org/wiki/Haskell_Curry

```
    return x * y;
  }
}
```

This function uses a closure to trap the first variable, x, inside a new function that's returned. This new function can then be used to provide the second argument. If both arguments are provided, the function simply multiplies them together:

```
multiplier(3,5);
<< 15
```

Let's have a look at what happens if only the first argument is passed to this function:

```
quadrupler = multiplier(4);
<< function (z){
    return x * z;
  }
```

We can see that a new function is returned that keeps the value of x that was provided to the `multiplier()` function:

```
quadrupler(5);
<< 20
```

Because the first call to a curried function returns another function, we can invoke the whole function by passing each argument in separate pairs of parentheses:

```
multiplier(8)(11);
<< 88
```

This works because `multiplier(8)` returns a function, and we're immediately passing the argument 11 to that function.

Currying allows you to turn a single function into a series of functions instead. This is useful if you find that you're constantly calling a function with the same argument. For example, if you were frequently using the same value in the `multiplier()` function to calculate a tax rate of 22%:

```
tax = multiplier(0.22,400); // calculate tax on 400
<< 88
```

If you found yourself doing this often, it would make sense to create a new curried function using 0.22 as the first argument:

```
calcTax = multiplier(0.22);
<< function (z){
     return x * z;
  }

calcTax(400);
<< 88
```

By currying the multiplier() function, we've created a new function, calcTax(), that is simpler to use.

A General Curry Function

In the last example, we hard coded the multiplier() function so that it could be curried. It's possible to use a curry() function to take any function and allow it to be partially applied. The curry function is the following:

```
function curry(func) {
  var fixedArgs = [].slice.call(arguments,1);
  return function() {
    args = fixedArgs.concat([].slice.call(arguments))
    return func.apply(null, args);
  };
}
```

This can now be applied to a more standard divider() function that returns the result of dividing its two arguments:

```
function divider(x,y) {
  return x/y;
}
```

```
divider(10,5);
<< 2
```

The curry() function can be used to create a more specific function that finds the reciprocal of numbers:

```
reciprocal = curry(divider,1);
<< function () {
       args = fixedArgs.concat([].slice.call(arguments))
       return func.apply(null, args);
    }

reciprocal(2);
<< 0.5
```

Quiz Ninja Project

Let's use the random() function that we created in this chapter to improve our quiz, so that the questions are chosen at random rather than just asking them in the order in which they appear in the array. Our first task is to add the random() function to our function definitions. It can go before or after the play() function:

```
//// function definitions ////

function random(a,b,callback) {
  if(b===undefined) {
    // if only one argument is supplied, assume the lower limit is 1
    b = a, a = 1;
  }
  var result = Math.floor((b-a+1) * Math.random()) + a;
  if(typeof callback === "function") {
    result = callback(result);
  }
  return result;
}
```

Next, we need to update the quiz object that contains the questions so that it includes an asked property. This will be set to false initially, but will change to true after a question has been asked. This enables us to avoid asking the same question twice:

```
quiz = {
"name":"Super Hero Name Quiz",
"description":"How many super heroes can you name?",
"question":"What is the real name of ",
"questions": [
{ "question": "Superman", "answer": "Clarke Kent", "asked": false },
{ "question": "Batman", "answer": "Bruce Wayne", "asked": false },
{ "question": "Wonder Woman", "answer": "Dianna Prince", "asked":
➥false }
]
}
```

You might like to add some extra questions to the questions array as well, as it will make the game more interesting to have more than three options!

Because we're no longer working through the questions one at a time, instead of using i to track which question we are asking, we'll use a variable called question to store the current question object. This means that we need to replace the following line:

```
var i = 0;
```

with this line that declares the question variable:

```
var question; // current question
```

This line only declares the question variable; it is set in the chooseQuestion() function that we'll update next:

```
function chooseQuestion() {
  console.log("chooseQuestion() called");
  var questions = quiz.questions.filter(function(question){
    return question.asked === false;
  });
  // set the current question
  question = questions[random(questions.length) - 1];
  ask(question);
}
```

Here we're using the filter() array method to return another array containing only the questions that have a value of false for their asked property, so they are yet to be asked. The `random()` function is then used to select a random number between 1 and the length of this array. We then subtract 1 from this value and use it as the index to select the question to ask by assigning it to the `question` variable. This is then passed to the `ask()` function as an argument.

The `ask()` function also needs updating, so that it provides a number of options for the player to select instead of just an input field for the player to fill in. This makes the `ask()` function quite a bit longer than it was before. It needs to be changed as follows:

```javascript
function ask(question) {
  console.log("ask() invoked");
  // set the question.asked property to true so it's not asked again
  question.asked = true;
  update($form,quiz.question + question.question + "?");
  // create an array to put the different options in and a button
➥variable
  var options = [], button;
  var option1 = chooseOption();
  options.push(option1.answer);
  var option2 = chooseOption();
  options.push(option2.answer);
  // add the actual answer at a random place in the options array
  options.splice(random(0,2),0,question.answer);
  // loop through each option and display it as a button
  options.forEach(function(name) {
    button = document.createElement("button");
    button.value = name;
    button.textContent = name;
    $form.appendChild(button);
  });

  // choose an option from all the possible answers but without
➥choosing the same option twice
  function chooseOption() {
    var option = quiz.questions[random(quiz.questions.length) - 1];
    // check to see if the option chosen is the current question or
➥already one of the options, if it is then recursively call this
➥function until it isn't
    if(option === question || options.indexOf(option.answer) !==
➥-1) {
      return chooseOption();
    }
```

```
    return option;
  }
}
```

In the code, we first set the `asked` property of the question to `true` to stop the question from being asked again later in the game. We then create an empty array called `options` to store the different options that will be presented to the player. Two options are chosen using the nested function called `chooseOption()`. This uses the `random()` function to pick a question at random from all the questions, and then checks to see if that question has already been chosen (and therefore already in the `options` array) or is currently being asked. If either of these are true, the function calls itself again and does this recursively until it eventually returns a valid option. After two options have been chosen, the actual question is inserted into the `options` array at a random place. This is done using the `splice()` array method with the return value of the `random()` function given as an argument.

The function then loops through each question held in the `options` array and creates a `button` element with a value attribute that corresponds to its `answer` property. Each button is then appended to the form as a child element, so three buttons will be presented to the player, one of which will present the correct answer.

The answer will be submitted when the player clicks on one of the buttons contained in the form. This means that we need to change the event listener to listen for `click` events instead of the `submit` event. Change the code for the event listener to the following:

```
// add event listener to form for when it's submitted
$form.addEventListener('click', function(event) {
  check(event.target.value);
  }, false);
```

Because the event listener is attached to the form, we can use the `target` property to identify which button was clicked. The `value` property corresponds to the answer given by the player, so this is given as an argument to the `check()` function, which will check to see if this is the correct answer.

In the `check()` function, the following line should be changed:

```
if(answer === quiz.questions[i].answer){
```

It needs to be modified as the question that was asked is now stored in the `question` variable, so we only need to check its `answer` property as follows:

```
if(answer === question.answer){
```

Since we are no longer using the variable `i` to keep track of the question being asked, we can also remove this line from the `check()` function:

```
i++;
```

Our last task is to remove the input and submit button from the form in the **index.htm** file as these are no longer used, so our form should look like this:

```
<form id="answer">
</form>
```

Have a go at playing the game by opening **index.htm** in a browser. The quiz now has a very different feel to it, and should look a little like the screenshot shown in Figure 11.1.

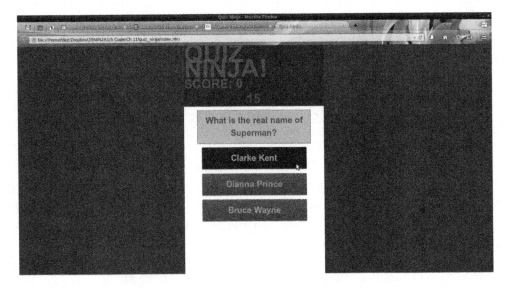

Figure 11.1. Quiz with random questions

The `random()` function has allowed us to provide options from which to choose, making the game much easier to play by not requiring any typing. It also means that each game produces questions in a different order (although it's a limited range, given that we only have three questions!)

Summary

In this chapter, we have learned the following:

- Functional programming involves breaking processes down into steps that can be applied as a series of functions.

- Functions can return other functions.

- Functions have built-in properties such as `length`, but can have custom properties added.

- All functions have `call()` and `apply()` methods that can be used to apply the function to different objects.

- A callback is a function that's provided as an argument to another function. They can be used to create event-driven asynchronous code that enables a program to continue running while waiting for an event to happen.

- A closure is the process of keeping a reference to a variable available outside the scope of the function it was originally defined in.

- Immediately Invoked Function Expressions or IIFEs are functions that are enclosed in parentheses and immediately followed by double parentheses so that they're invoked. They are useful for setting default values.

- Functions are able to dynamically redefine themselves in the body of the function, depending on certain conditions.

- A recursive function will keep invoking itself until a certain condition is met.

- Currying or partial application is the process of applying one argument at a time to a function. A new function is returned until all the arguments have been used.

In the next chapter, we'll be looking at the principles of object-oriented programming in JavaScript.

12

Object-oriented Programming in JavaScript

Object-oriented programming (OOP for short) is a style of programming that involves separating the code into objects that have properties and methods. Sound familiar? JavaScript obviously supports objects, as we saw in Chapter 5, so it also supports an object-oriented style of programming. In this chapter, we'll look at what object-oriented programming is and how to implement it in JavaScript.

In this chapter, we'll cover the following topics:

- an introduction to OOP

- constructor functions

- prototypes

- public and private methods

- inheritance

- creating objects from objects

- adding methods to built-in objects

- mixins

- chaining functions

- this and that

- borrowing methods from prototypes

- our project—create questions in an OOP way

Object-oriented Programming

Object-oriented programming is often used to model representations of objects in the real world. There are three main concepts in OOP: **encapsulation**, **polymorphism**, and **inheritance**. I'm going to use my juicer to illustrate how each of these concepts can be applied in a programming environment, since the juicer can be considered an object. It's a wonderful machine that makes fresh juice for me every morning. The juicer has properties such as speed and capacity, and also has methods or actions it can perform, such as juicing, switching on, and switching off.

Encapsulation

When I use my juicer, I put the fruit into the machine, press the "on" button and out comes the juice. I haven't a clue how it does it—only that it makes a very loud noise! This demonstrates the concept of **encapsulation**: the inner workings are kept hidden inside the object and only the essential functionalities are exposed to the end user, such as the "on" button. In OOP, this involves keeping all the programming logic inside an object and making methods available to implement the functionality, without the outside world needing to know *how* it's done.

Polymorphism

My juicer uses the same plug socket as other appliances in my kitchen. I can also place various types of fruit into it and it still juices them. These two examples demonstrate the concept of **polymorphism**: the same process can be used for alternative objects. In OOP, this means that different objects can have the same method, but they implement it in their own way.

Inheritance

I'd really like the next model up from my juicer, as it can deal with more types of fruit and it's a bit quieter. Even though it has these extra features, I'm sure that inside it uses many of the same parts that my juicer has. This demonstrates the concept of **inheritance**: taking the features of one object and then adding some new features. In OOP, this means that we can take an object that already exists and inherit all its properties and methods. We can then improve on its functionality by adding new properties and methods.

Classes

Many object-oriented languages, such as Java and Ruby, are known as **classical languages**. This is because they use the concept of classes to define a blueprint for an object. Objects are then created as an **instance** of that class and inherit all the properties and methods of the class. In my juicer example, the `juicer` class would represent the design of the juicer, and each juicer that's made on the production line would be instances of that class.

JavaScript doesn't use classes (although ECMAScript 6 will support them), but it does use the concept of object **prototypes,** which can be used as a blueprint for creating other objects. JavaScript is said to have a prototypal inheritance model. In the juicer example, this might involve building an actual prototype juicer and then using this prototype as the basis for making all the other juicers. The juicers based on the prototype would be able to do everything the prototype could do, with some being able to do even more.

Constructor Functions

In the objects chapter earlier in the book, we saw that it was possible to create new objects using the object literal notation. At the end of the chapter we created a `dice` object:

```
var dice = {
  sides: 6;
```

```
  roll: function () {
    return Math.floor(this.sides * Math.random() + 1)
  }
}
```

Another way to create objects is to use a **constructor function**, which is a function that returns an *instance* of an object that's defined in the function when it's invoked with the new operator. These are useful because they can be used to create instances of objects over and over again. This is similar to writing a class in a classical programming language.

Here is the dice example rewritten as a constructor function:

```
var Dice = function(){
  "use strict";
  this.sides = 6;
  this.roll = function() {
    return Math.floor(this.sides * Math.random() + 1)
  }
}
```

By convention, the names of constructor functions are capitalized, which is the convention used for classes in classical programming languages. A constructor function works in a similar way to a class, as it can be used to create lots of instances of the same object with all the properties encapsulated inside. The keyword this is used to represent the object that will be returned by the constructor function. In the previous example, we use it to set the sides property to 6 and create a method called roll. Each new object that's created using this constructor function will inherit these properties and methods.

To create an instance of the Dice object, invoke the constructor function using the new operator:

```
var red = new Dice();
<< {"roll": function () {
        return Math.floor(this.sides * Math.random() + 1)
     }, "sides": 6}
```

The function returned an object that was assigned to the variable red, which is said to be an instance of the Dice constructor function. We can confirm this using the instanceof operator:

```
red instanceof Dice
<< true
```

This means that it will have a sides property and roll() method:

```
red.sides;
<< 6

red.roll();
<< 4
```

 Use new

Make sure that you use the new operator when employing a constructor function to instantiate a new object. Otherwise, you'll actually just call the function itself, and will assign the variable to the return value of the function (which is usually undefined):

```
var yellow = Dice();
<< undefined

yellow.sides
<< Error: "yellow is undefined"
```

This can also have the unfortunate side effect of assigning all the properties and methods to the global object if strict mode isn't used:

```
window.sides
<< 6
```

One way around this is to add the following line to the beginning of a constructor function (in this example, the constructor function is called `Constructor`):

```
if((!this instanceof Constructor)) {
    return new Constructor;
}
```

This checks to see if `this` (the object that will eventually be returned) is an instance of the `Constructor`. If it isn't, it just invokes the constructor function again, but this time using the `new` operator.

Be wary that this method will rectify any mistakes where the `new` keyword has not been used, but it won't help to identify where the sloppy programming happened. An alternative would be to throw an error if this happens instead—which is what happens if strict mode is used and `new` isn't used.

 Built-n Constructor Functions

JavaScript contains a number of built-in constructor functions such as `Object`, `Array`, and `Function` that can be used to create objects, arrays, and functions instead of literals.

The easiest way to create a new object is to use the literal syntax:

```
literal = {};
<< {}
```

It is possible to use the `Object` constructor function:

```
constructedObject = new Object();
<< {}
```

A literal is still considered to be an instance of the `Object` constructor:

```
literal instanceof Object;
<< true
```

Similarly, the easiest way to create an array is to use the literal syntax like so:

```
var literalArray = [1,2,3];
<< [1, 2, 3]
```

But an alternative is to use the **Array** constructor function:

```
constructedArray = new Array(1,2,3);
<< [1, 2, 3]
```

Array constructor functions exhibit some strange behavior regarding the arguments supplied, however. If only one argument is given, it doesn't create an array with that argument as the first element as you might expect; it sets the array's **length** property instead!

```
new Array(5); // you might expect [5]
<< [undefined, undefined, undefined, undefined, undefined]
```

This results in an error being thrown if a floating point decimal number is provided as an argument because the length of an array must be an integer:

```
new Array(2.5);
<< Error: "invalid array length"
```

This behaviour is another reason why it is much better to use array literals when creating arrays.

All objects have a **constructor** property that returns the constructor function that created it:

```
red.constructor
<< Dice(sides)
```

When an object literal is used to create a new object, we can see that in the background the **Object** constructor function is being used:

```
var objectLiteral = {};
<< {}
objectLiteral.constructor;
```

```
<< function Object() {
  [native code]
  }
```

This can be used to instantiate a copy of an object, without having to reference the actual constructor function directly. For example, if we wanted to make another instance like the red dice, but if the name if its constructor was unknown, we could use the following:

```
var green = new red.constructor(10); // create a new Dice instance

green.instanceOf Dice
<< true
```

Prototypal Inheritance

JavaScript uses a prototypal inheritance model. To see how this works, let's make a constructor function for creating turtles:

```
var Turtle = function(name) {
  this.name = name;
  this.sayHi = function() {
    return "Hi dude, my name is " + this.name;
  }
}
```

This can then be used to create a new turtle instance:

```
var leo = new Turtle("Leonardo");
<< {"name": "Leonardo", "sayHi": function () {
    return "Hi dude, my name is " + this.name;
  }}
```

The variable leo points to an instance of the Turtle constructor. It has a name property and a sayHi() method that refers to the name property:

```
leo.name;
<< "Leonardo"

leo.sayHi();
<< "Hi dude, my name is Leonardo"
```

The Prototype Object

In the last chapter we saw that functions have properties and methods. All functions have a `prototype` property that returns an object, which is initially empty:

```
Turtle.prototype;
<< {}
```

When a new instance of the the `Turtle` object is instantiated using the new operator, all the properties and methods of the prototype will be added to the new instance. Since the prototype is just an object, we can add new properties by assignment:

```
Turtle.prototype.weapon = "Hands";
<< "Hands"
```

We can also add a method to the prototype object in a similar way:

```
Turtle.prototype.attack = function(){
  return this.name + " hits you with his " + this.weapon;
  }
<< function (){
  return this.name + " hits you with his " + this.weapon;
  }
```

Now if we create a new `Turtle` instance, we can see that it inherits the `weapon` property and `attack()` method from the `Turtle.prototype` object, as well as receiving the `name` property and `sayHi()` method from from the constructor function:

```
var raph = new Turtle("Raphael");
raph.name;
<< "Raphael"

raph.sayHi();
<< "Hi dude, my name is Raphael"
```

```
raph.weapon; // inherited from the prototype
<< "Hands"

raph.attack() // inherited from the prototype
<< "Raphael hits you with his Hands"
```

Notice that there's a reference to `this.name` in the prototype `attack()` method, and when the instance calls the `attack()` method, it uses the instance's `name` property. This is because `this` in the prototype object always refers to the instance that actually calls the method.

Finding Out the Prototype

There are a number of ways to find the prototype of an object. One way is to go via the constructor function's `prototype` property:

```
raph.constructor.prototype;
<< {"attack": function (){
   return this.name + " hits you with his " + this.weapon;
   }, "weapon": "Hands"}
```

Another way is to use the `Object.getPrototypeOf()` method, which takes the object as a parameter:

```
Object.getPrototypeOf(raph);
<< {"attack": function (){
   return this.name + " hits you with his " + this.weapon;
   }, "weapon": "Hands"}
```

Many JavaScript engines also support the secret __proto__ property. This is known as **dunder proto**, which is short for "double underscore proto." It is not an official standard, but it's supported in most modern browsers and is expected to be standardized in the next version of JavaScript:

```
raph.__proto__
<< {"attack": function (){
   return this.name + " hits you with his " + this.weapon;
   }, "weapon": "Hands"}
```

Every object also has a isPrototypeOf() method that returns a Boolean to check if it's the prototype of an instance:

```
Turtle.prototype.isPrototypeOf(raph)
<< true
```

Own Properties and Prototype Properties

In the previous example, the object raph had a name property that it inherited from the constructor function and a weapon property that it inherited from the prototype property. The object raph has access to both these properties, but the name property is considered to be its *own* property while the weapon property is inherited from the prototype object. Every object has a hasOwnProperty() method that can be used to check if a method is its own property, or is inherited from the prototype:

```
raph.hasOwnProperty('name');
<< true

raph.hasOwnProperty('weapon');
<< false
```

So what's the difference between own properties and prototype properties? Prototype properties are shared by *every* instance of the Turtle constructor function. This means that they'll all have a weapon property and it will always be the same value. If we create another instance of the Turtle constructor, we'll see that it also inherits a weapon property that has the same value of "Hands":

```
var don = new Turtle("Donatello");
<< {"attack": function (){
   return this.name + " hits you with his " + this.weapon;
   }, "name": "Donatello", "sayHi": function () {
     return "Hi dude, my name is " + this.name;
   }, "weapon": "Hands"
```

```
don.weapon;
<< "Hands"
```

Every time an instance of the `Turtle` constructor function calls the `weapon` property, it will return `"Hands"`. This value is the same for all the instances and only exists in one place—as a property of the prototype object. This means that it only exists in memory in one place, which is more efficient than each instance having its own value. This is particularly useful for any properties that are the same.

The Prototype Is Live!

The `prototype` object is live, so if a new property or method is added to the prototype, any instances of it will inherit the new properties and methods automatically, even if that instance has already been created. For example, we saw that the `raph` object had a `weapon` property and `attack()` method that it inherited from the `prototype` object. But the `leo` object that we created *before* we added these to the prototype will also gain access to them as well:

```
leo.weapon;
<< "Hands"

leo.attack();
<< "Leonardo hits you with his Hands"
```

If we now change the value of the prototype's `weapon` property, this will be reflected in *all* instances of the `Turtle` constructor:

```
Turtle.prototype.weapon = "Feet";
<< "Feet"

leo.attack();
<< "Leonardo hits you with his Feet"

raph.attack();
<< "Raphael hits you with his Feet"
```

```
don.attack();
<< "Donatello hits you with his Feet"
```

Redefining the Prototype

It is possible to completely redefine the prototype object by assigning it to a new object literal:

```
Turtle.prototype = {
    attack = function() {
        return this.name + " tickles you until you cry with
➥laughter";
        }
}
```

If you redefine the prototype, any child objects will retain the old properties and methods without receiving any new ones.

You should avoid redefining the prototype after any instances have been created, otherwise these instances will behave differently to any instances that are created later. Any properties and methods should be added to the prototype by assignment. The fact that the prototype is live means that all properties and methods added will be shared with *all* instances.

It is sometimes seen as a good idea to overwrite the prototype immediately after its creation, to add lots of properties in one go. But this also causes unexpected problems, as the prototype will lose its link to the constructor function:

```
Turtle.prototype.constructor
<< undefined
```

If you do use this method, be sure to reset the prototype's constructor function immediately after overwriting the prototype object:

```
Turtle.prototype.constructor = Turtle;
```

Adding multiple properties and methods at once can be made easier using a mixin function, which is covered later in the chapter.

Overwriting Prototype Properties

An instance object can overwrite any properties or methods inherited from its prototype by simply assigning a new value to it. For example, we can give our turtles their own weapons:

```
leo.weapon = "Katana Blades";
<< "Katana Blades";

raph.weapon = "Sai";
<< "Sai"

don.weapon = "Bo Staff";
<< "Bo Staff"
```

These will then become an "own property" of the instance and take precedence over the same `prototype` property:

```
leo.attack();
<< "Leonardo hits you with his Katana Blades"
```

When a property or method is called, the JavaScript engine will check to see if an object has its own property or method. If it does, it will use that one; otherwise, it will use the prototype's instead.

What Should the Prototype Be Used For?

The prototype can be used to add any new properties and methods after the constructor function has been defined. It should be used to define any properties that will remain the same for every instance of the constructor. The `weapon` example was unsuitable because all the turtles use a different weapon (we just needed it to demonstrate overwriting!). They do, however, like the same food—pizza! This makes a good candidate for a `prototype` property:

```
Turtle.prototype.food = "Pizza";
```

Methods are likely to be the same for all instances of a constructor, so all methods should be part of the prototype object rather than the constructor function itself:

```
Turtle.prototype.eat = function() {
  return "Mmm, this " + this.food + " tastes great!";
}
```

 Default Values in Prototype Objects Are Shallow

Be careful when using the prototype to set default values. They are shallow,[1] so any changes to an array or object made by an instance will be reflected in the prototype and therefore shared between all instances.

A golden rule to remember is: *Never use arrays or objects as a default value in prototype objects*.

An alternative would be to set the default value using the method of providing default values to functions that we saw in Chapter 4. For example, the default value of the **food** property could be set as **"pizza"** in the constructor function:

```
var Turtle = function(name,food) {
  this.name = name;
  this.food = food || "pizza";
}
```

To summarize, the following points should be considered when using constructor functions and prototype objects to create instances:

- Create a constructor function that deals with any initialization.

- Add any shared properties that remain constant and any shared methods to the prototype object.

- Add any individual properties to the instance by assignment (a mixin could be used for this, as we'll see later).

- Any extra methods and properties can be added to the prototype later, and will be added to *all* instances.

- Be careful when overwriting the prototype object completely—the constructor class needs to be reset.

---

[1] There's more about shallow and deep copies later in the chapter.

To demonstrate, let's create another `Turtle` instance. Use the constructor function to initialize an instance:

```
var mike = new Turtle("Michelangelo");
```

Verify that the new instance has inherited properties and methods from the prototype object:

```
mike.eat();
<< "Mmm, this Pizza tastes great!"
```

Augment the instance with individual properties:

```
mike.weapon = "Nunchuks";
<< "Nunchuks"
```

Public and Private Methods

By default, an object's methods are **public** in JavaScript. Methods and properties are said to be public because they can be queried directly and changed by assignment. The dynamic nature of the language means that an object's properties and methods can be changed after it has been created.

The `name` and `weapon` properties of our example object are said to be public:

```
raph.weapon
<< "Sai"
```

We can use the concept of variable scope to keep properties **private** and prevent them from being changed. A **getter** method can then be used to return their values. In this example, the `Turtle()` constructor function is modified to include a private `_color` property:

```
function Turtle(name,color) {

  this.name = name;
  this.sayHi = function() {
    return "Hi dude, my name is " + this.name;
  }
```

```
  // This property will only available inside the constructor
➥function
  var _color = color;

  this.getName = function() {
    return _name;
  }

  this.getColor = function() {
    return _color;
  }

}
```

Now it's impossible to change the values of _color, but they can be accessed using the getter methods:

```
raph.getColor();
<< "Red"
```

You could also add a setter method to allow private properties to be changed in a *controlled* way. This means that you can stop certain assignments from being made by screening the data before any changes are made to a property:

```
this.setColor = function(color) {
  if(typeof color === "string"){
      return _color = color;
    } else {
      throw new Error("Color must be a string");
    }
  }

raph.setColor("Pink");
<< "Pink";
```

```
raph.getColor();
<< "Pink"
```

Inheritance

The examples we've seen so far have all demonstrated inheritance by inheriting properties and methods from the prototype object. But the prototype object also has its own prototype object, which has its own prototype object ... and so on, creating a **chain of inheritance**.

The Prototype Chain

We can see an example of a prototype chain by looking at the prototype of the mike instance that we created in the last section, using the __proto__ property:

```
mike.__proto__
<< {"attack": function (){
        return this.name + " hits you with his " + this.weapon;
        }, "eat": function () {
        return "Mmm, this " + this.food + " tastes great!";
    }, "food": "Pizza"}
```

All objects have constructor functions, so we can look at what is the constructor function of the prototype object. As you'd expect, it's the Turtle() constructor function:

```
mike.__proto__.constructor === Turtle;
<< true
```

The prototype of the prototype is an apparently empty object literal (although it's actually not empty, as we'll see later):

```
mike.__proto__.__proto__
<< {}
```

The constructor for this is the built-in Object() constructor function:

```
mike.__proto__.constructor
<< function Object() {
    [native code]
  }
```

If we try find the next prototype, we receive `null`:

```
mike.__proto__.__proto__.__proto__
<< null
```

This demonstrates that all prototype chains end at the `Object` constructor function.

The Object Constructor Function

As we saw in the last example, all objects inherit from the `Object()` constructor function's prototype object.

When an object calls a method, the JavaScript engine will check to see if the object has that method. If it doesn't, it will check if the object's prototype has the method. If not, it will check whether the prototype's prototype has it. This continues until it reaches the `Object` constructor function's prototype, from which all objects in JavaScript inherit. If the `Object` prototype is without the method, an error will be returned saying the object doesn't exist:

```
window.unicorn;
<< Error: "window.unicorn is not a function"
```

But in the prototype chain example, the `Object` prototype was displayed as an empty object, so it has no methods—right? Er, actually, that's not the case.

The `Object` prototype object actually has a large number of methods that are inherited by all objects. The reason why the prototype appears as an empty object literal is because all of its methods are not enumerable.

Enumerable Properties

Properties that are not **enumerable** will not show up if you use a `for-in` loop to loop through an object's properties and methods. There is a method called `propertyIsEnumerable()` that every object has (because it's a method of the `Object` prototype) that can be used to check if a property is enumerable. We can see in the following example that the eat() method we created earlier is enumerable (in fact, all properties and methods that are created by assignment are enumerable):

```
Turtle.prototype.propertyIsEnumerable("eat");
<< true
```

All objects inherit a toString() method from the Object prototype, but as it's not enumerable, it won't show up in any objects:

```
Object.prototype.propertyIsEnumerable("toString");
<< false
```

In fact, the propertyIsEnumerable() method can be used to show that it isn't, itself, enumerable:

```
Object.prototype.propertyIsEnumerable("propertyIsEnumerable");
<< false
```

Good practice is for all built-in methods to be non-enumerable and any user-defined methods to be made enumerable. This is so that all the built-in methods don't keep showing up when looking at an object's methods, but user-defined methods are easy to spot.

Polymorphism

The Object constructor function prototype has a toString() method that's made available to all objects; however, different objects implement the method in different ways. Calling it on an array object will return each value in a comma-separated string:

```
[1,2,3].toString()
<< "1,2,3"
```

Calling it on a primitive number value will return a string containing that number:

```
2..toString; // remember 2 dot operators for integers!
<< "2"
```

 Primitive Object Wrappers

The number, string, and Boolean primitive types that we met way back in Chapter 2 [14] have their own corresponding constructor functions: `Number`, `String`, and `Boolean` respectively.

Rather bizarrely, though, these constructors don't produce primitive values:

```
new Number(2); // the return value looks like a primitive
<< 2;

typeof Number(2); // but it's actually an object!
<< "object"
```

Similarly, primitive values are not instances of these constructor functions:

```
2 instanceof Number;
<< false
```

In fact, the two things are not strictly equal:

```
Number(2) === 2;
<< false
```

Primitives are actually without their own methods. The primitive wrapper objects `Number`, `String`, and `Boolean` are used in the background to provide primitive values with methods. When a method is called on a primitive value, JavaScript creates a wrapper object for the primitive, which converts it into an object and then calls the method on the object. This means that it is possible to call methods on primitives such as we saw in Chapter 2:

```
2..toExponential(); // remember 2 dots to call methods on
➥integers!
<< "2e+0"
```

In the background, something similar to this is happening:

```
new Number(2).toExponential();
<< "2e+0"
```

Even custom objects that we've created have a `toString()` method:

```
mike.toString();
<< "[object Object]"
```

It may convey little information, but it does return a string representation of the object.

The `toString()` method is used by a number of built-in functions in the background. It can be used without fear of causing an error because *every* object has the method, as it's inherited from the `Object` prototype object.

One example of a function that uses the `toString()` method is the `alert()`. If an object is given as an argument to the `alert` function that isn't a string, it will call `toString()` on that object in the background and display the returned string. For example, the code:

```
alert([1,2,3]);
```

will display an alert dialog like the one shown in Figure 12.1.

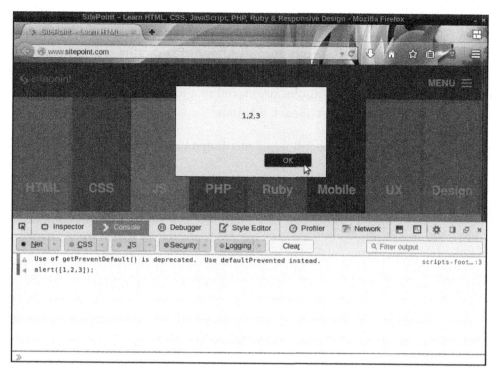

Figure 12.1. alert() uses toString()

It's often a useful exercise to override the toString() method using the prototype object, so that something more meaningful is displayed. For example, we could edit the Turtle() prototype object so that it's more descriptive:

```
Turtle.prototype.toString = function() {
  return "A turtle called " + this.name;
}

mike.toString();
<< "A turtle called Michelangelo"
```

The toString() method is a good demonstration of polymorphism, since different objects have the same method but implement it differently. The advantage of this is that higher-level functions are able to call a single method, even though it may be implemented in various ways.

Property Attributes and Descriptors

We've already seen that all objects are collections of key-value paired properties. It turns out that each property has a number of attributes that provide information about the property. These attributes are stored in a **property descriptor**, which is an object that contains values of each attribute.

All object properties have the following attributes stored in a property descriptor:

▪ `value` - this is the value of the property and is `undefined` by default

▪ `writable` — this Boolean value shows whether a property can be changed or not, and is false by default

▪ `enumerable` — this Boolean value shows whether a property will show up when the object is displayed in a `for in` loop, and is `false` by default

▪ `configurable` — this Boolean value shows whether you can delete a property or change any of its attributes, and is `false` by default

So far, we've just set properties by assignment, which only allows you to set the `value` attribute of the property. It's also possible to set each of the property attributes by using a property descriptor. For example, the following object has a property name:

```
var don = { color: "purple" }
```

The property descriptor for this property might look like this:

```
{ value: "purple", writable: true, enumerable: true,
➥configurable: true }
```

We've already seen how to add more properties by assignment:

```
leo.color = "blue";
```

The disadvantage with this is that it can only be used to set the `value` attribute of the property. Any property set by assignment will have attributes of `writable`, `enumerable`, and `configurable` set as `true` (note that these are the exact opposite of the default values for those attributes).

Getting and Setting Property Descriptors

The `Object()` function has a number of methods for getting and defining property descriptors. We can see these values using the `Object.getOwnPropertyDescriptor()` method:

```
Object.getOwnPropertyDescriptor(leo,'color');
<< {"configurable": true, "enumerable": true, "value": "blue",
➥"writable": true}
```

We can add properties to an object using the `Object.defineProperty()` method. This provides more fine-grained control when adding new properties as it allows each attribute to be set. The first argument is the object to which you want to add the property, followed by a property descriptor containing the attributes you want to set. Any attributes left out will take the default values:

```
Object.defineProperty(mike, 'color', { value: "orange",
➥writable: false, enumerable: true });
➥// configurable will be false by default
<< {"attack": function (){
  return this.name + " hits you with his " + this.weapon;
  }, "color": "orange", "eat": function () {
  return "Mmm, this " + this.food + " tastes great!";
}, "food": "Pizza", "name": "Michelangelo", "sayHi": function () {
    return "Hi dude, my name is " + this.name;
  }, "weapon": "Nunchuks"}
```

As you can see, the object is returned with the the new property added.

Getters and Setters

Every object property descriptor can also have `get()` and `set()` methods, which can be used to control how a property is set using assignment and which value is returned. For example, if we create an empty object and then add a new property to it, we can include `get()` and `set()` methods like so:

```
example = {}; // initialize an empty object literal

Object.defineProperty(example, 'sillyString', {
    get: function() {
```

```
      return "Craaazy!";
    },
    set: function(value) {
      return value;
    }
});
```

To test this out, we can assign a string to the `sillyString` property:

```
example.sillyString = "Hello";
<< "Hello"
```

This uses the `set()` method of the property descriptor. The argument of this is the value that's assigned to the property. In the example this value is simply returned, implying that the value of the `sillyString()` property has been set to the string `"Hello"`. We can check the value using the dot notation:

```
example.sillyString;
<< "Craaazy!"
```

This calls the `get()` method, which ignores the value returned by the `set()` method and returns the string `"Craaazy!"`, regardless of the value that was assigned to the property.

These methods give you much more power in controlling the way property assignment works; however, they should be used sparingly and with care, as changing the expected behavior of an assignment has the potential to cause a lot of confusion.

The `get` and `set` property descriptors are particularly useful for controlling the getting and setting of properties in constructor functions. In the example that follows, the `Dice()` constructor function has been rewritten so that `sides` is now a private variable. We can then use the `sides` property to create a `get` function that will return a description of the number of sides, rather than just the actual number and a `set` function that prohibits a non-positive number of sides to be set:

```
var Dice = function() {
  "use strict";
  var sides = 6;
```

```
    Object.defineProperty(this, 'sides', {
      get: function() {
        return "This dice has " + sides + " sides";
      },
      set: function(value) {
        if(value > 0) {
          sides = value;
          return sides;
        } else {
          throw new Error("The number of sides must be positive");
        }
      }
    });

    this.roll = function() {
      return Math.floor(sides * Math.random() + 1)
    }
}
```

The number of sides can now be assigned in the usual way, but it will act a little differently:

```
var yellow = new Dice(6);

yellow.sides;
<< "This dice has 6 sides"

yellow.sides = 10;
<< 10

yellow.sides;
<< "This dice has 10 sides"

yellow.sides = 0;
<< Error: "The number of sides must be positive"
```

Creating Objects from Objects

It's possible to avoid using constructor functions altogether and just use objects to create more objects. The Object constructor function has a method called create that can be used to create an object, using the object that is provided as an argument as a prototype. For example, we can create a `Human` object that will form the basis for other `Human` objects. This is simply created as an object literal:

```
var Human = {
  arms: 2,
  legs: 2,
  walk: function() { console.log("Walking"); }
}
<< {"arms": 2, "legs": 2, "walk": function ()
➥{ console.log("Walking"); }}
```

This will act as a prototype for all other `Human` objects. Its name is capitalized as it acts in a similar way to a class in classical programming languages, and it's only used to create `Human` objects. It should follow the same rules for prototype objects that we saw earlier—it will contain all the methods that `Human` objects uses, as well as any properties that won't change very often. In this case, the properties are `arms` and `legs`, and the method is `walk()`.

We can create an instance of the `Human` prototype object using the `Object.create()` method:

```
lois = Object.create(Human);
<< {"arms": 2, "legs": 2, "walk": function ()
➥{ console.log("Walking"); }}
```

Extra properties can then be added to each instance using assignment:

```
lois.name = "Lois Lane";
<< "Lois Lane"

lois.job = "Reporter";
<< "Reporter"
```

An alternative way is to add a second argument to the `Object.create()` method containing properties that are to be added to the new object:

```
jimmy = Object.create(Human, { name: { value: "Jimmy Olsen",
➡ enumerable: true }, job: { value: "Photographer",
➡enumerable: true } });
<< {"arms": 2, "job": "Photographer", "legs": 2, "name": "Jimmy
➡ Olsen", "walk": function () { console.log("Walking"); }}
```

This method is a little unwieldy as the properties have to be added using property descriptors, making the syntax awkward and overall verbose. It's often easier to create the object and then add each new property one by one. This can be made quicker using the `mixin()` method that is covered later.

Object-based Inheritance

The `Human` object can also act like a "super-class" and become the prototype of another prototype object called `Superhuman`. This will have all the properties and methods that the `Human` object has, but with some extra methods:

```
Superhuman = Object.create(Human);
<< {"arms": 2, "legs": 2, "walk": function ()
➡{ console.log("Walking"); }}

Superhuman.change = function() {
  return this.realName + " goes into a phone box and comes out as "
➡ + this.name;
}
<< function () {
  return this.realName + " goes into a phone box and comes out as "
➡ + this.name;
}
```

This method relies on the `name` and `realName` properties. It can be a good idea to create default values in the prototype so that the method will still work. In this case, we can use names that prompt some real data to be added:

```
Superhuman.name = "Name Needed";
<< "Name Needed"

Superhuman.realName = "Real Name Needed";
<< "Real Name Needed"
```

Now we can use the `Superhuman` object as a prototype to create lots of unique `Super-human` objects:

```
superman = Object.create(Superhuman);
<< {"arms": 2, "change": function () {
      return this.realName + " goes into a phone box and comes out
➥as " + this.name;
   }, "legs": 2, "name": "Name Needed", "realName": "Real Name
➥Needed", "walk": function () { console.log("Walking"); }}
```

Once a `Superhuman` object has been created, we can add specific properties by assignment:

```
superman.name = "Superman";
superman.realName = "Clarke Kent";
```

This method of adding custom properties is certainly more long-winded than using a constructor function, where the initial values are passed as an argument to the constructor function. This can be fixed by adding an `init()` method to the `Super-human` object that accepts initialization properties:

```
Superhuman.init = function(name, realName){
   this.name = name;
   this.realName = realName;
   this.init = undefined; // this line removes the init function, so
➥it can only be called once
   return this;
}
```

Now a new object can easily be created and initialized:

```
batman = Object.create(Superhuman);
batman.init("Batman","Bruce Wayne");
```

```
batman.name;
<< "Batman"

batman.realName;
<< "Bruce Wayne"
```

A new object can also be created and initialized in a single line using *chaining* (a technique that will be explained in more detail later in the chapter):

```
aquaman = Object.create(Superhuman).init("Aquaman", "Arthur Curry");
<< "arms": 2, "change": function () {
    return this.realName + " goes into a phone box and comes out as
➡" + this.name;
  }, "init": undefined, "legs": 2, "name": "Aquaman", "realName":
➡"Arthur Curry", "walk": function () { console.log("Walking"); }}
```

Object Prototype Chain

Creating objects from objects will create a prototype chain.

Every time a new object is created using the Object.create() method, the new object inherits all the properties and methods from the parent object, which becomes the new object's prototype. For example, we can see that the prototype object of the superman object is the Superhuman object using this code:

```
Object.getPrototypeOf(superman) === Superhuman;
<< true
```

And we can also see that the prototype of the Superhuman object is the Human object:

```
Object.getPrototypeOf(Superhuman) === Human
<< true
```

Additionally, we can verify that the Superhuman object is the prototype of any other objects created using it:

```
Superhuman.isPrototypeOf(batman);
<< true
```

 instanceof Will Fail Here

The `instanceof` operator will not work when objects have been created this way. It only works when using constructor functions to create objects.

This gives the following chain of inheritance:

```
superman -> inherits from -> Superhuman -> inherits from -> Human
```

Because of this chain, the `superman` object has all the properties and methods of the `Human` and `Superhuman` objects:

```
superman.walk();
<< "Walking"

superman.change();
<< "Clarke Kent goes into a phone box and comes out as Superman"
```

 These Objects Are Live!

Remember that the `Human` and `SuperHuman` objects are live prototypes. Any changes made to them will be reflected in other objects created this way.

Adding Methods to Built-in Objects

It is possible to add more methods to the prototype of JavaScript's built-in objects—such as `Number`, `String`, and `Array`—to add more functionality. This practice is known as **monkey-patching**, but it is mostly frowned upon in the JavaScript community, despite it being an incredibly powerful technique[2].

As an example, we can add `isOdd()` and `isEven()` methods to the `Number` wrapper object's prototype. These methods will then be available to number primitives:

---

[2] The Ruby programming community, on the other hand, generally embrace monkey-patching, so it is quite common in Ruby code examples.

```
Number.prototype.isEven = function() {
  return this%2 === 0;
}

Number.prototype.isOdd = function() {
  return this%2 === 1;
}
```

We can try a few more examples to check that these work:

```
42.isEven();
<< true

765234.isOdd();
<< false
```

Arrays are powerful objects, but seem to have some basic methods missing in JavaScript that are found in other languages. We can add a `first()` and `last()` methods that return the first and last items in the array:

```
Array.prototype.first = function() {
    return this[0];
  }

Array.prototype.last = function() {
  return this[this.length -1];
}
```

Again, we can check that these work with a couple of examples:

```
var jla = ["Superman", "Batman", "Wonder Woman", "Flash",
➥ "Aquaman"];

jla.first();
<< "Superman"

jla.last();
<< "Aquaman"
```

Another handy method that arrays lack is the `delete()` method. There is the `delete` operator that we met in Chapter 3, but the way this works is not very intuitive as it leaves a value of `null` in place of the item that's removed. In that chapter, we saw that it is possible to remove an item completely from an array using the `splice()` method. We can use this to create a new method called `delete()` that removes an item from the array at the index provided:

```
Array.prototype.delete = function(i) {
    return self.splice(i,1);
}
```

A useful example of monkey-patching is to add support for methods that are part of the specification, but not supported natively in some browsers. An example is the `trim()` method, which is a method of the `String` prototype object, so all strings should inherit it. It removes all whitespace from the beginning and the end of strings, but unfortunately this method is not implemented in Internet Explorer version 8 or below. This can be rectified using this polyfill code:

```
String.prototype.trim = String.prototype.trim || function() {
    return this.replace(/^\s+|\s+$/,'');
}

" hello ".trim();
<< "hello"
```

While monkey-patching built-in objects can seem a good way to add extra or missing functionality, it can also add unexpected behavior. You should think very carefully before monkey-patching any of the built-in object constructor prototypes. Further problems could occur if the method you've added is then implemented natively in the language.

If you do decide to do it, the suggested way is to check for built-in methods first and then try to mimic the built-in functionality from the specification. This can still be problematic, though, if the specification changes and is different from your implementation. Remember also that you can never guarantee that a method won't be implemented at some point in the future.

Mixins

A **mixin** method is a way of adding properties and methods of some objects to another object without using inheritance. It allows more complex objects to be created by "mixing" basic objects together. Below is a basic mixin method that is added as a property of the `Object.prototype` object. This means that *every* object will inherit this method and be able to use it to augment itself with the properties and methods from other objects:

```
Object.defineProperty(Object.prototype, 'mixin', {
    enumerable: false,
    writable: false,
    configurable: false,
    value: function(object) {
    for (var property in object) {
    if (object.hasOwnProperty(property)) {
      this[property] = object[property];
      }
    }
    return this;
  }
});
```

This appears to work as expected:

```
a = {};
<< {}

b = { name: "JavaScript" };
<< { name: "JavaScript" }

a.mixin(b);
<< { name: "JavaScript" };
```

There is a problem with this method, however. If any of the properties being mixed in are arrays or nested objects, only a shallow copy is made, which can cause a variety of issues (see note).

 Shallow and Deep Copies

When objects are copied by assignment, they are only copied by reference. This means that another object is not actually created in memory; the new reference will just point to the old object. Any changes that are made to either objects will affect both of them. Arrays and functions are objects, so whenever they're copied by assignment they will just point to the same object, and when one changes they'll all change. This is known as making a **shallow copy** of an object. A **deep**

or **hard copy** will create a completely new object that has all the same properties as the old object. The difference is that when a hard copy is changed the original remains the same, but when a shallow copy is changed so will the original.

This affects our mixin function when we try to copy a property that is an array or object, as can be seen in this example:

```
a = {};
b = { myArray: [1,2,3] };

a.mixin(b);
<< { myArray: [1,2,3] }
```

a now has a reference to the myArray property in the b object, rather than its own copy. Any changes made to either object will affect them both:

```
b.myArray.push(4);
<< 4

b.myArray;
<< [1,2,3,4]

a.myArray; // This has also changed
<< [1,2,3,4]
```

There is a simple way to sidestep that only a shallow copy is made. The mixin method is used to copy objects, so if a property is an array or nested object, we just call the mixin method recursively on it to copy its properties one at a time instead of using assignment. To do this, we'll change our code so that it checks to see if the property being copied is an object. If it is, the mixin method is called again on that property:

```
Object.defineProperty(Object.prototype, 'mixin', {
enumerable: false,
writable: false,
configurable: false,
value: function() {

for (var i = 0, max = arguments.length ; i < max ; i++) {
  if(typeof arguments[i] === "object") {
    var object = arguments[i];
```

```
      for (var property in object) {
        if (object.hasOwnProperty(property)) {
          if (typeof object[property] === "object") {
            this[property] = (object[property].constructor === Array)
➡ ? [] : {};
            this[property].mixin(object[property]);
          } else {
            var description = Object.getOwnPropertyDescriptor(object,
➡property);
            Object.defineProperty(this,property, description);
          }
        }
      }
    }
  }
return this;

}
});
```

Let's test this to see if it makes a deep copy:

```
a = {};
<< {}

b = { test: [1,2] };
<< { test: [1,2] }

c = { nest: { d: "nested" } };
<< { nest: { d: "nested" } }

a.mixin(b,c);
<< {"nest": {"d": "nested"}, "test": [1, 2]}

b.test.push(3);
<< 3

a.test
<< [1, 2]

b.test;
<< [1, 2, 3]
```

It works as expected—the changes only affect the object they are acted on.

The `mixin()` method is a particularly powerful way of dealing with objects, and has a number of uses.

Using Mixins to Add Properties

One use for the `mixin()` method is to add a large number of properties to an object all at once. For example, we can instantiate a new `Superhuman` object and then add all its individual properties in one go, instead of one at a time as we did earlier, while avoiding having to use the more verbose property descriptor notation:

```
wonderwoman = Object.create(Superhuman);
<< {"arms": 2, "change": function () {
   return this.realName + " goes into a phone box and comes out as "
➡ + this.name;
}, "legs": 2, "walk": function () { console.log("Walking"); }}
```

Instead of assigning each property, one at a time:

```
wonderwoman.name = "Wonder Woman";
<< "Wonder Woman"

wonderwoman.realName = "Diana Prince";
<< "Diana Prince"
```

We can just mix in an object literal and add both properties at once:

```
wonderwoman.mixin({ name: "Wonder Woman", realName: "Diana Prince"
➡});
<< {"arms": 2, "change": function () {
   return this.realName + " goes into a phone box and comes out as "
➡+ this.name;
}, "legs": 2, "name": "Wonder Woman", "realName": "Diana Prince",
➡"walk": function () { console.log("Walking"); }}
```

Using Mixins to Create a `copy()` Method

Another use of the `mixin()` method is to create a `copy()` method that is used to make an exact, deep copy of an object. This is added to the `Object` prototype object so that it's inherited by all objects. It uses the `Object.create()` method to create a new object that inherits from the same prototype as the object calling the method.

The `mixin()` method is then used to add all the properties and methods of the object calling the method to the new object, which is then returned:

```
Object.defineProperty(Object.prototype, 'copy', {
    enumerable: false,
    writable: false,
    configurable: false,
    value: function() {
      var object = Object.create(Object.getPrototypeOf(this));
      object.mixin(this);
      return object;
      }
})
```

Now we can create a clone of `superman`:

```
var bizarro = superman.copy();

bizarro.name = "Bizarro";
<< "Bizarro";

bizzaro.realName = "Subject B-0";
<< "Subject B-0"
```

Note that this is a deep copy and isn't copied by reference, so any subsequent changes to the `superman` or `bizzaro` objects will not affect the other.

Using the Mixin Method to Add Modular Functionality

The prototypal inheritance model allows us to add functionality to objects by inheriting properties and methods from other objects. While this is useful, it can be undesirable to create a chain of inheritance—sometimes we just want to add properties and methods without linking the two objects together. The `mixin()` method lets us encapsulate properties and methods in an object, and then add them to other objects without the overhead of an inheritance chain being created.

One way to think about the difference between inheritance from prototype objects and inheritance from mixin objects is to consider whether an object *is* something or whether it *has* something. For example, a tank *is a* vehicle, so it might inherit from a `Vehicle` prototype object. The tank *has a* gun, so this functionality could be added using a `gun` mixin object. This gives us extra flexibility since other objects might also use a gun but not be a vehicle, such as a `soldier` object, for example. The `soldier` object might inherit from a `Human` prototype object but also have the gun mixin.

We can use this idea to add super powers to our superhero objects used earlier. All the superheroes are superhuman, so they inherited any common traits from a `Super-human` prototype object. But they also have super-powers, and each superhero has a different mix of powers. This is a perfect use case for mixin objects: we can create some super-power mixin objects that can then be added to any of our super hero objects as required:

```
flight = {
  fly: function() {
    console.log(Up, up and away! " + this.name + " soars through the
➥air!");
    return this;
  }
}

superSpeed = {
  move: function() {
    console.log(this.name + " can move faster than a speeding
➥bullet!");
    return this;
  }
}

xRayVision = {
  xray: function() {
    console.log(this.name + " can see right through you!");
    return this;
  }
}
```

Now the relevant super powers can be added in a modular fashion to each of the super hero objects using the `mixin()` method:

```
superman.mixin(flight,superSpeed,xRayVision);

wonderwoman.mixin(flight,superSpeed);

superman.xray();
```

```
<< "Superman can see right through you!"

wonderwoman.fly();
<< "Up, up and away! Wonder Woman soars through the air!"
```

Chaining Functions

If a method returns `this`, its methods can be chained together to form a sequence of method calls that are called one after the other. For example, the `superman` object can call all three of the super-power methods that were mixed in earlier at once:

```
superman.fly().move().xRayVision();
<<    "Up, up and away! Superman soars through the air!"
      "Superman can move faster than a speeding bullet!"
      "Superman can see right through you!"
```

This is a technique that is commonly used by a number of JavaScript libraries, most notably jQuery. It helps to make code more concise by keeping multiple method calls on the same line, and with some clever method naming it can make the calls read almost like a sentence; the Jasmine testing library makes use of this.

A big drawback with this technique is that it can make code more difficult to debug. If an error is reported as occurring on a particular line, there is no way of knowing which method caused the error, since there are multiple method calls on that line.

It's worth keeping in mind that if a method lacks a meaningful return value, it might as well return `this` so that chaining is possible.

This and That

We saw earlier that the value of `this` points to the object calling a method. It allows us to create generalised methods that refer to properties specific to a particular object. Be aware of a certain problem when a function is nested inside another function, which can often happen when using methods in objects, especially ones that accept callback functions. The problem is that the value of `this` loses its scope and points to the global object inside a nested function, as can be seen in this example:

```
superman.allies = [batman,wonderwoman,aquaman]

superman.findFriends = function(){
  this.allies.forEach(function(friend) {
    console.log(friend.name + " is friends with " + this.name);
  }
  );
}

<<   "Batman is friends with "
     "Wonder Woman is friends with "
     "Aquaman is friends with "
```

It fails to produce the expected output because `this.name` is actually referencing the `name` property of the global `window` object, which in this case is empty so nothing is displayed. If strict mode is used, an exception would be thrown (this is a good example of how a silent fail may not be immediately spotted).

There are a couple of solutions to this problem.

Use that = this

A simple solution is to set the variable `that` to equal `this` *before* the nested function, and then refer to `that` in the nested function instead of `this`. Here is the example again, using `that`:

```
superman.findFriends = function(){
  that = this;
  this.allies.forEach(function(friend) {
    console.log(friend.name + " is friends with " + that.name);
  }
  );
}

superman.findFriends();
<<   "Batman is friends with Superman"
     "Wonder Woman is friends with Superman"
     "Aquaman is friends with Superman"
```

You might also see `self` or `_this` used to maintain scope in the same way.

Use bind(this)

The bind() method is a method for all functions and is used to set the value of this in the function. If this is provided as an argument to bind() while it's still in scope, any reference to this inside the nested function will be bound to the object calling the original method:

```
superman.findFriends = function() {
  this.allies.forEach(function(friend) {
    console.log(friend.name + " is friends with " + this.name);
  }.bind(this)
  );
}

superman.findFriends();
<<  "Batman is friends with Superman"
    "Wonder Woman is friends with Superman"
    "Aquaman is friends with Superman"
```

Borrowing Methods from Prototypes

It is possible to **borrow** methods from objects without having to inherit all their properties and methods. This is done by making a reference to the function that you want to borrow (that is, without parentheses so that it isn't invoked).

For example, the batman object does not have any of the super-power methods that the superman object has, but we can create a reference to them that can then be used by another object. For example, we can create a fly() function by referencing the superman object's fly method:

```
fly = superman.fly;
<< function () {
    return "Up, up and away! " + this.name + " soars through the
➥air!"
  }
```

This method can now be called on another object using the call method that all functions have:

```
fly.call(batman);
<< "Up, up and away! Batman soars through the air!"
```

Borrowing Array Methods

One of the most common uses of borrowing methods is from arrays. There are many *array-like* objects in JavaScript, such as the `arguments` object that's available in functions and the node lists that many of the DOM methods return. These act like arrays but are missing a lot of the methods arrays have—often it would be convenient if they had them.

For example, the `arguments` object can use the `slice` method from the `Array` constructor's prototype by assigning a variable that points to it:

```
slice = Array.prototype.slice;
```

This method can then be called on the `arguments` object using the `call` method:

```
slice.call(arguments, 1, 3)
```

The `call` method takes the object that the function is to be applied to as its first argument, and then the usual arguments come afterwards.

This can also be done directly from an array literal like so:

```
[].slice.call(arguments, 1, 3)
```

If you are finding that you need to call a lot of array methods on an array-like object, it might be worth turning it into an array using the `slice` method with no arguments:

```
Array.prototype.slice.call(arguments);
<<
```

This will return the `arguments` object as an array (since the `slice()` method returns an array).

Quiz Ninja Project

For the quiz project, we're going to replace the main play() function of the quiz with a Game() constructor function that will create a new Game instance every time it's invoked with the new operator. This will allow us to apply in our quiz some of the principles of OOP covered in this chapter.

The Game() constructor function is very similar to the first part of the play() function:

```
function Game(quiz){
  this.questions = quiz.questions;
  this.phrase = quiz.question;
  this.score = 0; // initialize score
  update($score,this.score);
  // initialize timer and set up an interval that counts down
  this.time = 20;
  update($timer,this.time);
  this.interval = window.setInterval( this.countDown.bind(this) ,
➡1000 );
  // hide button and show form
  hide($start);
  show($form);
  // add event listener to form for when it's submitted
  $form.addEventListener('click', function(event) {
    event.preventDefault();
    this.check(event.target.value);
    }.bind(this), false);
  this.chooseQuestion();
}
```

The main differences between the Game() constructor function and the play() function are:

▪ The variables score and time become this.score and this.time as they are properties of the Game instance.

▪ The variable interval changes to this.interval and the call to the countDown() function becomes a call to the this.countDown() method. It also has to be bound to the this object (otherwise the value of this in the this.countDown() method will be the window object).

▓ The event listener also needs to be bound to this so that it can call the
   this.check() method; otherwise the value of this will be the form element.

The nested functions that were inside the play() function now become methods
of the Game.prototype object. Most of these methods are the same as their equivalent
functions in the previous chapter, except that the variables that are properties of
the instance need this placing in front of them, such as this.questions, this.score
and this.time. The method calls also need this placing in front of them as they
are methods of the Game instance such as this.gameOver():

```
// Method definitions
Game.prototype.chooseQuestion = function() {
    console.log("chooseQuestion() called");
    var questions = this.questions.filter(function(question){
      return question.asked === false;
    });
    // set the current question
    this.question = questions[random(questions.length) - 1];
    this.ask(this.question);
  }
```

In the Game.prototype.ask() method we need to create a temporary variable called
quiz that is set equal to this. This allows us to refer to the Game object as quiz inside
the nested chooseOption() function because the value of this changes to the window
object inside nested functions.

```
Game.prototype.ask = function(question) {
  console.log("ask() called");
  var quiz = this;
  // set the question.asked property to true so it's not asked again
  question.asked = true;
  update($question,this.phrase + question.question + "?");
  // clear the previous options
  $form.innerHTML = "";
  // create an array to put the different options in and a button
➥variable
  var options = [], button;
  var option1 = chooseOption();
  options.push(option1.answer);
  var option2 = chooseOption();
  options.push(option2.answer);
  // add the actual answer at a random place in the options array
```

```
    options.splice(random(0,2),0,this.question.answer);
    // loop through each option and display it as a button
    options.forEach(function(name) {
      button = document.createElement("button");
      button.value = name;
      button.textContent = name;
      $form.appendChild(button);
    });

    // choose an option from all the possible answers but without
➥choosing the answer or the same option twice
    function chooseOption() {
      var option = quiz.questions[random(quiz.questions.length) - 1];
      // check to see if the option chosen is the current question or
➥already one of the options, if it is then recursively call this
➥function until it isn't
      if(option === question || options.indexOf(option.answer)
➥!== -1) {
        return chooseOption();
      }
      return option;
    }

}

Game.prototype.check = function(answer) {
  console.log("check() called");
  if(answer === this.question.answer){
    update($feedback,"Correct!","correct");
    // increase score by 1
    this.score++;
    update($score,this.score)
  } else {
    update($feedback,"Wrong!","wrong");
  }
  this.chooseQuestion();
}

Game.prototype.countDown = function() {
// this is called every second and decreases the time
  // decrease time by 1
  this.time--;
  // update the time displayed
  update($timer,this.time);
  // the game is over if the timer has reached 0
```

```
  if(this.time <= 0) {
    this.gameOver();
  }
}

Game.prototype.gameOver = function() {
  console.log("gameOver() invoked");
  // inform the player that the game has finished and tell them how
➥many points they have scored
  update($question,"Game Over, you scored " + this.score + " points"
➥);
  // stop the countdown interval
  window.clearInterval(this.interval);
  hide($form);
  show($start);
}
```

Finally, we need to change the event listener for the start button to create a new instance of the Game constructor function—instead of calling the play() function—as follows:

```
// Event listeners
$start.addEventListener('click', function() { new Game(test) } ,
➥ false);
```

If you have a go at playing the quiz by opening **index.htm** in your browser, you'll notice that nothing has changed in the way the game plays. We've made some very big changes to the code, though, as we have made the design much more object-oriented.

Summary

In this chapter, we have demonstrated that JavaScript supports the three main concepts of object-oriented programming: encapsulation, polymorphism, and inheritance. We have looked at using constructor functions to create multiple instances of objects, as well as using objects to create more objects. We have also seen how to use mixins to add modular functionality to objects.

The key points of the chapter are summarized here:

- Object-oriented programming (OOP) is a way of programming that uses objects as building blocks.

- The main concepts of OOP are encapsulation, polymorphism, and inheritance.

- Constructor functions can be used to create instances of objects.

- Inside a constructor function, the keyword `this` refers to the object returned by the function.

- All instances of a constructor function inherit all the properties and methods of its prototype object.

- The prototype object is live, so new properties and methods can be added to existing instances.

- The prototype chain is used to find an available method. If an object lacks a method, JavaScript will check whether its prototype has the method; if not, it will check that function's prototype until it finds the method or reaches the `Object` constructor function.

- Private properties and methods can be created by defining variables using `var` and defining a function inside a constructor function. These can be made public using getter and setter functions.

- Monkey-patching is the process of adding methods to built-in objects by augmenting their prototype objects. This should be done with caution as it can cause unexpected behavior in the way built-in objects work.

- A mixin method can be used to add properties and methods from other objects without creating an inheritance chain.

- Methods can be changed together and called in sequence if they return a reference to `this`.

- Polymorphism is when the same method is used by two unique objects in different ways.

- The value of `this` is not retained inside nested functions, which can cause errors. This can be worked around by using `that = this` or using the `bind(this)` method.

- Methods can be borrowed from objects.

In the next chapter, we'll be looking at how to send and receive data using JavaScript.

13

Ajax

Ajax is a technique that allows web pages to communicate asynchronously with a server and dynamically updates web pages without reloading. This enables data to be sent and received in the background, as well as portions of a page to be updated in response to user events, while the rest of the program continues to run.

The use of Ajax revolutionized how websites worked and ushered in a new age of web applications. Web pages were no longer static, but dynamic applications.

In this chapter, we'll cover the following topics:

- clients and servers

- a brief history of Ajax

- communicating with the server using the XMLHttpRequest object

- receiving data with Ajax

- sending data with Ajax

- form data

- Ajax timeouts

- JSON with padding

- our project—obtain questions using Ajax

Clients and Servers

The web of computers known as the Internet can be separated into two parts: clients and servers. A **client**, such as a web browser, will request a resource (usually a web page) from a **server**, which processes the request and sends back a response to the client.

JavaScript was originally designed as a **client-side** scripting language, meaning that it ran locally in the browser, adding dynamic features to the web page that was returned from the server. Ajax means that JavaScript can be used to request resources from a server on behalf of the client. The resources requested are usually JSON data or small fragments of text or HTML rather than a whole web page.

Consequently, a server is required when requesting resources using Ajax. Typically this involves using a **server-side** language such as PHP, Ruby, Node.js, or .NET to serve the data response following an Ajax request (usually from a back-end database). To practice using Ajax, you can either set up a local development server on your own computer, or request the files from an external website that uses cross-origin resource sharing (CORS) in order to avoid the same-origin policy that browsers enforce. All the examples in this chapter can be run without having to set up a local development server, although it may be worth looking into if you wish to do a lot of Ajax or server-side development.

 The Same-origin Policy and CORS

The **same-origin policy** in browsers stops any data being transferred from a domain that is different from the page making the request. This policy is enforced by all modern browsers and is to stop any malicious JavaScript being run from an external source. The problem is that the APIs of many websites rely on data being transferred across domains.

Cross-origin resource sharing (CORS)[1] is a solution to this problem as it allows resources to be requested from another website outside the original domain. The CORS standard works by using HTTP headers to indicate which domains can receive data. A website can have the necessary information in its headers to allow external sites access to its API data. Most modern browsers support this method and respect the restrictions specified in the headers.

A Brief History of Ajax

When the World Wide Web started, web pages contained static content. Any changes to the content on the page required a full page reload, often resulting in the screen going blank while the new page loaded. Remember, this was back in the 90s when dial-up modems were the norm.

In 1999, Microsoft implemented the XMLHTTP ActiveX control in Internet Explorer 5. It was developed initially for the Outlook web client, and allowed data to be sent asynchronously in the background using JavaScript. Other browsers implemented this technique, although it remained a relatively unknown feature and was rarely used.

Asynchronous loading techniques started to be noticed when Google launched Gmail and Google Maps in 2004 and 2005 respectively. These web applications used asynchronous loading techniques to enhance the user experience by changing the parts of the page without a full refresh. This gave them a much snappier and responsive quality that felt more like a desktop application.

The term "Ajax" was coined by Jesse James Garrett in 2005 in the article "Ajax: A New Approach to Web Applications,"[2] where he referred to techniques being used by Google in its recent web applications. Ajax was a neat acronym that referred to the different parts of the process being used: Asynchronous JavaScript and XML:

Asynchronous   When a request for data is sent, the program doesn't have to stop and wait for the response. It can carry on running, waiting for an event to fire when a response is received. By using callbacks to

---

[1] http://en.wikipedia.org/wiki/Cross-origin_resource_sharing
[2] https://web.archive.org/web/20080702075113/http://www.adaptivepath.com/ideas/essays/archives/000385.php

manage this, programs are able to run in an efficient way, avoiding lag as data is transferred back and forth.

JavaScript   JavaScript has always been considered a "front-end" language not used to communicate with the server. Ajax enables JavaScript to be used to send requests and receive responses from a server, allowing content to be updated in real time.

XML   When the term Ajax was originally coined, XML documents were often used to return data. Many different types of data can be sent, but by far the most commonly used in Ajax nowadays is JSON, which is more lightweight and easier to parse than XML. (Although it has never really taken off, the term Ajaj is sometimes used to describe the technique.)[3] JSON also has the advantage of being natively supported in JavaScript, so you can deal with JavaScript objects rather than having to parse XML files using DOM methods.

Ajax use really started to take off. Now users could see new content on web pages without having to refresh the page. Shopping baskets could be updated in the background, partial page content could be loaded seamlessly, and photo galleries could dynamically load images.

Today, it's unusual for Ajax not to be used when a partial web page update is required. The explosion in the use of public APIs also means that Ajax is used more then ever to transport data back and forth between sites.

 What is an API?

An application programming interface (API) is a collection of methods that allow external access to another program or service. Many websites allow controlled access to their data via public APIs. This means that developers are able to interact with the data and create mashups of third-party services. A weather site, for example, might have an API that provides methods that return information about the weather in a given location, such as temperature, wind speed, and so on. This can then be used to display local weather data on a web page. The information that's returned by APIs is often serialized as JSON. Since the data is being provided

---

[3] http://en.wikipedia.org/wiki/AJAJ

by an external site, CORS will have to be enabled in order to access information from an API. Some services may also require authentication in order to access their APIs.

The XMLHttpRequest Object

The XMLHttpRequest object was finally standardized by the WHATWG and W3C as part of the HTML5 specification, despite it originally being implemented by Microsoft many years earlier and already available in most browsers.

XMLHttpRequest2 was a draft API specification intended to extend the original XMLHttpRequest object. It added some useful features such as CORS and form data (covered later in this chapter). Since the end of 2011, the specifications were merged and are now simply known as XMLHttpRequest.

XMLHttpRequest is a constructor function that returns an object with methods for sending and receiving data. Older versions of Internet Explorer (before version 7) implemented this using an ActiveX object, but all modern browsers now support it natively.

To create a new XMLHttpRequest object, use the following code:

```
var xhr = new XMLHttpRequest();
```

readystate

The XMLHttpRequest object has a property called readystate. This is an integer value that corresponds to the status of the request:

0: UNSENT   the open() method has yet to be called

1: OPENED   after the open() method, but before the send() method has been called

2: HEADERS_RECEIVED   the send() method has been called and the HTTP headers and status code have been received

3: LOADING   the response is in the process of being received

4: DONE   the full response has been received

As the request progresses, this value is updated and the `onreadystatechange` event fires. The first task is to attach a callback function to the `onreadystatechange` event. This is the function that will be called every time the status of the response changes:

```
xhr.onreadystatechange = processResponse;
```

`processResponse` is the name of a callback function (without any parentheses as we don't want to call it at this point!). It can be called anything you like and can even be an anonymous function.

Opening the Request

Next we need to call the `open()` method. This method sets up the request and takes three parameters:

- The first parameter is the HTTP verb, which will be used to send the response. There are a number of HTTP verbs, but the most common are GET for retrieving data and POST for sending data.

 HTTP Verbs

The Web is built upon the Hypertext Transfer Protocol, or HTTP. When a client (usually a browser) makes a request to a server, it contains information about which HTTP **verb** to use. HTTP verbs are the language of HTTP and tell the server what type of request is being made, which determines how it will deal with the request.

The five most commonly used verbs when dealing with resources on the Web are:
- GET requests to retrieve resources
- POST requests, usually used to create a resource but can actually perform any task
- PUT requests to *upsert*, which means insert a resource or update it entirely
- PATCH requests to make partial updates to a resource
- DELETE requests to delete a resources

By default, a link in a web page will make a GET request and a form will send a POST request. When sending an Ajax request, the HTTP verb needs to be given explicitly as an argument to the `open()` method.

■ The second parameter is the URL address to which we are sending the request.

■ The last parameter is whether or not the request is to be sent asynchronously. This is almost exclusively set to `true`, as setting it to `false` can cause numerous problems:

```
xhr.open("GET", "path/to/resource", true);
```

 Avoid Synchronous Requests

It is possible to make a synchronous request using Ajax, but it should be avoided. If the response takes a long time, *everything* running in that browser tab will be blocked. This means that the browser menus, rendering, and downloads will all be stopped until the Ajax response is received—not a nice user experience!

Sending the Request

The last step is to actually send the request using the `send()` method:

```
xhr.send();
```

The `send()` method accepts any data that is to be sent with the request. If the request is a GET request, this can be left empty because we are requesting data rather than sending it. If the request is a POST request, the data can be sent in the form of a `key=value` query string, like so:

```
xhr.send("name=Superman");
```

Or a JSON string can be used:

```
xhr.send("name:Superman");
```

Receiving the Response

Once the request has been sent, the program can continue doing some other task while it waits for a response. Every time the the response status changes, the `on-readystatechange` event will fire and the callback function that we set up earlier will be called. This function can be used to process the response:

```
function processResponse() {
  if (xhr.readyState === 4 && xhr.status === 200) {
    // do something with the response
  }
}
```

Inside the callback function, we check to see if the request has completed. When this happens, the `readyState` property will have a value of 4 and the HTTP status is 200 (in other words, the request was okay). We can then place any code we want to run inside the code block.

 No Callback is Needed if the Request is Made Synchronously

A callback function is unnecessary if the request is made synchronously; that is, by setting the third parameter of the `open()` method to `false`. The code will pause after the `send()` method until the response is received, so any code can simply be placed after the `send()` method.

The `XMLHttpRequest` object has a number of properties that can be used to process the response:

- The `status` property returns the HTTP status code.[4] This will usually be 200 if the response was successful, 201 if a resource was created, or 204 when the request is successful but no content is returned.

- The `response` property returns the response sent back from the server. This can be text, HTML, JSON, a document, or a file.

- The `responseText` property returns a string representation of the response or `null` if nothing is returned. This can then be inserted into the document using the `innerHTML` property of an element or parsed into a JavaScript object if it's a JSON string.

- The `responseXML` property returns a document object that can then be parsed using the DOM methods that we saw in Chapter 6.

- The `responseType` property returns a string indicating the type of data contained in the response.

---

[4] http://en.wikipedia.org/wiki/List_of_HTTP_status_codes

Watch Out for Cookies

Each Ajax request is still a full HTTP request, so they will also download the cookies associated with that request. Even though cookies have a size limit they soon add up, causing each Ajax request to end up being larger than expected, making them slower and more cumbersome to deal with.

Receiving Information

To demonstrate how to update a page using Ajax, we'll need to set up a demonstration page. Create a file called **ajax.htm** that contains the following code:

ajax.htm

```
<!doctype html>
<html lang="en">
<head>
  <meta charset="utf-8">
  <title>Ajax Example</title>
</head>
<body>
  <button id="text">Request Text</button>
  <button id="html">Request HTML</button>
  <button id="api">Request API</button>
  <div id="output">
      Ajax response will appear here
  </div>
  <script src="scripts.js"></script>
</body>
</html>
```

This is a standard HTML5 web page that contains three buttons and a `div` element. Each button will be used to make a different type of Ajax request. The first will request a text file, the second will require an HTML file, and the third will request some JSON from an external API. The div with an `id` of `"output"` will be where we'll insert the response we receive from the Ajax request.

Ajax requests are usually made to files stored on a server, so we'll use a plain text file and an HTML file that are stored on SitePoint's Amazon Web Service (AWS) servers. These are to mimic files that would usually be stored on the same server as the website. If you've set up a local development server, you could create the files and serve them from your local server. The text file called **hello.txt** contains this string:

```
                                                                    hello.txt

Hello Ajax!
```

The HTML file is called **hello.htm** and contains the following:

```
                                                                    hello.htm

<h1>Hello Ajax!</h1>
```

For the external API we'll use the site JSON Test,[5] which provides a testing service for JSON data. The URL `http://ip.jsontest.com/` will return the IP address of the computer being used in JSON format.

 Enabling CORS

> The files stored on SitePoint's AWS servers and the JSON Test website allow CORS by setting `Access-Control-Allow-Origin` to `'*'` in the HTTP header. Hence, any domain can request data from its website using Ajax. In a real-world application, the files being requested will normally be hosted on the same server as the site requesting them, so CORS would be unnecessary.

Now we need a JavaScript file. This should be called **scripts.js** and can be saved in the same directory as the other files. It contains this code:

```
                                                            scripts.js (excerpt)

var text = document.getElementById("text");
var html = document.getElementById("html");
var api = document.getElementById("api");
```

It assigns a variable to each of the three buttons in the HTML file. Next, we'll add some code that will assign an event handler to each button:

---

[5] http://www.jsontest.com/

scripts.js *(excerpt)*

```
text.addEventListener("click", function(){ request("https://s3.amazo
➥naws.com/sitepoint-book-content/jsninja/hello.txt") }, false);
html.addEventListener("click", function(){ request("https://s3.amazo
➥naws.com/sitepoint-book-content/jsninja/hello.htm") }, false);
api.addEventListener("click", function(){ request("http://ip.jsonte
➥st.com/") }, false);
```

This calls the `request()` function when the button is clicked. This function is where the Ajax request will happen. It accepts a URL as a parameter, which is where the request is sent. Let's add this function to the end of the file:

scripts.js *(excerpt)*

```
function request(url) {
  var xhr = new XMLHttpRequest();
  xhr.onreadystatechange = function() {
    if (xhr.readyState === 4 && xhr.status === 200) {
      document.getElementById("output").innerHTML = xhr.
➥responseText;
    }
  }

  xhr.open("GET", url, true);
  xhr.send();
  document.getElementById("output").innerHTML = "Waiting for
➥ response ...";
}
```

Inside this function, we create a new `XMLHttpRequest` object and then assign an anonymous function to the `onreadystatchange` property. This checks the `readyState` property to see if the request is complete (when the `readyState` property is 4). Once complete it replaces the inner HTML of the output div with the response text. The `open()` method sets up an asynchronous GET request to the URL provided (depending on which button was pressed) and then the request is sent. Last of all, we update the output div with a message saying "`Waiting for response ...`". This demonstrates the asynchronous nature of an Ajax request because it will be shown *before* the response. The text and HTML files take very little time to be shown after they're downloaded the first time as they are cached by the browser, but the external API always takes a while before its response is returned. The "Waiting" message demonstrates that other code can run while we wait for the response.

Loading Spinners

In the previous example we displayed a message to say we were waiting for a response. It is common for sites to use spinners (or egg timers in the old days!) to indicate that the site is waiting for something to happen. Ajax Load[6] and Preloaders.net[7] are both good resources for creating a spinner graphic to be used on your site.

Let's try this out. Open **ajax.htm** in a browser and try pressing the buttons. You should see a similar sight to the screenshot in Figure 13.1.

Figure 13.1. A working Ajax example

Sending Information

We can also use Ajax to send information, usually as a JSON string. Back in Chapter 8, we created a form for entering information about a superhero. When the form was submitted the data was converted into a JSON string, which was then shown in an alert dialog. Using Ajax, this string could be saved to a database or sent to an external web API for processing.

Unfortunately, we're without a database to save this information to, but there's a very handy website that can be used for testing Ajax requests and responses, called Reqres.[8] It will accept a request containing JSON data and return a response that

---

[6] http://www.ajaxload.info/
[7] http://preloaders.net/
[8] http://reqr.es/

mimics making a save to a database, although it doesn't actually save any of the data that you send. We'll use it here to demonstrate the techniques.

The main difference when sending information is that the open() method's first argument needs to be the HTTP POST method, and the JSON string will be provided as an argument to the send() method.

To implement this in our superhero form example, all we do is change the last line of the makeHero() function from:

```
alert(JSON.stringify(hero));
```

to:

scripts.js (excerpt)

```
send(JSON.stringify(hero));
```

Now we add the send() function to the **scripts.js** file:

scripts.js (excerpt)

```
function send(hero) {
  var xhr = new XMLHttpRequest();
  xhr.open("POST", "http://reqr.es/api/users", true);
  xhr.setRequestHeader("Content-Type", "application/json");
  xhr.onreadystatechange = function(){
    if (xhr.readyState === 4 && xhr.status === 201) {
      console.log(xhr.responseText);
    }
  };
  xhr.send(hero);
}
```

Now if you open up the **hero.htm** file, fill in some form details about a superhero and submit it, you should receive a response from the Reqres website in the console similar to the one that follows. It indicates that the data has been saved as the returned object with the extra properties id and createdAt that have been added by a database (in reality, the data hasn't been saved, and these properties have just been added for demonstration purposes):

```
<<  "{"name":"Superman","realName":"Clarke Kent","powers":["Flight",
➥"Strength","Super Speed"],"type":"Hero","city":"Metropolis",
➥"origin":"Born as Kal-El on the planet Krypton, before being ...",
➥"age":"28","id":"242","createdAt":"2014-11-02T15:38:02.116Z"}"
```

Most forms will have an `action` attribute that specifies the URL to use if the form is sent without using Ajax. It will also have a `method` attribute that will specify the HTTP verb to use. These methods are available as properties of the `form` object, so the `open()` method can be generalized to work for any form as:

```
xhr.open(form.method, form.action, true);
```

FormData

One of the most useful additions to the XMLHttpRequest2 specification is the `FormData` interface. This is supported in all modern browsers and Internet Explorer from version 10 onwards, and makes it much easier to submit information in forms using Ajax.

A `FormData` instance is created using a constructor function:

```
data = new FormData();
```

If a form is passed to this constructor function as an argument, the form data instance will serialize all the data automatically, ready to be sent using Ajax. This is what the `makeHero()` function did in our last example, but it tooltook a lot of repetitive lines of code. The `FormData` interface helps to reduce the amount of code needed when submitting forms.

We can use this to cut down the size of our hero page. Edit the **scripts.js** file so that it contains the following:

scripts.js (excerpt)

```
var form = document.forms.hero;
form.addEventListener("submit", submitHero, false);

function submitHero(event) {
    event.preventDefault();
    var form = event.target;
```

```
    var data = new FormData(form);
    var xhr = new XMLHttpRequest();
    xhr.open("POST", form.action, true);
    xhr.setRequestHeader("Content-Type", "application/json");
    xhr.onreadystatechange = function(){
      if (xhr.readyState === 4 && xhr.status === 201) {
        console.log(xhr.responseText);
      }
    };
    xhr.send(data);
}
```

We now require a function named submitHero(), which is called when the form is submitted. In this function we grab a reference to the form using the event.target property (since it was the form that was submitted) and create a new instance of the FormData() constructor function, providing the form as an argument. This does all the hard work for us; after this, we submit the form using Ajax as before, but provide the form data instances (stored in the data variable) as an argument of the send() method.

It's also possible to add data to the form data instance as key-value pairs using the append() method:

```
data = new FormData(); // no form provided as an argument creates an
➥empty form data instance

data.append("height", 75);
```

The FormData interface interface really comes into its own when a form contains files to upload. This was a notoriously difficult task in the past, often requiring the use of Flash or another third-party browser plugin to handle the upload process. The FormData instance will automatically create the necessary settings required and take care of all the hard work if any file uploads are present in the form.

You can find more information about the FormData interface in this SitePoint article by Craig Buckler[9] and on the Mozilla Developer Network.[10]

---

[9] http://www.sitepoint.com/easier-ajax-html5-formdata-interface/
[10] https://developer.mozilla.org/en-US/docs/Web/API/FormData

Ajax Timeouts

Ajax requests can take different amounts of time for a response, depending on the server to which the request is made. This is why it's important to ensure the request is made asynchronously, so that the browser avoids being locked up while waiting for the response. But what if the server is down and the response never comes back?

The XMLHttpRequest object has a `timeout` property for setting the amount of time to wait for a response. This is measured in milliseconds and is set to 0 by default, which indicates no timeout period.

For example, to set a timeout of five seconds the following code can be used:

```
xhr.timeout = 5000;
```

If a response is not received after the specified amount of time, the request is automatically terminated. Alternatively, a function can be assigned to the `ontimeout` property that will be called when the request times out:

```
xhr.ontimeout = funciton() {
    console.log("request timed out");
}
```

Note that both these properties need to be set before the `xhr.send()` method is called.

JSON With Padding

JSONP or JSON with padding is a very common technique of transporting data as it allows the same-origin policy to be bypassed without using CORS. It involves sending a JSON string wrapped in a callback function that is then injected into a `<script>` tag. The same-origin policy doesn't apply to `<script>` tags, and because the callback function has already been defined in the domain requesting the data, all the data wrapped in the function will be available in that domain by referencing the callback function.

The Server Must Support JSONP

The server responding to the request must support JSONP requests and return a callback function. The technique will fail to work if normal JSON data is returned.

JSONP in Action

To demonstrate using JSONP, we'll create another small web page. In a new folder, create a file called **jsonp.htm** and add the following HTML code:

jsonp.htm

```
<!doctype html>
<html lang="en">
<head>
  <meta charset="utf-8">
  <title>JSONP Example</title>
</head>
<body>
  <button id="send">Request Text</button>
  <div id="output">
      Ajax response will appear here
  </div>
  <script src="scripts.js"></script>
</body>
</html>
```

This is similar to our earlier example FormData interface, but there is just one button that will make the JSONP request. To process this, we'll create a JavaScript file called **scripts.js** that's saved in the same directory as **jsonp.htm** and contains this code:

scripts.js (excerpt)

```
var send = document.getElementById("send");
send.addEventListener("click", update , false);
```

This gives us a reference to the button and then adds an event listener that will call the update() function when the button is clicked. This function, which makes the JSONP request, needs adding to the bottom of the **scripts.js** file:

```
                                                        scripts.js (excerpt)

function update() {
  var script = document.createElement("script");
  script.src = " http://echo.jsontest.com/name/superman/?callback=
➥process";
  document.getElementsByTagName("head")[0].appendChild(script);
}
```

This uses DOM methods to create a new `script` element. We then add the URL from which we'll be requesting the JSONP. In this example we're using the JSON Test site again, this time using its `echo` feature that returns a JavaScript object based on the URL provided. In this case, adding "**/name/superman**" results in this object being returned:

```
{
  name: superman
}
```

Notice at the end of the URL specified is the string **?callback=process**. This identifies the name of the callback that we want called when the data is returned. In this case, a function called `process()` will be invoked, so let's add this function to the bottom of **scripts.js**:

```
                                                        scripts.js (excerpt)

function process(response) {
  document.getElementById("output").innerHTML = response.name;
}
```

This callback function is automatically given the response data as an argument. We can then process the data in any way we like inside the function. In this case, we simply want to display the value of the `name` property in the output div.

Open **jsonp.htm** in a browser and try pressing the button. If everything is working properly, you should see a similar display to the screenshot shown in Figure 13.2.

Figure 13.2. A JSONP example

Quiz Ninja Project

We can use Ajax to fetch the questions from a server, instead of keeping them in an object inside our JavaScript file. First of all, we remove the object stored in the quiz variable at the start of the **scripts.js** file and transfer the information into a separate file. This information has to be in the JSON format, so the properties need to be strings. The file is saved on SitePoint's S3 account and can be found at the following URL (it also contains lots more questions than the three we've been using so far):

```
https://s3.amazonaws.com/sitepoint-book-content/jsninja/quiz.json
```

To access this JSON data, we need a function that will create an Ajax request to fetch the data. Add the following function just after the `"use strict"` line in the **scripts.js** file:

```
// gets the question JSON file using Ajax
function getQuiz() {
  var xhr = new XMLHttpRequest();
  xhr.onreadystatechange = function(){
    if (xhr.readyState === 4 && xhr.status == 200) {
      var quiz = JSON.parse(xhr.responseText);
      new Game(quiz);
    }
  };
  xhr.open("GET", "https://s3.amazonaws.com/sitepoint-book-content/
➥jsninja/quiz.json", true);
  xhr.overrideMimeType("application/json");
```

```
    xhr.send();
    update($question, "Waiting for questions...");
}
```

This function creates a new `XMLHttpRequest` object and then uses the `JSON.parse()` method to convert the JSON data in the response into a native JavaScript object. This object is then given as an argument to the `Game()` constructor function that we created in the last chapter to launch the game. After this, we use the `open()` method to request the data, the `overrideMimeType()` method to say that we're expecting JSON data to be returned, and the `send()` method to actually send the request. We then place a message in the `question` section to say that we're waiting for the questions to load.

The only thing to change now is our event listener that's attached to the start button so that it calls the `getQuestions()` function when clicked:

```
// Event listeners
$start.addEventListener('click', getQuiz , false);
```

Keeping the quiz data in a separate file and loading it using Ajax is beneficial as it keeps the question data separate from the actual application logic. It means that it's much easier to edit all in one place. It also means that we could potentially create lots of different JSON quiz files that could be linked to, enabling a variety of quizzes to be played.

Summary

In this chapter, we have seen how it's possible to use Ajax to update pages and exchange data asynchronously. This is a powerful feature that has transformed the way JavaScript is used.

In this chapter, we've learned the following:

- Ajax is a technique for sending and receiving data asynchronously in the background.

- The data can be sent in many forms, but it is usually inJSON.

- Ajax can be used for making partial page updates without having to do a full page reload.

- Ajax can be used for communicating with external APIs.

- Ajax requests are made using instances of the `XMLHttpRequest` object.

- Requests can receive data using a GET request or send data using a POST request.

- JSONP or JSON with Padding is a technique used to bypass the same-origin policy. It wraps the response data in a JavaScript callback function that is dynamically inserted the markup.

In the next chapter, we'll look at the new features in the HTML5 specification and how to implement them.

Chapter 14

HTML5 APIs

HTML5 is the latest iteration of the Hypertext Markup Language used to create web pages. This version goes beyond the actual markup language, however, and brings together a number of related technologies such as CSS and JavaScript. We've already seen in Chapter 8 some of the new form elements as well as the validation API that has been introduced. In this chapter, we'll be looking at some of the other APIs that have been made available in HTML5.

In this chapter, we'll cover the following topics:

- the development of HTML5 and the JavaScript APIs

- the `data-` attribute

- HTML5 APIs—local storage, geolocation, web workers, and multimedia

- drawing shapes with canvas

- shims and polyfills—how to make the most of HTML5 APIs, even when they're without browser support

The Development of HTML5

WHATWG

At the turn of the millennium, HTML was at version 4 and the World Wide Web Consortium (W3C)[1], the standards body that oversees the World Wide Web, decided that the future was in using XHTML, an extensible version of HTML. Version 1 of XHTML had been made a standard and development of version 2 was underway. A big problem with version 2 was that it would not be backwardly compatible with previous versions of HTML or XHTML. Because of this potential to "break the Web," the Web Hypertext Application Technology Working Group (WHATWG)[2] was set up by Apple, the Mozilla Foundation, and Opera Software in 2004 to develop a new version of HTML—one that made the most of the latest technologies while still being backwardly compatible. The pragmatic aim of WHATWG was to create a future-proof version of HTML that would also work in today's browsers, rather than being just a dream for the future (which is what XHTML version 2 turned out to be). New elements were introduced as well as new APIs for displaying media, such as play-ingvideos natively in the browser, which would have previously required a plugin such as Flash.

Working Together

In 2009, the W3C dropped development of XHTML 2.0 and officially endorsed HTML5. The W3C and WHATWG now work together in developing the HTML5 specification, although there are still some differences—the W3C are developing HTML5 as a "fixed" standard that will be frozen once the candidate recommendation is accepted. After this, the next version of HTML (presumably version 6) will be developed.

In contrast, WHATWG are working at developing HTML as a "living" standard with a specification in a constant state of evolution, so there are no specific versions. It's highly likely that W3C will base future versions of HTML on the state of the WHATWG HTML specification at the time.

---

[1] http://www.w3.org/
[2] https://whatwg.org/

In 2011, the W3C unveiled the official HTML5 logo. It was accompanied by a big explosion of interest as vendors such as Apple started using the term HTML5 to describe its latest web applications.

Adoption

Because browser vendors such as Apple, Mozilla, and Opera were part of the WHATWG, many of HTML5's features were implemented relatively quickly and it was soon being used in real-world applications. The speed of adoption in the wild has meant that it has become the de facto standard used to create all modern websites and applications.

Modules

A big feature of the HTML5 specification is that it is separated into **modules**. This allows different features to be developed at different paces and then implemented without having to wait for other features to be completed. It also means that when a previously unforeseen development occurs, a new module can be created to cater for it. Modules can be at different stages of maturity, from ideas to full implementation. A useful site that checks to see if a specific feature can be used is Can I Use _____?[3]

You can find out more about the HTML5 standard by reading _Jump Start HTML5 Basics_[4] by Tiffany Brown.

The `data-` Attribute

The `data-` attribute is a way of embedding data in a web page using custom attributes that are ignored by the browser. They're also private to a page, so shouldn't be used by an external service: their sole purpose is to be used by a JavaScript program. This means that they are perfect for adding data to be used either by an external API or as a hook that the program utilizes to access a particular element on the page.

The names of these attributes can be decided by the developer, but they must use the following format:

▨ start with `data-`

---

[3] http://caniuse.com/

[4] http://www.sitepoint.com/store/jump-start-html5-basics/

■ contain only lowercase letters

■ include an optional string value

Examples could be:

```
data-toppings="ham & pineapple"
data-hero="true"
data-dropdown
data-user="DAZ"
data-max-length="32"
```

The information contained in the attributes can be used to identify particular elements; for example, all the elements with an attribute of data-calendar could be identified as calendar widgets. The values of the attributes can also be used to filter different elements; for example, we could find all the elements that have a data-rating value of 3 or more.

Each element has a dataset property that can be used to access any data- attributes it contains. Here's an example of some markup:

```
<div id="pizza" data-toppings="cheese, tomato, mushroom">
Vegetable Deluxe Pizza
</div>
```

The data-toppings attribute can be accessed using the following code:

```
var pizza = document.getElementById("pizza");
var toppings = pizza.dataset.toppings;
<< "cheese, tomato, mushroom"
```

Notice that the data- prefix is dropped. To access the attribute, toppings is used as if it's a property of the dataset object. If a data- attribute's name contains hyphens, they are replaced with camel-case notation, so data-max-length would be accessed using maxLength.

 Browser Support

The support for the data- attribute is generally very good in modern browsers ... even Internet Explorer 8 has partial support! Some older browsers are unable to understand the dataset property, however, but any data- attribute can be found using the standard `getAttribute` method. So the previous code could be replaced with the following if you still need to support older browsers:

```
var toppings = pizza.getAttribute("data-toppings");
```

The restriction of only using a string value can be overcome by encoding any JavaScript object or value as a JSON string and then performing type-conversion later as required.

Data attributes provide a convenient way of adding data directly into the HTML markup, enabling a richer user experience. More information is available at Site-Point.[5]

HTML5 APIs

The HTML5 specification contains a number of APIs that help to gain access to the hardware, such as cameras, batteries, geolocation, and the graphics card. Hardware evolves quickly and APIs are frequently introduced to give developers access and control new features that appear in the latest devices.

In this section, we'll look at some of the more popular APIs that are already supported in most modern browsers; however, due to the ever-changing nature of most APIs, it is still best practice to use object-detection tests before using any of the API methods.

HTML5 Web Storage

The Web Storage API provides a key-value store on the client's computer that is similar to using cookies but has fewer restrictions, more storage capacity, and is generally easier to use. This makes it perfect for storing information about users, as well as storing application-specific information that can then be used during future sessions. It's supported in all modern browsers from Internet Explorer version 8 upwards, and each domain has its own separate storage area.

The Web Storage API has some crucial differences with cookies:

---

[5] http://www.sitepoint.com/use-html5-data-attributes/

■ information stored is *not* shared with the server on every request

■ information is available in multiple windows of the browser (but only if the domain is the same)

■ storage capacity limit is much larger than the 4KB limit for cookies[6]

If a browser supports the Web Storage API the `window` object will have a property called `localStorage`, which is a native object with a number of properties and methods used to store data. The information is saved in the form of key-value pairs and the values can only be strings. There is also a `sessionStorage` object that works in the same way, although the data is only saved for the current session.

Here is a basic example of storing information. To save a value locally, use:

```
if(window.localStorage) {
  localStorage.setItem(name, "Walter White");
}
```

This will illustrate that it's being saved locally. Try completely closing your browser, reopening the console, and entering the same line of code:

```
if(window.localStorage) {
  localStorage.getItem(name);
}
<< "Walter White"
```

To remove an entry from local storage use the `removeItem` method:

```
if(localStorage.name) {
  localStorage.removeItem(name);
}
```

Alternatively, this can be done by simply using assignment:

```
if(window.localStorage) {
  localStorage.name = "Jesse Pinkman";
}
```

---

[6] There is no actual limit in the specification, but most browsers have a limit set at 5GB per domain.

```
if(window.localStorage) {
 console.log(localStorage.name);
}
<< "Jesse Pinkman";
```

```
if(window.localStorage) {
 delete localStorage.name;
}
```

To completely remove everything stored in local storage, use the `clear()` method:

```
if(window.localStorage) {
 localStorage.clear();
}
```

Every time a value is saved to local storage, a `storage` event is fired. Note that this event is only fired on any *other* windows or tabs from the same domain, and only if the value of the item being saved changes. The event object sent by the event listener to the callback has a number of properties that provide information about the updated item:

- `key` tells us the key of the item that changed

- `newValue` tells us the new value to which it has been changed

- `oldValue` tells us the previous value before it was changed

- `storageArea` tells us if it is stored in local or session storage

The following piece of code will add an event listener that logs information about any changes to the Web Storage:

```
addEventListener('storage', function(event) {
 console.log("The " + event.key + " was updated from " +
➥event.oldValue + " to " + event.newValue " and saved in
➥" + event.storageArea) }, false);
```

That only strings can be saved might seem like a restriction at first, but by using JSON, we can store any JavaScript object in local storage. For example, we could save the superhero object that we created in the form in Chapter 8 by adding the following line of code to the to the end of the `makeHero()` function:

```
if(window.localStorage) {
  localStorage.setItem(hero.name, JSON.stringify(hero);
}
```

This will save the hero object as a JSON string using the name of the hero as the key. To retrieve the superhero as a JavaScript object:

```
if(window.localStorage) {
  superman = JSON.parse(localStorage.getItem("superman"));
}
```

The Web Storage API provides a useful way of storing various types of information on a user's computer without the restriction of cookies. More information about it is available at SitePoint.[7]

Geolocation

The Geolocation API is used to obtain the geographical position of the device. This means it can be used to find the user's exact location and then link to nearby places or measure the speed at which the user is moving. Because of privacy concerns, permission to use this has to be granted by the user first.

If geolocation is available it will be a property of the `navigator` object that we met in Chapter 9. This property has a method called `getCurrentPosition()` that will return a `position` object to a specified function, called `youAreHere()` in the example:

```
if(navigator.geolocation) {
  navigator.geolocation.getCurrentPosition(youAreHere);
}
```

The `position` object passed to the `youAreHere()` function has a `coords` property with a `latitude` and `longitude` property, which together give the coordinates of the device. These coordinates can then be used in conjunction with other applica-

---

[7] http://www.sitepoint.com/an-overview-of-the-web-storage-api/

tions or web services (such as a mapping service) to obtain the user's exact location. In this example, we simply show an alert dialog that displays the user's coordinates:

```
function youAreHere(position) {
  alert("Latitude: " + position.coords.latitude + ", Longitude:
➥ position.coords.longitude);
}
```

The `position` object has several other properties that can be used to find out information about the location and movement of the device:

- `position.speed` property returns the ground speed of the device in meters per second

- `position.altitude` property returns an estimate of the device's altitude in meters above the WGS84[8] ellipsoid, which is a standard measurement for the center of the Earth

- `position.heading` property returns the direction the device is moving in as a bearing in degrees, measured clockwise from North

- `position.timestamp` property returns the time that the position information was recorded

The `position` object also has properties that calculate the accuracy of the measurements. These can be useful as sometimes you only need to know the town or city users are in, while at other times you may need their exact position. `position.accuracy` property returns the accuracy of the `latitude` and `longitude` properties in meters. The lower the returned value the more accurate the measurements are, as is the case for the `position.altitudeAccuracy` property, which returns the accuracy of the `altitude` property in meters.

In addition, the `geolocation` object has a `watchPosition()` method that will call a callback function every time the position of the device is updated. This method returns an ID that can be used to reference the position being watched:

---

[8] http://en.wikipedia.org/wiki/World_Geodetic_System

```
if(navigator.geolocation) {
  var id = navigator.geolocation.watchPosition(youAreHere);
}
```

The `clearWatch()` method can be used to stop the callback being called, using the ID of the watch as an argument:

```
navigator.geolocation.clearWatch(id);
```

The Geolocation API provides a useful interface for adding location-based information to a website or application. More information can be found at the Mozilla Developer Network.[9]

Web Workers

We saw in earlier chapters that JavaScript is a single-threaded language, meaning that only one process can run at one time. **Web workers** allow processes to be run in the background, adding support for concurrency in JavaScript. The idea is that any processes that could take a long time are carried out in the background, so a website will continue to function without fear of the dreaded "script has become unresponsive" message that occurs when a script runs for too long, shown in Figure 14.1.

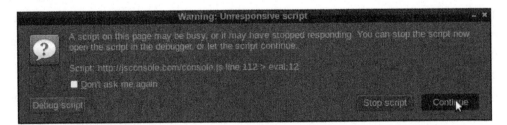

Figure 14.1. An unresponsive script

To get started, use the `Worker()` constructor function to create a new worker:

```
var worker = new Worker('task.js');
```

---

[9] https://developer.mozilla.org/en-US/docs/Web/API/Geolocation/Using_geolocation

This function takes the name of another JavaScript file as an argument. In the example, this is a file called **task.js**. If this file exists, it will be downloaded asynchronously. The worker will only start once the file has finished downloading completely. If the file doesn't exist, it will fail silently.

The variable that's assigned to the constructor function (`worker` in our example) can now be used to refer to the worker in the main program. In the worker script (**task.js**), the keyword `self` is used to refer to the worker.

Web workers use the concept of messages to communicate back and forth between the main script and worker script. The `postMessage()` method can be used to send a message *and* start the worker working. The argument to this method can send any data to the web worker. To post a message *to* the worker, the following code is used inside the main script:

```
worker.postMessage("Hello");
```

To post a message *from* the worker, the following is used in the worker script:

```
self.postMessage("Finished");
```

When a message is posted, a `message` event is fired, so they can be dealt with using an event listener. The data sent with the message as an argument is stored in the `data` property of the `event` object that's passed to the callback function. The following example would log any data returned from the worker to the console:

```
worker.addEventListener('message', function(event) {
    console.log(event.data);
}, false);
```

When a worker has completed its task, it can be stopped using the `terminate()` method from within the main script:

```
worker.terminate();
```

Or using the `close()` method from inside the worker script:

```
self.close();
```

A Factorizing Example

Back in Chapter 10, we created a function that found the factors of a given number. This works well, but can take a long time to find the factors of large numbers. If it was used in a website, it would stop any other code from running while it calculated the factors. To demonstrate this, save the following code in a file called **factors.htm**:

factors.htm

```
<!doctype html>
<html lang="en">
<head>
  <meta charset="utf-8">
  <title>Factorizor</title>
</head>
<body>
  <button id="rainbow">Change Color</button>
  <form>
      <label for="number">Enter a Number to Factorize:</label>
      <input type="number" name="number" min=1 value="20">
      <button type="submit">Submit</button>
  </form>
  <div id="output"></div>
<script src="js/scripts.js"></script>
</body>
</html>
```

This web page has a button that will change the background color of the page and an input field where a number can be entered. The factors will be displayed inside the output div. To get this working, create a folder called **js** in the same directory as **factors.htm**; then add a file called **scripts.js** that contains the following:

js/scripts.htm *(excerpt)*

```
var button = document.getElementById("rainbow");

var rainbow = ["red","orange","yellow","green","blue","indigo",
➥"violet"];

function change() {
  document.body.style.background = rainbow[Math.floor(7*
```

```
➥Math.random())];
}
button.addEventListener("click", change);
```

This first piece of code was covered way back in Chapter 1 and uses an event listener to change the background color if the button is clicked. We also need to factorize the number entered in the form, so add this code to the end of **scripts.js**:

js/scripts.htm (excerpt, incomplete)

```
var form = document.forms[0];
form.addEventListener("submit", factorize, false);

function factorize(event) {

  event.preventDefault(); // prevent the form from being submitted

  var number = Number(form.number.value);
  var factors = String(factorsOf(number));
  document.getElementById("output").innerHTML = factors;

}

function factorsOf(n) {

  if (n < 0) {
    throw new RangeError("Argument Error: Number must be positive");
  }

  if (Math.floor(n) !== n) {
    throw new RangeError("Argument Error: Number must be an
➥integer");
  }

  var factors = [];
  for (var i=1 , max = Math.sqrt(n); i <= max ; i++) {
    if (n%i === 0){
      factors.push(i,n/i);
    }
  }
  return factors.sort(function(a,b) { return a > b; });
}
```

This uses the same `factorsof()` function from Chapter 9 and adds a `submit` event listener to the form. When the form is submitted, it will find the factors of the number in the input field and then place the result inside the `output` div.

This works well, even coping with some large numbers, as can be seen in the screenshot in Figure 14.2.

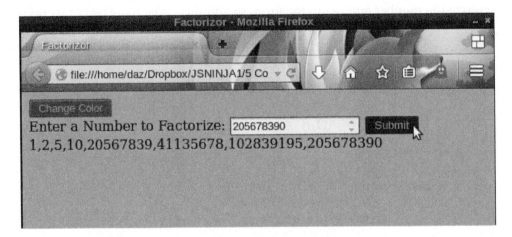

Figure 14.2. Our Factorizor in action

But if you enter a sizable number (around 18–20 digits), it takes longer to process the answer and the browser will display a warning, as shown in Figure 14.3.

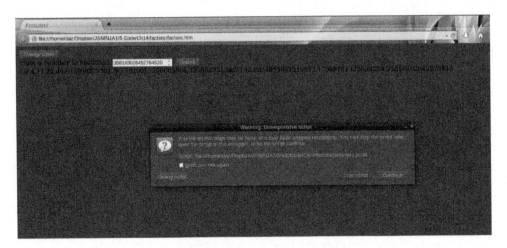

Figure 14.3. Factorizing an extremely large number

To make matters worse, it's impossible to click on the **Change Color** button while the factors are being calculated—the whole program freezes until the operation is complete. The good news is that we can use web workers to solve this problem. First of all we create a new file called **factors.js** that's saved inside the **js** folder. Remove the `factorsOf()` function from the **scripts.js** file and add it into this file. We'll be adding more to this file later, but first we need to edit the `factorize()` function in the **scripts.js** file so that it contains the following:

```
                                                          js/factors.js (excerpt)
function factorize(event) {

  event.preventDefault(); // prevent the form from being submitted

  var number = form.number.value;

  if(Worker) {
    worker = new Worker("link/to/file/factors.js");

    worker.postMessage(number);

    worker.addEventListener('message', function(event) {
      document.getElementById("output").textValue = event.data;
    }, false);

  }

}
```

After checking whether web workers are supported, it adds a new web worker. It then uses the `postMessage()` method to send a message to the worker, which is the number that we want to factorize. When the number has been factorized the worker will send a message back to say it has finished.

To deal with this, we set up an event listener that will fire when a message is received back from the worker. The information sent from the worker is stored in the `data` property of the `event` object, so we use the `textValue` property to insert the data into the `output` div.

Now we go back to the **factors.js** file and add this event listener code to the end of the file:

```
                                        js/factors.js (excerpt)
self.addEventListener('message', function(event) {

  var factors = String(factorsOf(Number(event.data)));
  self.postMessage(factors);
  self.close();

}, false);
```

This will fire when the worker receives a message, occurring when the form is submitted. The number to be factorized is stored in the `event.data` property. We use the `factorsOf()` function to find the factors of the number; then convert it into a string and send a message back containing the answer. We then use the `close()` method to terminate the worker, since its work is done.

Now if we test the code out, it will still take a long time to factorize a long number, but the page will not freeze. You can also continue to change the background color while the factors are being calculated in the background.

Use a Server

The file containing the worker code is expected to be hosted on a server. This is the best option, but if you want to run an example locally you need to turn off the *same origin policy*[10] setting in the browser.

Shared Web Workers

The examples we have seen so far are known as **dedicated web workers**. These are linked to the script that loaded the worker and are unable to be used by another script. You can also create **shared web workers** that allow lots of different scripts on the same domain to access the same worker object. Read more about shared web workers at SitePoint.[11]

Web workers allow computationally complex operations to be performed in a separate thread, meaning that the flow of a program won't suffer interruptions and an application will not freeze or hang. They are a useful feature that help to keep sites

---

[10] https://developer.mozilla.org/en-US/docs/Same-origin_policy_for_file:_URIs

[11] http://www.sitepoint.com/javascript-shared-web-workers-html5/

responsive, even when complicated operations are being carried out. You can find more information about them at the Mozilla Developer Network.[12]

Multimedia

Before HTML5 it was notoriously difficult to display audio and video in browsers, and plugins such as Flash often had to be used. HTML5 introduced the `<audio>` and `<video>` tags used to insert audio and video clips into a web page. It also introduced a Media API for controlling the playback of the clips using JavaScript.

An audio clip can be inserted into a page with the `<audio>` tag, using the `src` attribute to point to the audio file:

```
<audio src="/song.mp3" controls>
  Your browser does not support the audio element.
</audio>
```

A video clip can be inserted with the `<video>` tag, using the `src` attribute to point to the movie file:

```
<video src="http://movie.mp4" controls>
  Your browser does not support the video element.
</video>
```

Any content inside the `<audio>` or `<video>` tags will only display if the browser does not support them; hence, it can be used to display a message to users of older browsers without support for these features. The `controls` attribute can be added (without any value) and will display the browser's native controls, such as play, pause, and volume control, as can be seen in the screenshot in Figure 14.4.

---

[12] https://developer.mozilla.org/en-US/docs/Web/Guide/Performance/Using_web_workers

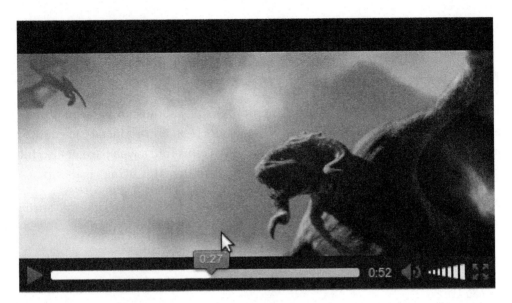

Figure 14.4. Browser video controls

The audio or video element can be referenced by a variable using one of the `document` methods we saw in Chapter 6:

```
video = document.getElementsByTagName("video")[0];
```

Audio and video elements have a number of properties and methods to control the playback of the clip.

The `play()` method will start the clip playing from its current position:

```
video.play();
```

The `pause()` method will pause the clip at its current position:

```
video.pause();
```

The `volume` property is a number that can be used to set the audio volume:

```
video.volume = 90;
```

The `muted` property is a Boolean value that can be used to mute the audio:

```
video.muted = true;
```

The `currentTime` property is a number value that can be used to jump to another part of the clip:

```
video.currentTime += 10; // jumps forward 10 seconds
```

The `playbackRate` property is used to fast-forward or rewind the clip by changing its value. A value of 1 is playback at normal speed:

```
video.playbackRate = 8; // fast-forward at 8 times as fast
```

The `loop` property is a Boolean value that can be set to `true` to make the clip repeat in a loop:

```
video.loop = true;
```

The `duration` property can be used to see how long the clip lasts:

```
video.duration;
<< 52.209
```

Audio and video clips also have a number of events that will fire when they occur, including:

- the `play` event, which fires when the clip starts and when it resumes after a pause

- the `pause` event, which fires when the clip is paused

- the `volumechange` event, which fires when the volume is changed

These events allow you to respond to any interactions the user has with the video. For example, the following event listener can be added to check whether the user has paused the video:

```
video.addEventListener("pause", function(event) {
    console.log("video has been paused"); }, false)
```

The audio and video elements bring native support for multimedia into the browser, and the API gives developers full control of the playback of audio tracks and video clips. You can learn much more about handling multimedia in HTML5 by reading *Jump Start HTML5: Multimedia* by Tiffany Brown.[13]

Other APIs

The list of APIs is constantly growing, and include APIs for accessing a device's camera, using WebSockets for multiple simultaneous connections, uploading files, accessing the battery status, handling push notifications, building drag and drop functionality, creating 3D effects with WebGL, and many more! A comprehensive list of HTML5 APIs can be found at the Mozilla Developer Network[14].

You can also read more about HTML5 standards and APIs in these SitePoint books:

- *Jump Start HTML5* by Tiffany Brown, Kerry Butters, and Sandeep Panda[15]

- *HTML5 and CSS3 for the Real World* by Alexis Goldstein, Louis Lazaris, and Estelle Weyl[16]

- *Jump Start HTML5: APIs* by Sandeep Panda[17]

Drawing with Canvas

The canvas element was introduced to allow graphics to be drawn onto a web page in real time using JavaScript. A canvas element is a rectangular element on the web page. It has a coordinate system that starts at (0,0) in the top-left corner. To add a canvas element to a page, the <canvas> tag is used specifying a height and width. Anything placed inside the tag will only display if the canvas element is unsupported:

---

[13] http://www.sitepoint.com/store/jump-start-html5-multimedia/
[14] https://developer.mozilla.org/en-US/docs/WebAP
[15] https://learnable.com/books/jump-start-html5
[16] https://learnable.com/books/html5-css3-for-the-real-world
[17] http://www.sitepoint.com/store/jump-start-html5-apis/

```
<canvas id="canvas" width="200" height="100">Sorry, but your
➥browswer does not support the canvas element</canvas>
```

This canvas can now be accessed in a JavaScript program using the `document.getElementById()` method:

```
var canvas = document.getElementById("canvas");
```

The next step is to access the **context** of the canvas. This is an object that contains all the methods used to draw onto the canvas. At the moment there's only a two-dimensional context, although there are plans to implement a three-dimensional context in the future. The `getContext()` method is used to access the context:

```
var context = canvas.getContext("2d");
```

Now we have a reference to the context, we can access its methods and draw onto the canvas. The fill and stroke colors can be changed by assigning a CSS color to the `fillStyle` and `strokeStyle` properties respectively:

```
context.fillStyle = "#0000cc"; // a blue fill color
context.strokeStyle = "#ccc"; // a gray stroke color
```

These colors will be utilized for everything that's drawn onto the canvas until they're changed.

The `lineWidth` property can be used to set the width of any line strokes drawn onto the canvas. It defaults to one pixel and remains the same until it's changed:

```
context.lineWidth = 4;
```

The `fillRect()` method can draw a filled-in rectangle. The first two parameters are the coordinates of the top-left corner, the third parameter is the width, and the last parameter is the height. The following produces a filled-in blue rectangle in the top-left corner of the canvas at coordinates (10,10) that is 100 pixels wide and 50 pixels high:

```
context.fillRect(10,10,100,50);
```

The strokeRect() method works in the same way, but produces a rectangle that is not filled in. This will draw the outline of a rectangle underneath the last one:

```
context.strokeRect(10,100,100,50);
```

Straight lines can be drawn employing the moveTo() and lineTo() methods. These methods can be used together to produce a path. Nothing will actually be drawn onto the canvas until the stroke() method is called. The following example will draw a thick red T shape onto the canvas by moving to the coordinates (150,50), then drawing a horizontal line 30 pixels long, and finally moving to the middle of that line and drawing a vertical line 40 pixels long:

```
context.beginPath();
context.moveTo(130, 50);
context.lineTo(180, 50);
context.moveTo(155, 50);
context.lineTo(155, 90);
context.strokeStyle = "#c00";
context.lineWidth = 15;
context.stroke();
```

The arc() method can be used to draw an arc of a given radius from a particular point. The first two parameters are the coordinates of the center of the arc; the next parameter is the radius, followed by the start angle, then the finish angle (note that these are measured in radians). The last parameter is a Boolean value that says whether the arc should be drawn counter-clockwise. The following example will draw a yellow circle of radius 30 pixels at center (200,200), since Math.PI * 2 represents a full turn:

```
context.arc(200, 200, 30, 0, Math.PI * 2, false);
context.strokeStyle = "#ff0";
context.lineWidth = 4;
context.stroke();
```

The fillText() method is used to write text onto the canvas. The first parameter is the text to be displayed, while the next two parameters are the x and y coordinates respectively. The font property can be used to set the font style used, otherwise the style is inherited from the `canvas` element's CSS setting (note that it needs to be changed *before* the `fillText()` method is used to draw the text). The following example will draw the text "Hello" in green at coordinates (20,50), as shown in Figure 14.5.

```
context.fillStyle = "#0c0"; // a blue fill color
context.font = "bold 26px sans-serif";
context.fillText("Hello", 20, 200);
```

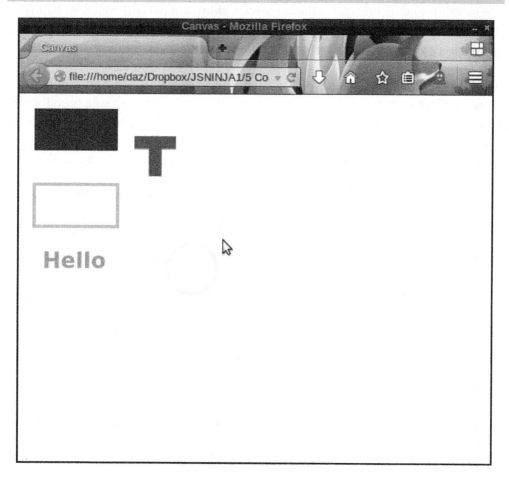

Figure 14.5. Drawing on a canvas

This is only a short introduction to what the `canvas` element can do. It is being used more and more in websites to draw data charts that are updated in real-time, as well as to animate HTML5 games. Much more information can be found in the excellent *Jump Start HTML5: Canvas and SVG* by Kerry Butters.[18]

Shims and Polyfills

HTML5 APIs progress at a rapid rate—new APIs are constantly being introduced and existing APIs often change. Modern browsers are very quick to update and implement many of the changes, but you can't always guarantee that users will have the most up-to-date browser. This is where a **shim** or a **polyfill** comes in handy. These are libraries of code that allow you to use the APIs as usual; they then fill in the necessary code that not provided natively by the user's browser.

The terms shim and polyfill are often used interchangeably. The main difference between them is that a shim is a piece of code that adds some missing functionality to a browser, although the implementation method may be differ slightly from the standard API. A polyfill is a shim that achieves the same functionality while also using the API commands that would be used if the feature was supported natively.

This means that as a ninja developer, your code can use the APIs as normal and it should work as expected in older browsers. The advantage here is that the same set of standard API commands can be used—you don't need to write additional code to deal with different levels of support. And when users update their browsers, the transition will be seamless as their experience will remain the same. Once you are confident that enough users have up-to-date browsers, you can remove the polyfill code without having to update any actual JavaScript code.

A comprehensive list of shims and polyfills is maintained by the Modernizr team.[19]

Quiz Ninja Project

We're going to use the Web Storage API to store the high score of the game. This will be stored locally even after the browser has been closed, so players can keep a record of their best attempt and try to beat it. To do this, we first add an extra paragraph to the header to show the high score. Add the following line between the score and `timer` paragraphs in the `<header>` element in **index.htm**:

---

[18] http://www.sitepoint.com/store/jump-start-html5-canvas-svg/
[19] https://github.com/Modernizr/Modernizr/wiki/HTML5-Cross-Browser-Polyfills

```
<p id="hiScore"></p>
```

Now we need to write a method of the Game.prototype object to update the high score. Add the following to the end of the Game constructor function::

```
Game.prototype.hiScore = function() {
  if(window.localStorage) {
    // the value held in localStorage is initally null so make it 0
    var hi = localStorage.getItem("hiScore") || 0;
    // check if the hi-score has been beaten and display a message
➥if it has
    if(this.score > hi || hi === 0) {
      localStorage.setItem("hiScore", this.score);
    }
    return localStorage.getItem("hiScore");
  }
}
```

This function checks to see if window.localStorage is supported first. If it is, it sets a local variable called hiScore to the value that's stored inside the object under the key hiScore. If a high score is yet to be set already, it will be null, so we'll initialize it to 0 in this case. Next, we check to see if the score that's provided as an argument to the function is bigger than the current high score that we just retrieved. If it is, we show a message to congratulate the player, and also update the value stored in localStorage using the setItem() method.

Have a go at playing it by opening up **index.htm**, as shown in Figure 14.6, and try to get a new high score.

Figure 14.6. Our quiz with high scores

Summary

In this chapter, we've learned the following:

- HTML5 is the latest incarnation of the Hypertext Markup Language. It covers a variety of technologies, including several APIs that are accessible using JavaScript.

- `data-` attributes help to embed custom data into a web page that can then be used to enhance the user experience with JavaScript.

- The Web Storage API allows key-value pairs to be stored on the user's device in a similar way to cookies, but without the same storage restrictions.

- The Geolocation API allows you to access the geographic coordinates of the user's device, as long as the user gives permission.

- The Web Worker API can be used to perform computationally intensive tasks in the background, which helps to avoid websites becoming unresponsive.

- The `<audio>` and `<video>` elements can be employed to embed audio tracks and video clips in a web page. They also have aMedia API that can help control the playback using JavaScript.

- The `canvas` element can be used to dynamically draw geometric shapes, fonts, and images on a web page in real-time using JavaScript.

- A shim or polyfill is a piece of code that adds support of missing features to older browsers.

In the next chapter, we'll cover how to organize and optimize your code.

Organizing Your Code

As you build more and more complex JavaScript projects, you'll find the amount of code you are using increases into hundreds and then thousands of lines. This can be difficult to manage without some sort of organizing. The first step is to break the code into separate files, but this presents its own problems, such as how to include all the files on a web page and which code to put in which files. Indeed, how do you ensure that a file has access to the code in another file?

Just as real-life ninjas have lots of nifty weapons such as nunchakus and shuriken stars, there are lots of cool tools that a JavaScript ninja can use to help organize code and make it run more efficiently. In this chapter, we'll look at the various frameworks and tools that can be employed to improve the quality of your code. In turn it will make it more organized and easier to maintain, promoting reuse. We'll also look at how to make your applications ready for production.

In this chapter, we'll cover the following topics:

▓ frameworks

▓ using modules

- MVC libraries such as Backbone.js, AngularJS, and CanJS

- template libraries such as Mustache, Jade, Underscore, Handlebars, EJS, and Hogan

- optimizing your code with minification

- build processes using Grunt and Gulp

- our project—create a build process, employ templates, and use MVC architecture

Frameworks

A **framework** is a library of JavaScript code that provides several methods that make it easier to achieve common tasks. JavaScript is an extremely flexible language that can accomplish most programming tasks ... but not all undertakings are as easy to do as they should be. A framework will abstract functionality into easier-to-use functions and methods. These can then be used to achieve common assignments without having to use lots of repetitive code.

DOM Manipulation Example

A good example of how frameworks can help save time is in DOM manipulation. The DOM API provides all the tools required to manipulate the DOM, but some can be verbose and take several lines of code to attain even the most basic of tasks.

For example, if we wanted to add a class to a paragraph element stored in the variable para, then append another paragraph on the end, we could do it using the following:

```
para.classList.add("important");
var newPara = document.createElement("p");
newPara.textContent = "Another Paragraph";
para.appendChild(newPara);
```

Yet by using the jQuery framework, we can achieve the same result using a single line of code:

```
$(para).addClass("important").append("<p>Another Paragraph</p>");
```

So you can see how using a framework can reduce the amount of code you have to write, as well as making common tasks easier to implement.

jQuery

jQuery is the most popular of all the JavaScript frameworks used today, as seen in these statistics on W3Techs[1] and Built With.[2] It is used in a huge number of commercial websites and has a plugin system that makes it easy to build common web page elements, such as a lightbox or carousel widget.

jQuery was released in 2006, originally as a DOM manipulation framework. It has grown into a bigger framework today that now provides methods for selecting nodes and traversing the DOM, animation effects, Ajax, and events. It also has its own testing framework: QUnit[3].

jQuery is a very powerful and polished framework that provides a considerable number of useful methods. It has become so popular that many online tutorials assume that you're using jQuery rather than just JavaScript. You can learn more about jQuery by reading the excellent *jQuery: Novice to Ninja: New Kicks and Tricks*[4] by Earle Castledine and Craig Sharkie.[5]

The $ Symbol

The jQuery framework uses the $ symbol as a global namespace object. It is actually a convenient alias for the the global `jQuery` object of which all jQuery's methods are methods. This prevents the global scope from being polluted with any of jQuery's methods. Other frameworks use the $ sign in a a similar way since only a single character is needed to access any methods; however, this can cause method name clashes if more than one of them are used in the same project.

---

[1] http://w3techs.com/technologies/overview/javascript_library/all
[2] http://trends.builtwith.com/javascript/jQuery
[3] http://qunitjs.com/
[4] http://www.sitepoint.com/store/jquery-novice-to-ninja-new-kicks-and-tricks/
[5] http://www.sitepoint.com/store/jquery-novice-to-ninja-new-kicks-and-tricks/

Advantages and Disadvantages of Frameworks

A big advantage of utilizing a popular library is that it will be used by lots of people and thoroughly tested. It will probably have been optimized and battle-tested for nearly every eventuality. Using a framework means that you can be confident that your code will be as bullet-proof as possible in many browsers. In addition, there will usually be lots of online documentation and a strong community ready to help out if you become stuck. The popularity of frameworks often means that others will have encountered the same problem as you, often making it easy to find a solution by searching on the Internet.

There are some disadvantages to using frameworks, however. You need to include the code for the framework as well as your own code. This increases the amount of code that needs to be downloaded by a website, which in some cases can cause performance issues. Thankfully, most modern frameworks are relatively small once server-side optimizations are made (such as gzip compression), minimizing any latency issues. Another problem with frameworks is that it might fail to implement the functionality in the precise way that you want it to perform. This might not be a problem, but sometimes you'll have to get your hands dirty and write your own functions in order to achieve the functionality for which you are looking. Using a framework can also make your code slower than using plain vanilla JavaScript. This is because there are often more lines of code in using the abstracted functions in a framework rather than writing a direct implementation in just JavaScript, which is "closer to the metal," so to speak. These speed differences can be barely noticeable, although there are occasions when using a framework is a poor choice for some operations. Using plain JavaScript can be significantly faster than a framework, as seen in these examples in this post by Craig Buckler.[6]

The debate about whether to use a framework or not is a big one that stretches back to the start of programming and refuses to go away. Indeed, there has been a movement towards using plain JavaScript in recent years. Additionally, the Vanilla JS[7] website showcases plain JavaScript as if it were a framework, highlighting that many tasks can be accomplished with a similar amount of code but much better performance.

---

[6] http://www.sitepoint.com/jquery-vs-raw-javascript-1-dom-forms/
[7] http://vanilla-js.com/

You only need to look at any professionally produced website to see that some sort of framework has been used in its production. Frameworks are often the pragmatic choice to complete a project in a realistic time frame, especially when working in a large team. They can also be useful in supporting older browsers, and when performance isn't the most important factor (when prototyping sites, for example).

When to Use a Framework

It can be helpful to use a framework, but you should certainly question whether it's worth the extra work. You have to learn the framework's notation, which can either be similar or very different to standard JavaScript. Every framework you use will add to the total file size that's downloaded so you need to assess whether the extra overhead is worth it.

It's also advisable to consider that the popularity of frameworks is in a constant state of flux, meaning they can be "here today, gone tomorrow." Some of the most popular frameworks of the past have fallen out of favor and lost support, even discontinued. This can potentially cause problems if you've relied on one particular framework in most of your projects.

Many frameworks have become monolithic, with a plethora of methods that try to do everything. An example of this is jQuery; while it is a useful framework, it provides lots of features that are often unnecessary. If you find that you're not using many of the methods a framework offers, you should consider using a lighter alternative that only focuses on solving one problem (some suggestions are given below). And if you're only using a handful of methods, maybe avoid using a framework altogether and try using plain old JavaScript. You could even package useful functions you have created together and produce your own personal framework.

Some Useful Frameworks

It is certainly worth considering using a framework to make some common tasks easier. Below is a list of popular frameworks and the tasks with which they can assist:

- Query selectors: Qwery,[8] jQuery[9]

---

[8] https://github.com/ded/qwery
[9] http://jquery.com/

- DOM manipulation: jQuery,[10] Bonzo[11]

- Cookie handling: Jar,[12] CookieJS,[13] Easy Cookie[14]

- Testing: Jasmine,[15] Mocha,[16] QUnit[17]

- Events: Hammer[18] (touch events only), Bean[19]

- Ajax: reqwest,[20] jQuery,[21] Bull,[22] MicroAjax[23]

- Animation and graphics: KineticJS,[24] Move.js,[25] jsAnim,[26] Raphael[27]

- Functional programming: underscore[28]

In addition, JSDB[29] is a website that features a large number of high-quality JavaScript libraries and frameworks, while MicroJS[30] is a high-quality repository of small JavaScript libraries that focus on specific tasks.

Be careful not to rely on a framework and find that you're learning the framework rather than the language. A framework should not be used because of a lack of understanding JavaScript; instead, it should be used to speed up JavaScript develop-

---

[10] http://jquery.com/
[11] https://github.com/ded/bonzo
[12] https://github.com/amccollum/jar
[13] http://www.codephun.com/cookiejs-small-javascript-cookie-framework/
[14] http://pablotron.org/software/easy_cookie/
[15] http://jasmine.github.io/
[16] http://mochajs.org/
[17] http://qunitjs.com/
[18] http://hammerjs.github.io/
[19] https://github.com/fat/bean
[20] https://github.com/ded/reqwest
[21] http://jquery.com/
[22] http://sourceforge.net/projects/bull/
[23] https://code.google.com/p/microajax/
[24] http://kineticjs.com/
[25] http://visionmedia.github.io/move.js/
[26] http://jsanim.com/
[27] http://raphaeljs.com/
[28] http://underscorejs.org/
[29] http://www.jsdb.io/
[30] http://microjs.com/

ment by making it easier to complete common tasks. Using a library can sometimes make your code more sloppy; it's easy, for example, to write short jQuery expressions that look concise but are spectacularly inefficient. And even if you do choose to use a framework or library, remember that a ninja should always be inquisitive as to how things work. In fact, reading a framework's source code is a great way of learning some powerful JavaScript programming techniques.

Modules

A **module** is a self-contained piece of code that provides functions and methods that can then be used in other files. This helps to keep code organized in separate, reusable files, which improves code maintainability. The code in a module should have a single purpose and group together functions with distinct functionality. For example, you might keep any functions used for Ajax in their own module. This could then be used in any projects where Ajax was required. Keeping code modular helps to make it more *loosely coupled* and interchangeable, meaning you can easily swap one module for another without affecting other parts of a project. Indeed, small single-purpose modules are the exact opposite of large monolithic frameworks as they enable developers to use only the modules that are needed, avoiding any wasted code.

 Tightly And Loosely Coupled

The **coupling** of code refers to how dependent cetain elements or modules of code are on each other. Two pieces of code are said to be tightly coupled if one relies on the other to run. This often occurs if a piece of code makes hard coded references to another piece of code, requiring it to be used. This will often mean that changes to one piece of code will necessitate changes in the other. On the other hand, two pieces of code are said to loosely coupled if one piece of code can be easily substituted by another without affecting the final outcome. This is often achieved by referring to common methods (often provided in an API) that are used by many different pieces of code. It is considered good design to keep code as loosely coupled as possible as this allows for the most flexibilty in developing sytems of code as different modules can be used independently and in a variety of different applications, rather than being restricted to a single use-case.

When you start to use more and more modules, you'll find that some modules depend on other modules to work. These are known as **dependencies**. Dependency management is the process of ensuring that all the dependencies a module requires are met. This can be difficult to do manually once a project becomes large.

JavaScript lacks a built-in way of creating modules,[31] but it is possible to create modules using the tools that JavaScript provides. A popular way of doing this is using Christian Heilmann's Revealing Module pattern[32]. This uses an IIFE to return the module as an object that's stored in a global variable. This keeps the module in its own private namespace (the variable it is assigned to), which helps stop any methods from clashing with other methods having the same name.

For example, we could create a `Stats` module based on the `sum()`, `mean()`, and `standardDeviation()` functions we created in Chapter 11:

```
var Stats = (function() {
  "use strict";

  // square and sum are private functions
  function square(x) {
    return x * x;
  }

  function sum(array, callback) {
    if (typeof callback === "function") {
      array = array.map(callback);
    }
    return array.reduce(function(a,b) { return a + b; });
  }

  function mean(array) {
    return sum(array) / array.length;
  }

  function sd(array) {
    return sum(array,square) / array.length - square(mean(array));
  }

  // public functions are exported as methods of an object
  return {
    mean: mean,
```

---

[31] This will change in the next version, see Chapter 16.
[32] http://christianheilmann.com/2007/08/22/again-with-the-module-pattern-reveal-something-to-the-world/

```
    standardDeviation: sd
  };
}());
```

This function will return an object that's assigned to the variable `Stats`. It has two public methods, `mean()` and `standardDeviation()`. The module also has two private functions, `square()` and `sum()`, that are not returned, so are not publicly available to the module (they are just used internally by other methods). The public methods are called using the `Stats` object:

```
Stats.mean([1,2,3]);
<< 2

Stats.standardDeviation([1,2,3]);
<< 0.666666666666667
```

To use a module in a web page, include the file in which it's saved in script tags on the page:

```
<script src="stats.js"></script>
<script src="scripts.js"></script>
```

Two standard ways of implementing JavaScript modules have emerged: the CommonJS Module pattern and the Asynchronous Module Definition pattern. Unfortunately, these patterns are incompatible with each other. An example of each follows, where they are both capable of keeping modules in their own namespace, and adding multiple methods as well as submodules and dependencies on other modules.

CommonJS Modules

CommonJS Modules have a compact syntax that is designed for synchronous loading. It is how modules are implemented in Node.js.

A module is created in a separate file and the `module.exports` method is used to make any functions available to other files. For example, we could create a module for the `random()` function that we created in Chapter 11 by first placing the following code in a file called **random.js**:

```
module.exports = function(a,b) {
  if(b===undefined) b = a, a = 1; // if only one argument is
➥supplied, assume the lower limit is 1
  return Math.floor((b-a+1) * Math.random()) + a;
}
```

This is simply the `random()` function written as an anonymous function that's assigned to `module.exports` as if it was a variable.

To use the module, it needs to then be required inside the main **scripts.js** file. This is done using the `require()` method, and takes the file that contains the module as an argument and returns the function that was exported:

```
var random = require('./random');
```

The function that was exported in the module is now assigned to the variable `random`, which is then used to call the function:

```
random(6);
<< 4
```

Asynchronous Module Definitions

Asynchronous Module Definitions (AMD) modules are most commonly used by RequireJS,[33] which is a file and module loader designed for use in the browser. The AMD module syntax is slightly more complicated than the CommonJS module, but it's designed to support asynchronous loading of any modules and their dependencies.

AMD modules are written in a separate file and provided as an argument to the `define()` function. The following code is an example of how the `random()` function would be defined as an AMD module in a file called **random.js**:

```
define({
    random: function (a, b) {
        if (b===undefined) b = a, a = 1; // if only one argument
➥is supplied, assume the lower limit is 1
```

---

[33] http://requirejs.org/

```
        return Math.floor((b - a + 1) * Math.random()) + a;
    }
});
```

The same process is used to require the module as in the Common JS Module syntax. This code would be placed in the main `scripts.js` file:

```
var random = require('./random');
```

To use Require.js, you only need to use a single `<script>` tag in your HTML file:

```
<script data-main="js/scripts.js" src="lib/require.js"></script>
```

This uses a `data-` attribute to specify the name of the main JavaScript file to be loaded first. Inside this script you can configure Require.js and also use the `requireJS()` function to require any modules:

```
requirejs.config({
    //Any configuration goes in here
});

requirejs(['jquery', 'random']);
```

Package Managers

As modules have become more widely used in JavaScript, there's been a need for tools to manage them. Package managers help to organize code into modules. They can also handle dependency management between modules.

Browserify

A tool that uses the CommonJS Module pattern is Browserify.[34] It can be used to package your own modules or third-party modules downloaded and installed using the Node Package Manager (npm). It creates a single *bundle* file requiring all the necessary modules, including any dependencies. This means that you can organize all your code into separate modules, but only need add one bundle file in your HTML file:

---

[34] http://browserify.org/

```
<script src="bundle.js"></script>
```

npm packages normally require Node.js to run, but Browserify can also be used to compile npm packages into code that runs in a browser. Any of the popular libraries of code available as npm packages can be used in web-based projects. Note that to do this, you'll need to install Node.js and the npm package manager on your own machine.

 Node Package Manager

If you install Node.js[35] (which is increasingly useful to do as a modern JavaScript developer), the Node Package Manager will be included in the installation. This is thepackage manager for installing modules written in Node.js. It includes a huge number of modules that can be used for a variety of tasks.

Browserify makes it much easier to use popular frameworks such as jQuery. Instead of downloading the framework code and then adding a script tag in the HTML file, all you need to do is install jQuery on your system using npm and the following line in a terminal:

```
npm install jquery
```

Then it can be included in any project by using a `require` statement at the start of any file that uses jQuery. For example, the following line will include the jQuery library in the bundle file that Browserify creates:

```
var $ = require('jquery');
```

More information about getting started with Browserify can be found in this post by Patrick Catanzariti.[36]

Bower

Bower is a package manager,[37] developed by Twitter, that can be used for managing versions of libraries employed in a project. Installed Bower using npm:

---

[35] http://nodejs.org/download/

[36] http://www.sitepoint.com/getting-started-browserify

[37] http://bower.io/

```
bower install jquery
```

You can also install a specific version of a package:

```
bower install jquery#1.11.1
```

And keep these packages up to date:

```
bower update
```

All Bower packages have a **bower.json** specification file that outlines the package's dependencies; for example, the backbone package depends on the underscore package. So if you were to install Backbone, Bower will automatically install Underscore as a dependency.

Ender

Ender[38] is a package manager created by Dustin Diaz that can install packages and manage dependencies. It lets you select just the packages you require and then mix and match them into a custom-built framework containing only the functionality needed. All the methods from the different frameworks and modules are all put together under the $ namespace, so any methods can be called using the $ notation, just like using jQuery.

Ender is also installed using npm, so it requires Node.js to run. Once it has been installed, you can use it to build a normal and minified file containing all the modules and frameworks you specify; these will all be installed locally along with any dependencies.

MVC Libraries

Model-View-Controller (MVC) is a design pattern that's been used for a long time in server-side languages. It is a common way of designing software and used by server-side frameworks such as Ruby on Rails and Django. In recent years it has been used in JavaScript code to make it easier to organize large-scale web applications.

---

[38] http://enderjs.com/

MVC separates an application into three distinct, independent components that interact with each other, as shown in Figure 15.1:

- **Models** are objects that implement the functionality for creating, reading, updating, and deleting (known as CRUD tasks), specific pieces of information about the application, as well as any other associated logic and behavior. In a to-do list application, for example, there would be a task model providing methods to access all the information about the tasks such as names, due dates, and completed tasks. This data will often be stored in a database or some other container.

- **Views** provide a visual representation of the model showing all the relevant information. In a web application, this would be the HTML displayed on a web page. Views also provide a way for users to interact with an application, usually via forms. In a to-do list application, the views would display the tasks as an HTML list with check boxes that a user could tick to say a task had been completed.

- **Controllers** link models and views together by communicating between them. They respond to events, which are usually inputs from a user (entering some data into a form, for example), process the information, and then update the model and view accordingly. In a to-do list application, the controller functions would respond to the event of a user clicking on a check box and then inform the model that a task had been completed. The model would then update the information about that task.

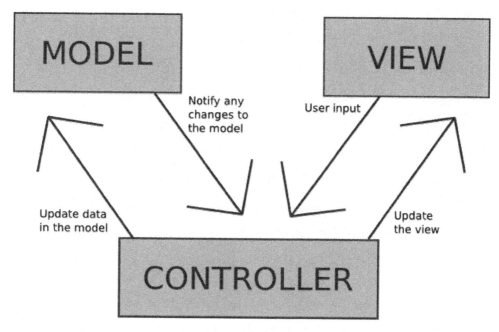

Figure 15.1. The MVC architecture

 MV*

It is quite common to see the acronym MV* used to describe JavaScript frameworks, rather than MVC. This is because many JavaScript implementations do not strictly follow the controller pattern. Sometimes controller code is mixed into the views, and sometimes other patterns are used such as Model-View-Presenter (MVP), Model-View-ViewModel (MVVM), and Angular, which calls itself a Model-View-Whatever (MVW) framework. These tend to be only slight variations on the MVC pattern, but for simplicity MV* is used as a catch-all term.

A Quick List Example

Here's an example of how the MVC architecture can be implemented using JavaScript. It will be a simple list creator that allows the user to add items to a list by entering them into a form field.

To start, create a folder called **MVC** and save the following as **list.htm**:

```
                                                              list.htm
<!doctype html>
<html lang="en">
<head>
  <meta charset="utf-8">
  <title>MVC List</title>
</head>
<body>
    <form id="input">
      <label for="name">Name:</label>
      <input type="text" name="name" autofocus required >
      <button type="submit">Submit</button>
    </form>
    <ul id="list"></ul>
    <script src="js/scripts.js"></script>
</body>
</html>
```

This is a basic HTML5 web page containing a form with a single input field for entering a list item. It also contains an empty <ul> element in which to place the list items. Now we need to create the JavaScript file. Create a file called **scripts.js** inside a folder called **js**.

In JavaScript, a model is often represented by a constructor function that can create new instances of an object. This will keep track of any properties the list item has, as well as any methods. In this example, we'll create an Item() constructor function that only has a name property provided as an argument to the constructor function. Add this code to **scripts.js**:

```
                                                    js/scripts.js (excerpt)
"use strict"

function Item(name) {
  this.name = name;
}
```

Each new list item that is created will be an instance of this constructor function.

Next we'll create a controller object. This will be responsible for adding an event listener to the form to see when the user adds information. When this happens, it will create a new instance of the model and then render the updated view. Add the following code to **scripts.js**:

js/scripts.js *(excerpt)*

```
controller = {
  watch: function(form) {
    form.addEventListener("submit", function(event){
      event.preventDefault(); // prevent the form from being
➥submitted
      this.add(form.name.value);
    }.bind(this), false); // binding this to the controller instead
➥of the form
  },

  add: function(name) {
    var item = new Item(name);
    view.render(item);
  }
}
```

After this we create a view object with a render() method. This is used to produce an HTML fragment that shows the instance's name (from the name property stored in the model). It is dynamically inserted into the list using DOM API methods. Add the following code to the **scripts.js** file:

js/scripts.js *(excerpt)*

```
view = {
  render: function(item) {
    var list = document.getElementById("list");
    var li = document.createElement("li");
    li.textContent = item.name;
    list.appendChild(li);
  }
}
```

Finally, we have to call the watch() method of the controller. This keeps an eye on the form and checks when it is submitted. Add the following line to the end of the **scripts.js** file:

js/scripts.js *(excerpt)*

```
controller.watch(document.getElementById("input"));
```

Open up **list.htm** in your browser and have a go at adding some items to the list. It should look a little like the screenshot shown in Figure 15.2.

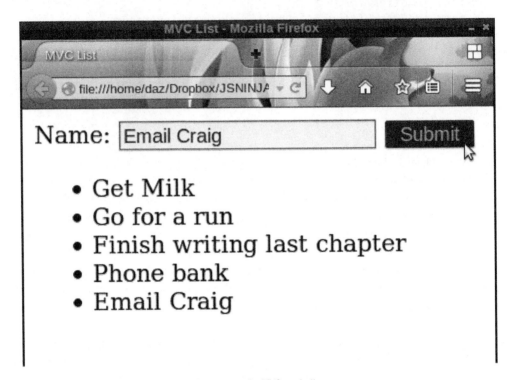

Figure 15.2. An MVC to-do list

This is just a small and simple example of the MVC pattern to give an idea of how it works. In reality the model would contain many more properties and methods; the controller would also contain more methods for editing and deleting instances of the model. There's also likely to be more views to display the different states of the model, and there would need to be more robust code used in order for the controller to monitor the changes that may happen in the views. Most MVC implementations also tend to be more generalized in their implementation and avoid hard coding details about which elements are being updated on the page (such as the reference to the "list" id in the example). Despite this, I hope the example demonstrates how to separate code into the three distinct components of MVC.

Saving Data

Most web applications will need some form of **persistence** to save the information held in the models in order to maintain state. This could be done using the Web Storage API that we covered in the last chapter. Another option that's often used in real-world applications is to send a JSON representation of the model to a back-end database using Ajax whenever a model changes.

MVC Frameworks

MVC can take a lot of code to implement, and many frameworks have emerged that take care of much of the setup code for you. One of the main features of MVC frameworks is **data binding,** which is the process of linking the model and view together. As a result, a large amount of boilerplate controller code is not needed as the framework takes care of it all in the background for you. **One-way data binding** is when a change in the model will automatically result in the view being updated, and **two-way data binding** is when a change in the view automatically updates the model.

These methods are often accessed by a user via **routes** using the hashtag notation. The controller will look for anything after a hashtag in a URL for information about what to do. For example, the URL http://ninjatasks.com/user/23#add might be used to add a task, whereas the URL http://ninjatasks.com/user/23#edit-task32 would be used to edit the task with an id of 32.

The views are simply web pages written in HTML, although it is common to use templating languages so that dynamic data can be inserted into the page (more about these in the section that follows):

▣ Ember[39] is a framework designed to make building large web applications easier. It does this by using common conventions that avoid the need for lots of set-up code, though it can become more difficult if you don't follow these conventions.

▣ AngularJS[40] is a powerful framework by Google to make creating dynamic web applications easier. This is done by extending the HTML language using custom ng- attributes.

---

[39] http://emberjs.com/
[40] https://angularjs.org/

■ CanJS[41] is a fast and lightweight framework that supports live data-binding.

■ Backbone.js[42] is a lightweight MVC framework created by Jeremy Ashkenas. It is less opinionated about how to perform tasks, making it quite flexible, but it often requires more code to achieve what could be done in a few lines in other frameworks.

The website TodoMVC[43] has lots of examples of to-do list applications written in many of the popular MVC frameworks.

Templates

Many MVC frameworks use **templating languages** to insert dynamic data into the page. Templating languages can be written in HTML or another language, such as markdown, that compiles into HTML. They can be whole web pages, but are often just **partials**—parts of a page. This means that the application can update part of the page without having to make a request to the server, saving an HTTP request. This is usually done by dynamically inserting the fragment of HTML into the DOM.

Templating languages allow HTML to be separated from the JavaScript program, making maintenance easier because they are no longer tightly coupled. The templates are often stored in separate files or inside their own script tags, so they can be reused and quickly edited in one place if changes need to be made. It also means that inserting large strings of HTML into a document (which can have adverse effects on performance) is avoided. All that is needed is a reference to the relevant file that contains the template.

Templating languages often have a mechanism for inserting dynamic data into the HTML. These tend to fall into two camps: placing dynamic code inside curly braces (the "mustache" symbol) or inside the special <% %> tags made popular by Embedded Ruby (ERB).

For example, Mustache and Handlebars would use this to insert the value of the variable name into a heading tag:

```
<h1>Hello {{ name }}</h1>
```

Underscore and EJS, on the other hand, would use the following to achieve the same result:

```
<h1>Hello <%= name %></h1>
```

Templating languages also enable you to insert basic programming logic into views, allowing you to conditionally show different messages or use loops to show multiple pieces of similar code.

For example, say we wanted to display the following array of to-do objects:

```
var tasks = [
   { name: "Get Milk" },
   { name: "Go for a run" },
   { name: "Finish writing last chapter" },
   { name: "Phone bank" },
   { name: "Email Craig" }
]
```

Mustache implements "logic-less" templates that don't require any lines of logic to be explicitly written in JavaScript; instead, it is inferred from the context. This is how it would iterate over the `task` array to display a list of tasks:

```
<ul>
{{#tasks}}
  <li>{{name}}</li>
{{/task}}
</ul>
```

EJS uses more explicit JavaScript coding to achieve the same result. Each line of JavaScript code is placed inside the special `<% %>` tags. If any values need to be evaluated, they are placed inside `<%= %>` instead:

```
<ul>
<% tasks.forEach(function(task) { %>
<li><%= task.name %></li>
```

```
<% }); %>
</ul>
<% } %>>
```

Both of these templates would return this HTML code:

```
<ul>
  <li>Get Milk</li>
  <li>Go for a run</li>
  <li>Finish writing last chapter</li>
  <li>Phone bank</li>
  <li>Email Craig</li>
</ul>
```

There are a number of popular templating languages to choose from, a selection of some of the most popular are shown in the list below:

- Handlebars[44]
- Jade[45]
- Underscore[46]
- EJS[47]
- Hogan[48]
- Mustache[49]
- Nunjucks[50]
- React[51]

Web Components

The W3C are working on developing a standard called *Web Components* that attempts to extend HTML and introduce new features such as templates, custom tags, the ability to import HTML partials, and a shadow DOM. The idea is to use

---

[44] http://handlebarsjs.com/
[45] https://github.com/jadejs/jade
[46] http://underscorejs.org/
[47] http://www.embeddedjs.com/
[48] https://github.com/twitter/hogan.js
[49] https://github.com/janl/mustache.js
[50] http://mozilla.github.io/nunjucks/
[51] http://facebook.github.io/react/

it to develop modular and self-contained components that can be reused in different applications. An example of implementing these standards is the Polymer project,[52] allowing anything from small widgets to a full application to be developed. Web Components is a fast moving area of development that is likely to be used much more in developing web applications.

Minification

Minification is the process of removing any unnecessary characters from your code to reduce the file size. This includes all comments, whitespace, and other characters that are superfluous.

Tools are available to do this, known as *minifiers*. Some popular choices include:

- YUI Compressor[53]
- Google's Closure[54]
- UglifyJS[55]

These tools can also change variable and function names to single letters. This is often referred to as **code obfuscation** as it can make the code more difficult to read. They will also try to employ optimizations to make the code run faster. For example, here is the Stats module that we created earlier in the chapter after it is minified using UglifyJS:

```
var Stats=function(){function e(e){return e*e}function t(e,t){if(typ
➥eof t==="function"){e=e.map(t)}return e.reduce(function(e,t){retur
➥n e+t})}function n(e){return t(e)/e.length}function r(r){return t(
➥r,e)/r.length-e(n(r))}return{mean:n,standardDeviation:r}}()
```

As you can see, it is significantly smaller in size, but much more difficult to read and make sense of!

Minifying your code can have a major effect on the overall size of your files, making them download and run faster. It also means that your code can use descriptive naming conventions and be well-commented, as these will be stripped away by the

---

[52] https://www.polymer-project.org/

[53] https://www.npmjs.org/package/yui

[54] https://developers.google.com/closure/compiler/

[55] https://github.com/mishoo/UglifyJS

minifier tools. As a general rule, you should aim to use well-commented and descriptive code in development and minified code in production (since there is no need for end users to read comments).

Files can also be compressed on the server using a file-compression tool such as gzip, which can have a dramatic effect reducing the file size. Using both minification and compression in production means that JavaScript files are a mere fraction of their original size, making them much quicker to download.

Task Runners

A **task runner** is a piece of software that automates tasks that can be tiresome to carry out by hand. These include the following tasks:

- minifying code

- linting

- testing code

- compiling modules into a single file

- compiling CSS preprocessor files (such as Sass, Less, or Stylus) into standard CSS files

Grunt

Probably the most popular task runner at the time of writing is Grunt.[56] It can be used for a variety of tasks and has a plugin system, so many common tasks are already available to use as plugins. Grunt needs Node.js to run and is installed using npm with this line of code:

```
npm install grunt -g
```

Note that the `-g` flag is used to install Grunt globally, makings it available in all projects on your system. It can be run using `grunt` rather than `node grunt`.

---

[56] http://gruntjs.com/

npm will also require a **package.json** file. This is a configuration file that lists all the npm packages required to run the task, including Grunt itself. A basic **package.json** file can be created using the `npm init` command. Here is an example of a **package.json** file:

```
{
  "name": "ninja project",
  "version": "1.0.0",
  "devDependencies": {
    "grunt": "~0.4.5",
    "grunt-contrib-uglify": "~0.5.0"
  }
}
```

A Grunt file is then needed to create a custom task. This contains all the configuration for the task to be completed and is always saved as **Gruntfile.js**. The following example shows a Grunt file that can be used to create a default task; this will minify any JavaScript files in the **src** folder and output the minified files into the **js** folder.

It uses the uglify plugin[57] to minify the code. All Grunt files are placed inside a wrapper function that uses the CommonJS Module `exports` syntax:

```
module.exports = function(grunt) {
  // configuration goes at the start
  grunt.initConfig({
    pkg: grunt.file.readJSON('package.json'),
  uglify: {
    build: {
      src: 'src/*.js', // where to find the JavaScript files to
➡minify
      dest: 'js/' // where to put the minified files
    }
  }
  // These methods will load and register the tasks to do
  grunt.loadNpmTasks('grunt-contrib-uglify');
  grunt.registerTask('default', ['uglify']);

};
```

---

[57] https://www.npmjs.org/package/grunt-contrib-uglify

To run the default task, simply enter the following command in a terminal:

```
grunt
```

Gulp

Gulp[58]is another task runner that appeared more recently than Grunt, but is gaining in popularity. gulp also requires Node.js to run and is installed using npm. It also has its own plugin system, although there are fewer plugins available than for Grunt.

Gulp uses a **package.json** file and a Gulp file (which is always saved as **gulpfile.js**) to create tasks, but it uses a different notation to the Grunt file. Gulp uses code to accomplish tasks, rather than configuration as Grunt does. Gulp works by using the concept of streams of data provided from files that are piped from one plugin to the next, where the end result is piped to a given destination. For example, the minification plugin will take a stream of files from the **src** folder and pipe them into the minifier, which will then pipe the minified code into a folder called **js**. This means it can run faster than Grunt, as intermediary files don't need to be created.

Gulp tries to keep its plugins streamlined so that they only complete a single task. As a result more plugins are often needed to accomplish a set of tasks. Gulp also has the ability to watch files using the `gulp.watch()` method. This will watch a file or collection of files and run a function whenever a file changes. This can be useful if you want to, for example, automatically run tests as soon as any file changes to quickly spot any errors.

The following is an example of a Gulp file that can be used to minify a group of files. It uses the `gulp-minify` plugin, which uses UglifyJS to minify any JavaScript files that are in the **src** directory:

```
var gulp = require('gulp'), // requires gulp
    minify = require('gulp-minify'); // loads the minify plugin

var
  source = 'src/*', // this specifies where the source files are
  dest = 'js/'; // this specifies the destination of the output

gulp.task('default', function(){
```

---

[58] http://gulpjs.com/

```
    gulp.src(source) // the stream to read
    .pipe(minify()) // pipe the stream to the minify plugin
    .pipe(gulp.dest('./js/')); // where the stream is written to
});
```

To run this default task, enter the following command in a terminal:

```
gulp
```

At the time of writing, Grunt is the most popular task runner and has more documentation and plugins available. Gulp is gaining popularity due to its leaner and more concise syntax. Additionally, there are alternatives available, such as Broccoli[59] and Brunch,[60] and there are sure to be more popping up in the future.

Deploying JavaScript

When it comes to deploying your JavaScript program, it's time to think about optimizing the code. If you've used multiple external libraries and lots of modules, you might have a large number of files that need to be included in your HTML file. One way of doing this is to simply include a different `<script>` tag for each JavaScript file; however, this is not optimal for a number of reasons:

- the scripts must be included in the correct order
- each file represents a separate request to the server
- the files will be large

The solution is to combine all the scripts into a single minified and compressed file. There are a number ways to achieve this, some of which we have already looked at in this chapter. You can use a package manager such as Bower, Ender, or Browserify to deal with dependency management; Browserify will also bundle everything together into a single file for you. Alternatively, you can use Grunt or Gulp to automate the process of bundling the files together and minifying them at the same time. There are a number of options that will do this for you on the server side as well.

---

[59] https://github.com/broccolijs/broccoli
[60] http://brunch.io/

Once you've combined all the files into a single file, then minified and compressed it, adding it to the HTML file is the next step. The optimal position for the `<script>` tag is right at the end of the page just before the closing `<body>` tag, which we have used in all our examples:

```
<!doctype html>
<html lang="en">
  <head>
    <meta charset="utf-8">
    <title>Ninja JavaScript</title>
  </head>
  <body>


    ...


    <script src="js/scripts.js"></script>
  </body>
</html>
```

This will ensure that the page has finished loading before the JavaScript code is processed.

If you have a large amount of JavaScript (even after minification), there are further optimizations that can be made such as lazy loading and preloading. **Lazy loading** is the process of loading just the critical code that will be needed right away, then loading any other code later by dynamically inserting another script tag into the DOM. **Preloading** is the process of loading any code that might be required on future pages. This way, the code will have already been downloaded by the time the user visits the relevant page.

Quiz Ninja Project

We'll now put some of the ideas we've learned in this chapter into practice in our quiz project. Our first task is to move all the view logic into a self-contained module using an IIFE. This includes all the variables that refer to elements (those with names that start with the $ symbol) and the update(), hide(), and show() functions. We'll move all of these into an anonymous IIFE that returns an object assigned to the global variable view. Add the following code to the beginning of the **scripts.js** file (right after the "use strict" declaration):

```
var view = (function () {
  function update(element,content,klass) {
    var p = element.firstChild || document.createElement("p");
    p.textContent = content;
    element.appendChild(p);
    if(klass) {
      p.className = klass;
    }
  }

  function hide(element) {
    element.style.display = "none";
  }

  function show(element) {
    element.style.display = "block";
  }

  return {
    question: document.getElementById("question"),
    score: document.getElementById("score"),
    feedback: document.getElementById("feedback"),
    start: document.getElementById("start"),
    form: document.getElementById("answer"),
    timer: document.getElementById("timer"),
    hiScore: document.getElementById("hiScore"),
    update: update,
    hide: hide,
    show: show
  }
}());
```

This defines the functions and then returns an object that has references to the DOM elements as its properties and the function definitions as its methods.

Everything to do with the view is now self-contained. To access the form element, we would now use view.form and to call the update() function we'd use view.update(). We now need to go through the rest of our code and update it to use these new names, which requires making the following changes:

- update becomes view.update

- hide becomes view.hide

▓ `show` becomes `view.show`

▓ all the $ symbols become `view.` (for example, `$timer` becomes `view.timer`)

By separating the view logic into a separate module, we are moving towards an MVC-style structure. The `Game` object acts as the model and the event handlers act as controllers that take care of all the different interactions with the player.

Deployment

The final task we'll do with our quiz game is prepare it for deployment. This will involve removing the `console.log` statements and minifying the code. To make this easier, we'll use a Gulp task to automate the process.

In order to use Gulp, you'll need to install Node.js. Then use npm to install Gulp via the terminal as follows:

```
$ npm install --g gulp
```

From your project folder, you must then initialize the project using:

```
$ npm init
```

You will be prompted for parameters such as the project name, version, author, and so on. Hit **return** to accept the defaults. Your folder will now contain a **package.json** file that defines which dependencies you require. First, you must install a local version of Gulp as a development dependency:

```
$ npm install --save-dev gulp
```

Next, you'll to install the necessary Gulp plugins. These are the `gulp-strip-debug` plugin to remove any `console.log()` statements and the `gulp-uglify` plugin to minify the code. To install these, enter the following commands in a terminal prompt:

```
$ npm install --save-dev gulp-strip-debug gulp-uglify
```

Gulp and the plugins will now be shown in the `devDependencies` section of your **package.json** file:

```
{
  "name": "Quiz Ninja",
  "version": "1.0.0",
  "description": "My first JavaScript project",
  "main": "index.html",
  "devDependencies": {
  "gulp": "^3.8.10",
  "gulp-strip-debug": "^1.0.1",
  "gulp-uglify": "^1.0.1"
  }
}
```

You'll also have a **node_modules** folder where Gulp and the plugins have been installed.

 Sharing Your Project

Our **node_modules** folder only contains development dependencies, so it need not be distributed with the code. If you're using Git, you could add **node_modules/** to the **.gitignore** file.

If you want to pass the project to another developer, just ensure that the **package.json** file is included. The developer could then install all project dependencies using:

```
$ npm install
```

The main JavaScript files that are written in development should be moved into a new folder named **src**. The Gulp task will take the JavaScript file in this folder and pipe them through the `stripdebug` and `uglify` plugins before saving the output in the **js** folder.

We now need to create the Gulp file that will run the task. Create a file called **gulpfile.js** that contains the following lines of code and save it in the same directory as **index.htm**:

```
var
  gulp = require('gulp'),
  stripdebug = require('gulp-strip-debug'),
  uglify = require('gulp-uglify');
```

```
var
  source = 'src/*',
  dest = 'js/';

// strip debugging and minify JS
gulp.task('js', function() {
  return gulp.src(source)
    .pipe(stripdebug())
    .pipe(uglify())
    .pipe(gulp.dest(dest));
});

// default task
gulp.task('default', ['js'], function() {

  // watch for javascript changes
  gulp.watch(source, ['js']);

});
```

This file contains two tasks: the js task and the default task. The js task will use the stripdebug plugin to remove the debugging console.log commands, and then use the uglify plugin to minify the code. Run this task using this terminal command:

```
$ gulp js
```

After running the task, you should find a file called **scripts.js** inside the **js** folder. The contents of this file should contain the minified code and be smaller in size than the original file.

There is also the default task. This runs our js task and then watches for any file updates. If a file is added, removed, or modified in the **src** folder, the js task is run again. Run the default task using the following command:

```
$ gulp
```

More plugins and tasks can be added to **gulpfile.js**. For example, if our project JavaScript was contained in several separate, smaller files, we could use a Gulp task to concatenate together, or we could add a CSS preprocessor such as Sass to compile SCSS to normal CSS. You can even write a Gulp task that would watch for changes to the files, and run a JS Lint test on it whenever these changes signalled any mistakes made in the code.

Although we haven't changed the functionality of the quiz game in this chapter, we have made it more modular and therefore easier to maintain in the future, as well as optimizing the file size, ready for deployment. These are both important tasks to consider when writing JavaScript that will be deployed to a server.

Summary

In this chapter, we have learned the following:

- A framework is a JavaScript library of code that provides methods to make common tasks easier to achieve.

- Frameworks can make programming much easier, but you should think carefully about whether you require a framework and which one is best for your needs.

- A module is a self-contained piece of code that provides functions and methods that can then be used in other files.

- JavaScript does not support modules, but there are patterns available that can mimic them.

- CommonJS Modules and AMD modules are two popular module patterns. CommonJS modules are used by npm while AMD Modules are used by RequireJS.

- Browserify and Bower are two popular package managers that can be used to install modules and frameworks, as well as manage dependencies.

- The MVC pattern is used to organize code into distinct sections that are responsible for different elements of an application.

- Template files can be used to separate view code from JavaScript; they also enable dynamic code and programming logic to be inserted into the markup.

- Minification is the process of removing any redundant characters from the code in order to reduce its file size.

- Files can be compressed on the server using the gzip compression tool.

■ A task runner can be used to automate common tasks such as minifying code, running tests, and concatenating multiple files into one.

■ Grunt and Gulp are two of the most popular task runners whose approaches slightly differ, but which both have a large amount of plugins for automating common tasks.

■ Before code is deployed it should be concatenated into a single file, minified, and compressed. The script tag should be placed just before the closing </body> tag to ensure that all elements on the page have loaded before the script runs.

In the next chapter, we'll be looking at some of the features in the next version of JavaScript, as well as some ideas of what you can build using JavaScript.

Next Steps

We are nearing the end of the road to becoming a JavaScript ninja. But as one journey finishes, a new one begins. Now it's time to level up your JavaScript ninja skills. In this final chapter, we're going to see what's in store in the next version of JavaScript. We'll also look at how to be a better programmer, as well as offer some ideas of what to do with your newfound JavaScript programming skills.

In this chapter, we'll cover the following topics:

- ECMA6 and Harmony
- key ninja skills
- project ideas for JavaScript development

What's Next: ECMA6, Harmony

The next version of ECMAScript will be version 6. The code name "Harmony" is used to describe the features that are likely to appear in either version 6 or 7 of ECMAScript. This section introduces some of the exciting new features under discussion that will help to make JavaScript a more powerful and expressive language.

Block Scope

The `let` and `const` key words are being introduced as an alternative to using `var` to declare variables.

`let` works in a similar way to `var`, but it has block scope, so the variable will only exist inside the block it was created in:

```
if(a < 10) {
    var b = 2;
    let c = 3;
}
// b exists here, but c doesn't
```

`const` works in a similar way, but is used for declaring constant values. Once a value is declared using `const`, it cannot be redefined or changed:

```
const PI = Math.PI;
```

Most modern browsers already support these keywords, so it's possible to try using them today.

Classes

Harmony includes a new notation for declaring classes in JavaScript. It actually works in the background in the same way as creating a constructor function and prototype object, such as we saw in Chapter 12, but the syntax has been changed so that it looks more like a classical language. It is hoped that this will reassure programmers who come from a classical language background, as they are often confused by the lack of classes in JavaScript.

Here's an example of how the `Turtle` example from Chapter 12 would look:

```
var Turtle = function(name) {
    this.name = name;
    this.sayHi = function() {
        return "Hi dude, my name is " + this.name;
    }
}
```

```
Turtle.prototype.attack = function(){
  return this.name + " hits you with his " + this.weapon;
}
```

Harmony will introduce a class definition that would look like the following:

```
class Turtle {
  constructor(name) {
    this.name = name;
  }

  sayHi() {
    return "Hi dude, my name is " + this.name;
  }

  attack() {
    return this.name + " hits you with his " + this.weapon;
  }
}
```

Inside the class definition, there's a constructor method where all the initialization code goes. Instead of assigning methods to the prototype object, they can simply be listed inside the class definition. The advantage here is that all the code is kept in one place, rather than having to use a separate prototype object.

Inheritance will also be supported using the `extends` keyword. Back in Chapter 12, we created a `Superhuman` object that inherited all the properties from the `Human` object. This can be achieved in Harmony using the following code:

```
class Superhuman extends Human {
  // Superhuman specific properties and methods go here
}
```

 Syntactic Sugar

Harmony is not implementing anything different from what already exists in previous versions of ECMAScript in terms of supporting classes. All that's changing is the notation used to implement them. This is known as **syntactic sugar**, as it allows us to write an existing piece of code in a nicer, more succinct way.

Arrow Notation

Harmony will introduce a new arrow notation that can be used as syntactic sugar to write anonymous callbacks more concisely. For example, the following code uses the map() method and a callback function to square each value in an array:

```
[1,2,3].map( function(x) { return x * x } );
```

This can be written using the arrow notation:

```
[1,2,3].map(x => x * x);
```

Instead of needing the function keyword, all that's required is to place the parameters before the => symbol, followed by the return value of the callback.

The arrow notation also fixes the scope problem associated with the keyword this (discussed in Chapter 12). Any nested functions that are written using the arrow notation will keep the scope of this.

Default Parameters

Harmony will allow default parameters to be specified in a function definition. This means that the following workaround that we covered in Chapter 4 using the || operator will be unnecessary:

```
function hello(name) {
  var name = name || "JavaScript";
  return "Hello " + name;
}
```

Instead, we can save the line of code at the beginning of the function and set the default value when the parameter is defined by assigning a value inside the parentheses:

```
function hello(name = "JavaScript") {
  return "Hello " + name;
}
```

Now if no argument is provided, the default value will be used:

```
hello("Ninja");
<< "Hello Ninja"

hello();
<< "Hello JavaScript"
```

Promises

Harmony will introduce a new notation for using **promises**. The increase in the use of asynchronous programming in JavaScript has meant that more and more callbacks are used. This can result in messy and confusing "spaghetti code" when more than one callback is used in the same function. A promise is used to call a piece of asynchronous code without having to use multiple callbacks. Promises don't do anything that can't already be achieved using callbacks, but they aim to simplify the process and avoid the convoluted code that can result from using multiple callbacks.

A promise deals with these phases of an operation's execution:

- pending—the operation hasn't failed or been fulfilled
- fulfilled—the operation was successful
- failed—the operation didn't work

These phases allow you to specify which code to run for each part of the operation.

A promise is created using a constructor function. This takes a function called an **executor** as an argument where it's possible to state the conditions for success and failure:

```
var promise = new Promise(
    function (resolve, reject) {
        ...
        if (...) { // condition for success goes here
            resolve(value); // success
        } else {
```

```
            reject(reason); // failure
        }
    });
```

Now the promise is stored in a variable—called promise in this case—where it's possible to call methods on the promise. The then() method gives a readable way of specifying what needs to be done once the operation is successful:

```
promise.then(
    function (value) {
        // success code here
    }
);
```

The catch() method is used to specify what to do if the operation fails:

```
promise.catch(
    function (reason) {
        // failure code here
    }
);
```

Generators

Harmony will also introduce support for **generators**. These are special functions used to produce iterators that maintain the state of a value.[1]

To define a generator function, an asterisk symbol (*) is placed after the function declaration, like so:

```
function* exampleGenerator() {

}
```

Calling a generator function doesn't actually run any of the code in the function; it returns a new generator object. This can then be used to implement an iterator. For example, we can create a generator to produce a Fibonacci-style number series (a

---

[1] We used a closure to create an iterator function in Chapter 11.

sequence that starts with two numbers and the next number is obtained by adding
the two previous numbers together) using the following code:

```
function* fibonacci(a,b) {
  let [ prev,current ] = [ a,b ];
  for (;;) {
    [prev, current] = [current, prev + current];
    yield current;
  }
}
```

The code starts by initializing an array with the first two values of the sequence,
which are provided as arguments to the function. A for loop is then used without
any conditions (hence the ;; inside the parentheses) as none are needed; the loop
will continue indefinitely every time the iterator's next() method is called. Inside
this loop is where the next value is calculated by adding the previous two values
together.

Generator functions employ the special yield keyword that is used to return a value.
The difference between the yield and the return keywords is that by using yield,
the state of the value returned is remembered the next time yield is called. Hence,
the current value in the Fibonacci sequence will be stored for use later.

To create a generator object based on this function, we simply assign a variable to
the function:

```
let sequence = fibonacci(1,1);
```

The generator object is now stored in the sequence variable. It inherits a method
called next(), which is then used to obtain the next value produced by the yield
command:

```
sequence.next();
<< 2

sequence.next();
<< 3
```

```
sequence.next();
<< 5
```

It's also possible to iterate over the generator:

```
for (n of sequence) {
    // stop the sequence after it reaches 100
    if (n > 10)
        break;
    console.log(n);
}
<< 8
<< 13
<< 21
<< 34
<< 55
<< 89
```

Note that the sequence continued from the last value that had been produced using the next() method. This is because a generator will maintain its state throughout the life of a program.

Modules Using Export and Import

Harmony will support modules natively. The main implementation of modules so far has been in CommonJS and RequireJS; the notation used by Harmony tries to use the best features of both these approaches. The notation uses **named exports** to highlight anything in a library that's to be exported. This is done by placing the keyword export in front of any declaration. For example, if we had a script called average.js containing the sum() and mean() functions that we wrote in Chapter 11, we could declare these functions as named exports:

```
export function sum(array, callback) {
  if(typeof callback === "function") {
    array = array.map(callback);
  }
    return array.reduce( function(a,b) { return a + b });
}
```

```
export function mean(array) {
  return sum(array)/array.length;
}
```

To then import this in the main **scripts.js** file, you'd add this line of code:

```
import  { sum, mean } from averages;
```

Now the sum() and mean() functions can be used in the **scripts.js** file.

Everything in a module file can be imported using this notation:

```
import * as averages from 'averages';
```

This will then import all the functions from the **averages.js** file and they'll be given a namespace of averages. So, the mean function could be used as follows:

```
averages.mean([2,6,10]);
```

Ready to Use Today

Certain browsers have already started implementing the new features in Harmony, although it might be some time before they're all fully supported. It is possible to implement these features now using a **transpiler**, which converts code written in ECMAScript 6 into JavaScript code to work in modern browsers. One example of a transpiler is the Google project Traceur,[2] which supports many features of ECMAScript 6 and generates code that runs reasonably well on modern browsers. If you're using Node.js to run any JavaScript, it is possible to add the --harmony flag to get support for most of the new features.

The ECMAScript 6 compatibility table[3] contains up-to-date information about which features have been implemented in different browsers and transpilers.

The next version of JavaScript promises to deliver some powerful new features, so it is worth learning about them now—even using them in some cases—so that you're comfortable using them when they're part of the main language. You can find out

---

[2] https://github.com/google/traceur-compiler
[3] http://kangax.github.io/compat-table/es6/

more about this by reading the excellent *Preparing for ECMAScript 6 series* by Aurelio De Rosa[4] on SitePoint and the book *Understanding ECMAScript 6* by Nicholas C. Zakas.[5]

Ninja Skills

At this stage of the book, you should be well on your way to becoming a proficient JavaScript programmer. But a Ninja programmer needs to do more. A Ninja programmer doesn't just know the language, they have further skills that set them apart from regular programmers. This section outlines a few key skills that are well worth mastering to help take your programming to the next level.

Version Control

Version control software allows you to track all the changes that are made to your code, because every version of your code is kept and can be recalled at any time. Many people use a crude form of version control by saving different versions of code with different file names such as **projectV1.js**, **projectV2.js**, **projectV3.js** ... and so on. This is a reasonable method, but it can be error-prone. (If you've used this method before, how many times have you forgotten to change the name before saving?) It also doesn't offer the same benefits that can be gained by using a source control management tool.

One of the most popular source control management tools is Git,[6] written by Linus Torvalds, the creator of Linux. Git enables you to **roll back** to a previous version of your code. You can also **branch** your code to test new features without changing the current stable codebase. Git is a distributed source control system, which means that many people can **fork** a piece of code, develop it independently, then merge any of their changes back into the main codebase.

Git uses the command line to issue commands, but there are a large number of GUI front ends that can be installed to give a visual representation of the code.

Source control is invaluable if you're working in a team, as it means that different developers can work on the same piece of code without worrying about causing

---

[4] http://www.sitepoint.com/preparing-ecmascript-6-map-weakmap/
[5] https://leanpub.com/understandinges6/read/
[6] http://git-scm.com/

any errors in the main codebase. If any mistakes do accidentally end up in the main codebase, they can easily be rectified by rolling back to the last stable version.

There are a number of online services that can host Git repositories, including Git-Hub,[7] Kiln,[8] Bitbucket,[9] and Codeplane.[10] They can be used to host an online Git repository that can then be forked by other developers, making it particularly useful for team projects. Some of these services make all the code public and so they are often used by open source projects to host source code; others keep the code private, and are used to host personal or business projects.

As a ninja JavaScript developer, your life will be made much easier by integrating Git into your everyday workflow. To get started with Git, a very useful mini book is *Git Fundamentals*, available on Learnable.[11]

Keep Your Knowledge Up to Date

The world of JavaScript is fast-moving and, if anything, it's getting faster. You need to ensure that you keep up to date with recent developments and best practices. Here are some suggestions of how you can keep your knowledge current:

- subscribe to blogs such as SitePoint's JavaScript channel[12]

- write your own blog

- follow other JavaScript developers on Twitter

- attend conferences or local meetups

- read magazine articles

- contribute to an open-source project

- join a local or online user group

---

[7] https://github.com/
[8] https://www.fogcreek.com/kiln/
[9] https://bitbucket.org/
[10] https://codeplane.com/
[11] https://learnable.com/books/git-fundamentals
[12] http://www.sitepoint.com/javascript/

- sign up for the SitePoint newsletter, *Versioning*.[13]

- read books on more advanced topics such as *Functional JavaScript* by Michael Fogus[14] and *Human JavaScript* by Henrik Joreteg[15]

Use Common JavaScript Coding Patterns

A **pattern** is a piece of code that solves a common problem and represents best practice. In the time that JavaScript has existed, a number of patterns have emerged that help to write maintainable code that's proven to work. In JavaScript development, a pattern is the generally accepted way of achieving a specific goal, often because it's the best way of doing it.

Another advantage of using standard coding practices is that it makes sharing code between developers a cinch. If you use the same style and terminology, developers will find it much easier to follow your code. Patterns often have names attached to them (for example, the IIFE pattern that we've seen previously). This makes it easier to discuss different patterns, since the name can be referred to explicitly.

An **antipattern** is a piece of code that's accepted bad practice. It generally causes more problems than it solves and should be avoided.

As you write more JavaScript, it's a good idea to try and follow as many patterns as possible. They'll save you from having to reinvent the wheel and help you to write reusable code that is easier for others to read. A good resource for learning more about JavaScript patterns is *Learning JavaScript Design Patterns* by Addy Osmani.[16]

Build Things

You can learn all the theory you want, but the only way you'll actually develop your coding style it to go out and build things. By putting ideas into practice and solving real problems, you'll really start to get a feel for the language. There is nothing better for improving your technique than writing code. So get writing! In the next section, there are some ideas for what you can build.

---

[13] http://www.sitepoint.com/versioning/
[14] http://shop.oreilly.com/product/0636920028857.do
[15] http://humanjavascript.com/
[16] http://addyosmani.com/resources/essentialjsdesignpatterns/book/

JavaScript Development Ideas

Now that you've learned how to program in JavaScript, you might be thinking what next? You need a project! But what? In this section, we'll look at what you can do with your newly acquired programming skills.

JavaScript has evolved so much in recent years. It's no longer considered to be just an easy scripting language used to add a drop-down menu and a few effects to a web page, although it is still perfectly fine to use it for this.

The following ideas are intended to get your creative juices flowing and, I trust, spark an idea for a project. It is by no means a complete list of what you can do with JavaScript—the possibilities are endless and only limited by your imagination.

HTML5 Game Development

The advent of HTML5 has heralded a massive growth in online games written in JavaScript and using other HTML5 technologies. Previously, most online games were written using Flash as JavaScript was considered too slow. The adoption of Canvas as well as faster JavaScript engines now means that HTML5 games can compete with native applications. The development of WebGL and browser GPUs means that fast, rendered 3D games in the browser are now a realistic possibility.

For the launch of Internet Explorer 9, Microsoft teamed up with Zepto labs to create a brilliant version of Cut the Rope[17] that could run in a browser using only HTML5 technologies. This is a terrific example of what can be done, but games need not be overly complex; the success of Flappy Bird[18] shows that a good idea that's well implemented can be incredibly popular. There are lots of examples of different styles of game at js13kGames,[19] an annual competition where all the games must be written in 13 kilobytes or less (including all the code, graphics, and sounds!).

There are many libraries that help to write HTML5 game code. A couple of excellent ones are Jaws[20] and Phaser.[21]

---

[17] http://www.cuttherope.net/
[18] http://flappybird.io/
[19] http://js13kgames.com/
[20] http://jawsjs.com/
[21] http://phaser.io/

If you're interested in writing an HTML5 game, you can find lots of useful information at the HTML5 Game Development website.[22]

Single-page Web Applications

A single-page web application is an application that, as the name suggests, runs on a single web page in a browser. The idea is to create a seamless experience as users navigate around the application and avoid the feeling that they are moving from one page to another. This is frequently achieved by preloading data in the background. The data might be stored in a back-end database and retrieved as JSON using Ajax, or it may be stored locally using the Local Storage API. An MVC framework will often be used to ensure that the interface is updated quickly. Many applications are now using the single-page web application model, a good example of which is the Strike to-do list app.[23]

App Development

Firefox OS is an ambitious project launched by the Mozilla Foundation that aims to create an open-source mobile operating system solely using web technologies to create applications.[24] This means that JavaScript is the primary programming language used to write the software for any Firefox OS devices. If you have an idea for a smartphone or tablet app, you already have the tools needed to produce one. Just create your app using HTML, CSS, and JavaScript and then test it using the Firefox OS simulator in a browser.[25] You can then submit your app to the Firefox Marketplace,[26] where users of the operating system will be able to install it on their devices.

If you want to develop an app for Firefox OS, a good place to start is by reading this "Firefox OS Application Primer" by Preetish Panda,[27] as well as the official documentation on the Mozilla Developer Network.[28]

Android and iOS don't use JavaScript as their native programming language; however, it's still possible to build an application using HTML5 technologies and

---

[22] http://www.html5gamedevelopment.com/

[23] http://www.strikeapp.com/

[24] There are some extra APIs available for interfacing with the phone's hardware and services.

[25] https://developer.mozilla.org/en-US/docs/Tools/Firefox_OS_Simulator

[26] https://marketplace.firefox.com/

[27] http://www.sitepoint.com/firefox-os-application-primer/

[28] https://developer.mozilla.org/en-US/Firefox_OS

JavaScript and then use a conversion tool such as CocoonJS,[29] Cordova,[30] or PhoneGap.[31] These will convert an HTML5 application into native code that can be run on the Android and iOS platforms. So you can build using just HTML5 technologies and JavaScript, but then deploy on multiple devices.

Node.js Development

JavaScript has been traditionally thought of as a front-end programming language used for client-side programming in the browser. That all changed when Node.js was released and transformed the JavaScript landscape. Node.js means that JavaScript can be run without using a browser, so JavaScript can now be used to write server-side code or command-line tools that interact with the file system.

As a JavaScript ninja, you'll probably install Node anyway to use the many tools that will make your life easier (such as Grunt, which we saw in the previous chapter). Node.js can be used to write your own tools that help to automate your workflow, or to build server-side applications (such as full stack), scalable web applications, dynamic websites that link to back-end databases, and web API services. Node.js is increasingly being used to develop large-scale websites and applications, with companies such as PayPal, Groupon, and Yahoo using it to deliver parts of their sites.

Due to the asynchronous nature of JavaScript, Node.js has a number of advantages over traditional server-side languages such as PHP, Python, and Ruby. It's ideally suited for real-time update applications with lots of concurrent users as it's able to quickly deal with requests in a non-blocking way.

If you want to learn more about Node.js, why not take a look at *Jump Start Node.js* by Don Nguyen.[32]

And There's More!

And it doesn't stop there—JavaScript is becoming the language of choice for communicating with devices via APIs provided by the manufacturers. The so-called

---

[29] https://www.ludei.com/cocoonjs/

[30] http://cordova.apache.org/

[31] http://phonegap.com/

[32] http://www.sitepoint.com/store/jump-start-node-js/

"Internet of Things[33]" includes a range of devices, from watches and virtual-reality headgear to home automation devices and even robots! Knowledge of JavaScript will enable you to program an ever-growing list of electronic devices.

This brilliant article[34] by Patrick Catanzariti lists a large number of devices that use JavaScript as their scripting language.

Summary

In this chapter, we've learned the following:

- The next version of ECMAScript is version 6, which is codenamed Harmony. It introduces several exciting new features that will help to make JavaScript even more expressive and easier to use.

- A ninja JavaScript developer should use version control such as Git to keep any projects.

- A ninja JavaScript developer's knowledge can be kept up to date by subscribing to mailing lists, attending talks and conferences, following developers on Twitter, and reading books and blog posts.

- A ninja JavaScript developer should use common JavaScript coding patterns that are proven best practice. This also makes it easier to communicate about code.

- A ninja JavaScript developer should write lots of code and build things!

- There are many different uses for JavaScript, such as HTML5 games, server-side development using Node JS, app development for Firefox OS, and building single-page web applications.

- JavaScript is increasingly being used as a scripting language for the Internet of Things (IoT), meaning it can be used to program a variety of devices.

And that brings us to the end of our journey! I hope you have enjoyed learning JavaScript and will continue to develop your skills in the future.

---

[33] http://en.wikipedia.org/wiki/Internet_of_Things
[34] http://www.sitepoint.com/javascript-beyond-web-2014/

JavaScript has moved beyond its humble beginnings as a basic scripting language for adding effects to web pages. It now occupies a unique position as a powerful language that can be used to program on the client-side *and* the server-side. JavaScript is now becoming increasingly available on several other platforms, extending its reach beyond the Web. The future certainly seems bright for the language as it offers various opportunities to interact with technology. The only limit to what you can do is your imagination. So what are you waiting for? Get programming, ninja!

CPSIA information can be obtained at www.ICGtesting.com
Printed in the USA
BVOW08s1458171214

379835BV00016BA/51/P